DISTINCTION

ENGLISH
FOR ADVANCED
LEARNERS

MARK FOLEY ▪ DIANE HALL

Nelson

Nelson English Language Teaching
100 Avenue Road
London NW3 3HF

A division of Thomas Nelson and Sons Ltd

An International Thomson Publishing Company

London • Bonn • Boston • Madrid • Melbourne • Mexico City •
New York • Paris • Singapore • Tokyo

© Mark Foley and Diane Hall 1993

First published by Thomas Nelson and Sons Ltd 1993

ISBN 0-17-556395-0
NPN 9 8 7 6 5 4 3

Printed in China

Acknowledgements
The authors and publishers would like to thank the following for their co-operation in the production of this book.

For piloting:
The staff and students of Kingsway College of Further Education and the Wimbledon School of English; the students of
the European Business School, London; King's College, University of London; and the School of Oriental and African
Studies (SOAS), University of London.

Thanks to Neville Britten for permission to include *The Murder of Michael Roe* (page 22) and *The Strange Case of the
Mulahabad Diamonds Fraud* (page 95) and to the many teachers who piloted the material worldwide.

For taking part in recorded interviews:
Mike Down (London Zoo), Jon Elkon, Dr Martin Lee, Ken Miki, Jill Murphy, Hamish Pringle (Leagas Delaney) and Jamie
Shambaugh.

For permission to reproduce text:
Academic Press, BBC Enterprises Ltd, Capital Radio, André Deutsch, Daily Express, David Higham Associates, Doubleday,
Faber & Faber, Fire and Safety Department, George Weidenfeld & Nicholson Ltd, Grisewood & Dempsey Ltd, Guinness
Publishing, Heinemann, Impact Books, JM Dent & Sons Ltd, Macmillan, Michael Joseph, Murray Pollinger, New English
Library, Newsweek International, Pan Books, Pelican Books, Penguin Books, Rogers Coleridge & White Ltd, Sidgwick &
Jackson, The Sunday Times, The Times, Transworld.

For permission to reproduce photographs and ephemera:
Academy of Applied Science, Boston, Massachusetts, USA, Allsport, Amtrak Express, BFI Stills, Posters and Designs, John
Birdsall Photography, BMP DDP Needham Agency, BMW, British Library, Brooke Bond Food Ltd, Cadbury Schweppes,
Crown Paints, Cricketer Holidays, Egypt Tourism Authority, Tony Ellis, Mark Foley, Fortean Picture Library, Tony Garside,
Hulton Picture Agency, Jamaica Tourist Board, Japanese Embassy, Kellogg's, Levi Strauss, the Louvre, Nestlé, Philips,
PG Tips Family Campaign, Bill Potter, Princess Cruises, Rijksmuseum, Rolex, Shelter, Spanish Embassy Press Office,
Syndication International, Turkish Tourist Authority, Madame Tussaud's, Virgin Atlantic, Josie Williams, Zefa.

The publishers made every effort to contact copyright holders, but in some cases this was not possible. They apologise for
any omissions and will be glad to rectify these when the title is reprinted.

Designed and set by ELA and ARC Design.

Illustrations by Charlotte Devulder, John Foley, Kate Palmer, Carol Popjoy, Josephine Sumner, Richard Wileman.

Introduction to the student

Distinction is a comprehensive course which will take you to the level necessary to follow advanced examination courses or allow you simply to pursue your English studies at an advanced level. You may recently have taken the Cambridge First Certificate Examination (or a course at that level) and now wish to consolidate and extend the English you have learnt so far. The main aim of **Distinction** is to help you improve your English in a way that you will find accessible, informative, interesting and enjoyable. It provides practice in all areas of the language. While there is an emphasis on grammar (most units contain two main grammar points), there is also extensive coverage of vocabulary, development of all the skills (including a carefully constructed writing syllabus) and work on areas such as register and language awareness.

Distinction Student's Book is accompanied by a Workbook which provides support and practice in reading, vocabulary, grammar and writing. It is intended that this is used mainly at home. The Workbook also provides practice in the type of exercises currently found in the Cambridge Certificate in Advanced English Examination, which will be of particular use to students intending to take this exam at a later date.

We would like you to get the most out of **Distinction**. The following information will help you to do so:

- The majority of the reading texts and listening passages are examples of real English, i.e. they have not been simplified or specially written for students. This means that you cannot expect to understand immediately everything you read or listen to. Don't worry. Try to understand the general meaning at first; the exercises you then do will lead you to understanding the important points of the text.
- At this level you will find it useful to use a good dictionary – but try not to overuse it. Try to guess meanings of words from context first, and only look up unfamiliar words after you have completed the exercises related to the text.

- In **Distinction** you will often be asked to look at information at the back of the book. Don't read ahead or look at this until your teacher asks you to, as this material is usually part of communicative tasks in which each student has only part of the information.
- **Distinction** contains a lot of groupwork and pairwork. This is to ensure that you get as many opportunities as possible to use the language in tasks which are based on the 'real' world. When using the information at the back of the book, don't show it to your partners, but make the most of the opportunities to develop your communication skills. Try not to work with the same partners all the time; you will benefit more from working with different people whenever possible.
- A number of exercises in **Distinction** are intended to help you learn independently. These concentrate on areas such as vocabulary acquisition and organisation, analysing the language, analysing text and constructing different types of text. Try to think of these exercises as providing techniques which help you to learn language effectively, and try to apply these techniques in different situations.
- Pages 184 to the end of the book contain a reference section with information about the structures presented in **Distinction**. Use this section if you are not sure about any of the structures in the course.
- Four units of **Distinction** concentrate on topics connected with language. These are included for two reasons: to help you understand the way language works and to provide subjects for thought and discussion in which you are currently involved.

Finally, we have written this book with you, the advanced learner, very firmly in our minds. Language learning at advanced level should be a stimulating and enjoyable experience, and we hope that you enjoy the time you spend learning with **Distinction**.

Contents

Contents

Writing	Speaking _Pronunciation_	Vocabulary	Language awareness/Study skills
Writing a film review	Comparing a spoken and written review _Attitudinal intonation_	Film Finding categories	Word formation and suffixes
Narrative accounts	Persuading and convincing _Assimilation_	Words with negative connotations Idioms of reality and illusion	Analysing and gap-filling
Hypothesising Expressing cause and effect	Speculating _Sentence stress_	Positive and negative bias Environment, climate and geography Multi-word verbs with particle _down_	
Writing an expository essay	Describing people	Parts of the body Categorising	Dictionary work
Comparing and contrasting (3)	Comparing and contrasting _Sound-spelling correspondences (1)_	Matching words with definitions	
Editing and error correction	Reciting poetry _Rhythm and stress in poetry_	Gap filling	
Writing a song review	Telling jokes	Fashion: fabrics, patterns and colours	
Writing a discursive essay Writing advertisements	False starts _Linking sounds_	Buying and selling	
Expressing attitude indirectly	Expressing annoyance and regrets/ complaining	Architectural styles Matching and expanding	
Using textual references Writing a chronological summary	Giving a formal speech _Sound-spelling correspondences (2)_	Scanning a text for specific words	Similarities in words: words with similar meanings; homonyms, homographs and homophones

Introduction

1 What do you know about unusual and dangerous sports? Look at these photographs and names of sports. Match the photos to the correct names and then match all the names to the definitions below.

Name of sports

*abseiling boxing bullfighting
bungy jumping hang-gliding
parascending pot holing
speed skiing stock-car racing
tobogganing*

Definitions

1 exploring underground caves
2 fighting with the fists
3 skiing down high, steep slopes at great speed
4 flying an unpowered aircraft which consists of a cloth wing stretched over a light framework
5 descending a cliff or wall using a rope
6 racing specially adapted cars round a circuit, crashing into other cars when necessary in order to get past them
7 jumping from a high building or structure when attached to it only by elastic
8 steering a specially designed sledge down icy slopes at high speed
9 fighting a bull in a ritualised way
10 being pulled out of the water and through the air by a speedboat and parachute

In groups, rank these sports 1 – 10 in order of their level of danger.
(1 = most dangerous)

Reading skills

2 *Matching headings and texts*

Even some very unlikely sports have their dangers. The stories on the right come from *The Book of Heroic Failures*, and they all concern failures in sporting activities.

A Read them quickly and decide what the activity is in each case. Then match each story with an appropriate heading from the list a – f on the right.

a The worst boxer
b The worst homing pigeon
c The worst boat race
d The worst bet
e The least successful balloon flight
f The worst save

B Work out which story each cartoon depicts. What do you think is being said in each one? Work in pairs to choose a caption. For **A** choose one of the three captions below it, then write your own for the others. Compare captions as a class and choose the best ones.

3 Work in groups of four. Choose one story each from Stories 1, 4, 5 and 6 and read it again carefully. Underline any words associated with the activity described. Use a dictionary to help you if necessary. Now put the words in the chart below the texts as appropriate.

In your groups, pool information to complete the chart. Explain your words to the other students.

- Oh look! There's Boswell. I must have a word with him.
- Still in with a chance – hang on to the boat.
- I wonder if the rules specify breaststroke or crawl.

1   In 1823 Mr Charles Green, the pioneer balloonist, climbed into his basket and lit the takeoff fire. The balloon rose slowly, but due to oversight or a practical joke the ropes were inadequately tied. The result was that the basket stayed behind on the ground. Rather than remain in it, Mr Green and a colleague clung on to the balloon hoop. Thus dangling, they floated over Cheltenham.

2   This historic bird was released in Pembrokeshire in June 1953 and was expected to reach its base that evening. It was returned by post, dead, in a cardboard box, eleven years later from Brazil. 'We had given it up for lost,' its owner said.

3   Ralph Walton was knocked out in ten-and-a-half seconds at Lewiston, Maine, USA, on 29 September 1946. It happened when Al Coutre struck him as he was still adjusting his gum shield in the corner. The ten-and-a-half seconds includes ten seconds while he was counted out.

4   This honour falls to Senhor Isadore Irandir, goalkeeper for the Brazilian team Rio Preto, who let in a goal after three seconds. From the kick-off in the soccer match between Corinthians and Rio Preto at Bahia Stadium, the ball was passed to Roberto Rivelino who scored instantly with a left-foot drive from the halfway line. The ball went past the ear of Senhor Irandir, where he was on his knees finishing pre-match prayers in the goalmouth.

5   The greatest ever Oxford and Cambridge boat race was held in 1912. Both crews sank. Oxford rowed into an early lead but their boat was soon taking water on board. 'We decided,' said the cox, 'to make for the river bank.' Once there they all hopped out, upturned the boat and hopped back in again. At this moment, one of their oarsman saw a friend and disappeared into the crowd for a chat. The cox explained to him that they were actually having a race, if he wouldn't mind getting in. No sooner were they waterborne again than they saw the Cambridge crew go past. They were, however, swimming, as their boat was underwater. Rescue boats appeared and the race was abandoned.

6   Just before the First World War Mr Horatio Bottomley, the British politician and horse owner, carefully devised what he considered to be a sure way of winning a fortune. His plan was beautifully simple: prior to a race at Blankenberghe in Belgium, he bought all six horses entered. He then hired six English jockeys who were given strict instructions as to the order in which they should cross the finishing line. Leaving nothing to chance, Bottomley backed all the horses, as a final precaution. Halfway through the race, a thick sea mist blew inshore and engulfed the whole course. The jockeys could not see each other, the judges could not see the horses, and those that finished did so in a jumble. Mr Bottomley lost a fortune.

story	activity	people involved	groups involved	equipment etc.	related verbs	related nouns
1		balloonist				
4			team		pass	kick-off
5	rowing					
6					finish	

Study skills

4 Categorising

Over the last three exercises you have been talking about activities. In pairs, look at Exercises 1 and 2 again and list the activities. Is each one a sport, a game or something else? What do you think is the difference between a game and a sport?

Compare your categories with another pair and add the following activities to your list.

> aerobics   badminton   chess   dominoes
> rugby   lacrosse   Scrabble   snooker
> mountain climbing   ice skating

Now add any more activities you can think of.

Complete the tree diagram below by adding all your games and sports to it.

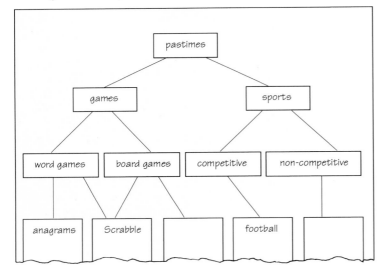

Listening skills

5 Listening for individual words

Listen to a group of friends discussing their ideas on how to define a sport. Which three of the following words do you think you won't hear in the conversation?

> joking   football   skill   moving   swimming
> pastime   result   weightlifting   competitive
> tiddlywinks   healthy   fit

Listen and list the sports you hear.

Listen to the discussion again. Next to the sports you have listed, make a note of whether each one is considered a sport by the group, or whether they can't agree, and why or why not.

Example
Golf: not a sport – not physical, player doesn't hit a moving ball, but it is competitive.

Compare your lists with one or two students. Do you want to make any changes to your tree diagram now? If so, do.

Pronunciation

6 Stress in contradictions

When making contradictions, the placing of stress is as important as the words used.

A Listen to the following extract from the discussion and underline the stressed words.

MARK *What about things like, em, say aerobics, or body-building or weightlifting?*
LOUISE *Oh, I wouldn't call that a sport.*
MARK *They're not competitive, are they?*
JANET *Yeah, it's strange. Yes, but I would consider some of those as sport, because if people say to me ...*

There are two contradictions in this extract. How do people contradict each other? Which words do they stress?

The words which mark the contradiction (i.e. the elements which are different) are usually stressed.

B Study the short dialogues and mark the stresses in each response.

1 I think that stock-car racing is really exciting, don't you?
  – No, I don't. I think it's positively dangerous.

2 I love watching Graham play tennis. He moves so well.
  – Do you think so? I think he's rather wooden. I'd rather watch Alan.

3 Jane's been lazing around for too long. She can join us in the next game.
  – No, I can't! I enjoy lazing around.

4 Um, the answer to two down must be football.
  – No, it's not, two down's got seven letters, not eight.

Listen to check and then practise the dialogues with a partner.

C Work in pairs. Swap roles after number 3.

Student A: Use the prompts below to make sentences.
Student B: Disagree or contradict.

1 You think chess is interesting.
2 Your favourite sports person is ...
3 You want to stop playing ... now; you're bored.
4 You can't stand ... (actor).
5 You think cricket is exciting.
6 You think B has watched enough TV today.

D Work in groups of three. According to your role, discuss whether you feel the following activities are sports, contradicting where necessary.

> sailing   chess   mountain-climbing   snooker
> swimming   table tennis   horse racing   football

Student A: Turn to page 163.
Student B: Turn to page 169.
Student C: You believe that a sport has to be something physical, involving a lot of exercise.

Reading skills

7 Finding similarities and differences

In pairs, you are each going to read about the history of one of two fairly modern games.

A Find the following information in your text and tell your partner about your game.

- What is the name of the game now?
- How successful was the game at first?
- When did the game become successful?

Student A: Read the passage below.
Student B: Read the passage on page 169.

THE HISTORY OF SCRABBLE

During the next few minutes, while you are reading this text, many thousands of people worldwide will be playing games of one type or another, and a large proportion of them will be playing Scrabble. It is one of the most popular word games ever invented. Indeed, in 1953, when people had been enjoying the game for only six years, *Life Magazine* stated that no game had ever sold so rapidly as Scrabble. However, despite the millions of sets sold since its invention, Scrabble has made almost no money for its inventor, one Alfred Butts.

Alfred Butts was an out-of-work architect in the USA with a passion for mind games, who, in the Depression of the 1930s, decided that he was going to invent a game to make him rich. He researched the kind of games that people were playing at the time – card games, dice games, number games and word games – and decided that he would take a simple form of the latter – anagrams – and improve on it. He produced a simple version of the game with lettered tiles and racks, and a draughts board covered with paper to give an impression of the board he wanted. He called it Criss-crosswords. He then took his game to the major games manufacturers of the time, all of whom rejected it as 'too highbrow', 'too serious' or 'too complicated'. Although Butts persevered in his determination to sell his idea from 1933 to 1938, it was universally rejected, and eventually Butts made fifty sets by hand which he sold at cost to friends and acquaintances. The companies which rejected the idea at the time must now be kicking themselves in much the same way as the film companies that rejected *Gone with the Wind*, and the music companies that turned down The Beatles.

Had it not been for the appearance of James Brunot, a business acquaintance of Butts', in 1947, the story of Scrabble might have ended with the fifty hand-made sets. However, Brunot saw the game's potential and bought the rights from Butts, who had lost faith in the game and so didn't bother to negotiate a percentage of future profits for himself. Brunot changed the name to Scrabble, manufactured the game and started marketing it himself, experiencing at first the same cynicism as Butts, but eventually placing it with American distributors Selchow and Righter. He thus generated a business which had produced more than fifty million sets by 1955. The game is now played and enjoyed by people from all walks of life, including the British Queen Mother, Sophia Loren and Dustin Hoffman.

B In your pairs, complete the chart.

	Scrabble	Trivial Pursuit
inventor		
nationality		
reason for inventing it		
original name of game		
first rejected because		
first marketed in USA		
person/company to launch it		
American distributor		
people who play it		

8 Work in the same pairs.

A Match these words and phrases from the texts with the definitions.

1 highbrow
2 collating
3 at cost
4 founder
5 kicking themselves
6 takes
7 walks of life
8 never looked back
9 unviable
10 time capsule

a not possible
b were successful from then on
c fail
d for the price of production only
e short bursts of filming
f angry that they had acted so stupidly
g putting together
h a container in which objects typical of a certain historical period are preserved for future generations
i intellectual
j parts of society

B Now complete the mind map, helping each other where necessary. Use the words below and any others you can think of.

*number games   word games   card games
anagrams   tiles   racks   board
question cards   dice*

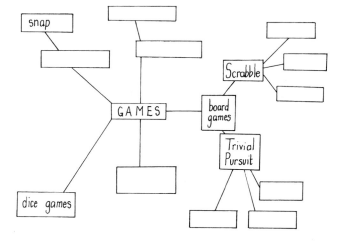

Language work

9 *The continuous tenses*

English has six continuous tenses. Can you remember which ones they are?

A Look at the examples below. Which continuous tenses are not represented?

1 *... thousands of people will be playing games ...*
2 *... in 1953, when people had been enjoying the game for only six years ...*
3 *He researched the kind of games that people were playing at the time ...*
4 *The pair were playing Scrabble when they started to wonder ...*
5 *... the master game is selling across the world ...*
6 *... a cast of a film or a TV show may well be acting the story of Chris Haney and Scott Abbott.*

Now answer the questions below.

1 What other tense is included in Example 4? Why?
2 What function does the past simple tense have here?
3 Example 6 is slightly different from the others. Why?

Continuous tenses are often used to express one of the following functions. Match some of sentences 1 – 6 above with functions a and b below.

Continuous tenses are used:
a to express an action starting before a point in time and possibly continuing after that point.
b to emphasise the duration of an action up to a point in time.

B Look at the two texts and underline other examples of the continuous tenses. Which function does each express?

C Each of the pairs of sentences below contrasts a continuous and a simple tense. Discuss the differences in meaning between the two sentences in each case.

1 Hundreds of people are playing Scrabble at this moment.
 Hundreds of people play Scrabble every day.
2 They were playing a dominoes tournament.
 They played a dominoes tournament.
3 He was finishing the match when I arrived.
 He finished the match when I arrived.
4 I've won every game this season.
 I've been winning the games all season.
5 They'd been playing Trivial Pursuit for two hours when the call finally came.
 They'd played three games of Trivial Pursuit when the call finally came.
6 I'll be going to the games room later. What do you want?
 What do you want from the games room? I'll go and get it.

D Complete this text with verbs in the continuous form of the correct tense.

I never imagined I'd be so successful. I didn't plan on creating a commercial game. One evening I (1) ... computer games with my son, John, when I realised I could improve one of them. I (2) ... a course in computer programming at the time so I decided to have a go.

John, who was then only eleven, (3) ... computers at school. He came home one day and said that they (4) ... code games on the computer that afternoon and that codes might be an idea for my game. We wrote the programme together and sent it to about three companies. Well, we (5) ... only a few weeks when one of the companies expressed interest. That was two years ago; the game (6) ... for about six months now and we're astonished at the size of the cheque we (7) ... soon. We (8) ... another game now which we (9) ... to the company next month if it's ready. But I don't think success will change us; this time next year we (10) ... in the same house, John (11) ... the local comprehensive school and I (12) ... at the bank.

Listening skills

10 *Completing a text*

You will now hear some people talking about a sport called lacrosse. It is a sport which was invented about 500 years ago by the American Indians, as a way of preparing their men for war. In this discussion, Louise describes the sport and talks about its aims and objectives. Complete the text below with a few words in each gap to write a description of lacrosse.

Lacrosse is an unusual sport. In Britain it is not played by all the population but is considered a (1) ... . The game is played on a pitch, like (2) ..., with teams of (3) ..., and it's played with a special 'racket', which consists of a stick with a (4) ..., and a ball. Unlike football or hockey, where the ball is kicked or hit, in lacrosse it (5) ... from one player to another. Lacrosse is similar to football and hockey in that the objective is to (6) ... . The goalpost is similar to a hockey goalpost: it consists of a (7) ... but it is a bit (8) ... a hockey goalpost. Lacrosse is a fast and aggressive game; in fact, there are quite a few (9) ... because the sticks are usually in the air, as the players (10) ... from the challenges of the opposing team as they try to get the ball. Also, the ball is made of (11) ... and can be dangerous if it is travelling fast. Professional lacrosse players now protect themselves with (12) ..., although many people wear no protection.

Louise believes that lacrosse is quite a dangerous sport. What do you think?

Language work

11 *Instructions and descriptions*

A   🔲 Complete these phrases from the tape.

1   It ——— with a stick …
2   … and ——— the stick and ——— the ball …
3   … it ——— on a large pitch …
4   … rather than throwing the ball with your hands ——— to each other …
5   ——— keep the stick close to your head …

* Which of these sentences describe the game?
* Which give instructions on how to play it?
* What language forms are used in each case?

B   Read the rules for badminton and label the doubles court.

B A D M I N T O N
Rules of play (singles)

Equipment
Badminton is played on a court with a net separating the two halves of the court. The only other equipment necessary is a racket for each player and a shuttlecock.

Object of the game
The object is to score points by causing the shuttlecock to touch the floor in the opponent's court. The winner is the player to reach 15 points first.

The court
Each half of the court is bounded by a baseline (at the back of the court), two tramlines down each side and a service line in front of the net. The service court, bounded by the baseline and the inner tramlines, is divided into two halves.

Rules of play
Players usually spin a racket to determine who starts. The player who starts continues to serve until he or she loses a point. The serve then passes to the other player. The play court is bounded only by the baseline and the inner tramlines.

Serving
Service always takes place from one half of the service court and is played into the diagonally opposite half of the opponent's court. Service starts from the right-hand court and changes side each time a point is won on the serve. If the opponent fails to return the serve, the shuttlecock must land in the correct service court, or the point is lost.

Scoring
A player can score points only while serving. As soon as he or she loses a point, the serve is dropped and passes to the opponent. Play starts at love (nil) and proceeds one point at a time until the game is won.

What are the differences between the language forms used in the spoken instructions for lacrosse and the language forms used in the written instructions here?

Writing skills

12 *Describing rules and giving instructions*

Work in pairs. Think of a sport or game you both know and discuss its rules, thinking about the headings given in the text above. Change partners and describe your game to your new partner. Take notes of the game your partner describes to you.

Now write a description of the game your partner described. Use the headings and language from Exercise 11 above. When you have finished, give your description to your partner to read and check.

13 *Discussion*

Read this proverb: *All work and no play makes Jack a dull boy.* What does it mean? Is *play* important in modern life? Is it more important than it used to be? What role does it play today? (Think about your personal life, health, politics etc.) Discuss the questions in groups of four or five. Contradict people if you disagree with them.

Vocabulary

14 *Idioms: sports and games*

Use your imagination and your knowledge of sport to complete idioms 1 – 10 with the 'sport' words below.

sport   game (x2)   ball (x2)   cards   skate   swim   deep   play

1 the … is in your court
2 to be thrown in at the … end
3 to give the … away
4 to … on thin ice
5 two can play at that …
6 to show one's …
7 to sink or …
8 to keep the … rolling
9 to be a good …
10 to … the game

Do you think any of these idioms refer to particular sports? Match the idioms above with the definitions below.

a to act in a manner that you know is risky
b to make sure that progress continues on a project
c to reveal one's plans (usually intentionally)
d to behave fairly
e it's your turn to do something
f to be given a new job/task without being prepared
g to be fun, to be cheerful and easy-going
h one person can behave exactly as another does
i to manage or not in a difficult situation
j to reveal something that is happening, inadvertently

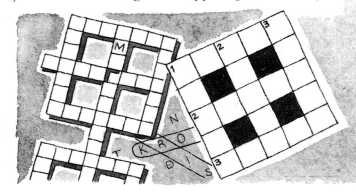

Final task

15 *Word games*

Do you enjoy playing word games? What word games do you play in your language? Here are two word games you can play in English.

A *Words within words*
This is a very common game. The aim is to make as many words as possible from one word. You can only use the letters from that word, and use each letter only once in the new word. For example, from the word STRANGER, you can make the following new words: *strange, range, great, grate, grant, anger, stag, gnat, seat, stage, rage* and so on. Can you think of any others?

How many words can you make from the following words?

EXAMINATION   UNIVERSAL   INSTITUTION

B *Anagrams*
An anagram uses all the letters of a word and rearranges them to make another word, for example: READ = DARE, DEPART = PARTED. Anagrams are often used as clues in crosswords. Can you work out from the clues what these anagrams are?

LEAP   not very dark
MELONS   feeling rather serious and subdued
PRAISED   hopelessness
CARTHORSE   a number of people making music
EXCITATION   to make someone drunk

Introduction

1 What is this leaflet advertising?
What can be found in the Chamber of Horrors?

Find out how much you know about famous crimes, criminals and victims with this game.

Work in groups of three or four to make nine sentences about famous historical crimes. Each of you has the first part of three of the sentences, plus the mixed up second and third parts. Compare your information (without showing it to your partners) and see how quickly your group can work out the nine complete sentences.

Student A: Turn to page 163.
Student B: Turn to page 169.
Student C/D: Turn to page 176.

2   Reading

- Why do people find stories of violent crime fascinating, do you think?
- Can you think of any places where notorious crimes have taken place?
- Why do some people want to visit these places?

The extract below is from a London guide to sites of violent crime. It includes a description of the crimes committed by John Haigh. From the title, can you guess exactly what his crimes were?

Now read the text and complete the tasks on the next page.

The Vampire of South Kensington

The acid-bath murders

1 In the basement of a house in South Kensington, John Haigh would conduct his 'experiments': into a bath of sulphuric acid he would drop live mice and watch them as they slowly disintegrated. Here between 1944 and 1949 Haigh murdered at least four people and drank their blood before disposing of their bodies in the acid bath. His trial at Lewes Assizes in July 1949 attracted enormous publicity and his wax-work effigy is still looked for avidly in the Chamber of Horrors at Madame Tussaud's.

2 Haigh was born in 1909. His parents were both members of the Plymouth Brethren religious sect to whom all human pleasure was sinful and even the reading of newspapers frowned upon. John was brought up under the strictest discipline and often subjected to paternal punishment. He developed a strong sense of 'self control' and recalled in later life, 'I remained superficially quiet while I was being punished, but inside I was a boiling cauldron. I used to feel bitterly resentful but I learnt not to show my feelings.' As a child he had frequently recurring nightmares, often involving blood and violence.

3 He married in 1934 but soon left his wife after serving his first prison sentence for fraud. During the following years he was in and out of prison on a series of petty thefts. In 1943, he settled at the Onslow Court Hotel, Queen's Gate, South Kensington, where he remained for the next six years.

4 Haigh committed his first murder in 1944 when he killed young Donald McSwann, whose father had previously employed him as a secretary and chauffeur. He met Donald at The Goat public house, Kensington High Street, and took him back to his Gloucester Road basement where he hit him on the head with a cosh. 'Then I went out', said Haigh, 'and fetched a drinking glass, made an incision in his body with a penknife, and collected a glass of blood which I drank. He was dead within five minutes or so. I then put him in a forty-gallon tank into which I poured sulphuric acid. I later disposed of his remains down a manhole in the basement.' Haigh subsequently murdered Donald's mother and father in exactly the same way.

5 A few months after killing Donald McSwann, Haigh met a young woman about thirty-five years of age on Hammersmith Bridge and invited her back to his 'flat' in Gloucester Road. 'She came with me to the basement where I duly knocked her on the head with a cosh and tapped her for blood.' She, too, was disposed of in the acid bath.

6 Haigh also had a 'workroom' in Leopold Road, Crawley. Here, too, he had an acid bath in which he dissolved several more victims.

7 In February 1949, Haigh invited a fellow guest at the Onslow Court Hotel, a Mrs Durand-Deacon, to visit his Crawley workroom. He shot her through the head, drank her blood and put her body in the acid tank. Accompanied by another hotel guest he went to the police to report Mrs Durand-Deacon missing. Following this report the police became suspicious of Haigh, and their investigations led to his Crawley workroom where they found traces of a human body that the acid had failed to obliterate, including a set of false teeth. They also found the handbag Mrs Durand-Deacon had been carrying on the night of the murder.

8 On his arrest, Haigh admitted to the murder but pleaded insanity. He was convicted, however, and hanged at Wandsworth Prison on 6 August 1949.

9 The site of Haigh's gruesome crimes can still be seen by those tourists intrepid enough to explore the back streets of London's South Kensington.

A   Use the information in the text to put the events below into the correct chronological sequence.

- ☐ the murder of the woman from Hammersmith Bridge
- ☐ the murder of Donald McSwann
- ☐ Haigh's imprisonment for fraud
- ☐ Haigh's arrest for murder
- ☐ the murder of Mrs Durand-Deacon
- ☐ the murder of Mr and Mrs McSwann
- ☐ Haigh's separation from his wife
- ☐ the discovery of traces of a human body in the Crawley workroom

B   Now read the text again more carefully and answer the questions.

1   Do we know exactly how many people Haigh murdered?
2   Why did Haigh use sulphuric acid?
3   How did Haigh know Donald McSwann?
4   What evidence connected Haigh to the crimes?
5   What was Haigh's response to the accusation of murder?
6   What was Haigh's punishment?
7   How do you think Haigh's childhood affected his personality?
8   Do you think he was insane?

Vocabulary

3   Matching words with meanings

Find words and phrases in the text which mean the following.

1   broke up into small parts *(paragraph 1)*
2   model or representation of a person *(para 1)*
3   small group of people following a particular religion *(para 2)*
4   disapproved of *(para 2)*
5   large container for heating liquid *(para 2)*
6   the stealing of small items of limited value *(para 3)*
7   a heavy piece of rubber or metal used to hit people, often on the head *(para 4)*
8   a cut *(para 4)*
9   a hole with a metal cover, a pavement cover giving access to a drain *(para 4)*
10 very small remains *(para 7)*
11 found guilty in court *(para 8)*
12 horrific, bloodthirsty, disgusting *(para 9)*

Now find these phrases in the text and write a short explanation for each of them.

1   *strictest discipline* (para 2)
2   *paternal punishment* (para 2)
3   *frequently recurring* (para 2)
4   *failed to obliterate* (para 7)
5   *pleaded insanity* (para 8)

Language work

4   Linking words showing sequence

A   *The Vampire of South Kensington* contains a number of linking words which show the sequence of events. Read this example, in which the linking word is underlined.

Haigh murdered at least four people <u>before</u> disposing of their bodies in the acid bath.

Now draw an arrow from each event to the time line so that the diagram shows the correct sequence of events. Which event came first?

He disposed of the bodies in the acid bath.   *Haigh murdered four people.*

time ——————————————————————→

Find and underline all the linking words showing sequence in the text.
Use the words you have underlined to complete the five statements about the diagram below. (More than one linking word may be possible in some cases.)

```
              A                    B
              ↓                    ↓
time  ——————————————————————————————→
              |←————————→|
                    C
```

1   A happened _____ B happened.
2   A happened. _____ B happened.
3   B happened _____ A.
4   A happened _____ C.
5   _____ A, B happened.
6   B happened. _____ A had happened.

B   Use appropriate linking words to complete this summary of the story of John Haigh.

John Haigh moved to London in 1943 (1) … a number of years in which he had been in and out of prison. (2) … the next five years he was to murder at least four people. The first was in 1944: (3) … meeting Donald McSwann in a pub, Haigh took him back to his basement flat and killed him with a cosh. (4) … he drank his blood and disposed of the body in an acid bath. (5) … this incident Haigh went on to kill McSwann's parents, for whom he had (6) … worked as a chauffeur. It seems that Haigh (7) … killed at least three or four more people, one of whom is known as the 'woman from Hammersmith Bridge'. Haigh's final murder took place in February 1949. He enticed a Mrs Durand-Deacon to his workroom in Crawley and (8) … he had shot her, he proceeded to drink her blood and put her body in the acid bath.

(9) … he went to the police to report her missing. This was his fatal mistake. The police became suspicious and (10) …their investigations they discovered the Crawley workroom and the remains of Mrs Durand-Deacon.

5 *Review of past tenses*

A   Study these extracts from *The Vampire of South Kensington*.

1   *... into a bath of sulphuric acid he <u>would drop</u> live mice and watch them as they slowly disintegrated.*
2   *'I remained superficially quiet while I <u>was being punished</u>, ...*
3   *...but inside I was a boiling cauldron. I <u>used to feel</u> bitterly resentful but I learned not to show my feelings.'*
4   *... they <u>found</u> traces of a human body that the acid...*
5   *... <u>had failed</u> to obliterate ...'*
6   *They also found the handbag Mrs Durand-Deacon <u>had been carrying</u> on the night of the murder.*

Complete this chart by matching the underlined examples above with the verb forms and the appropriate uses from the list below.

REVIEW OF PAST TENSES		
verb form	example	use
past perfect	5	
past perfect continuous		
past simple		
past continuous		
would + infinitive		
used to + infinitive		

a   a repeated or habitual action, situation or state in the past
b   an action at a particular time in the past
c   an action or situation which continued until a specified time in the past (or until another action or situation began)
d   a continuous action or situation in the past, or a background situation to another event or story
e   a repeated or habitual action in the past
f   an action in the past which happened before another action in the past

B   Study these sentences and explain the differences in meaning between them.

1   When the police went to the workroom they found some human remains.
2   When the police went to the workroom some human remains were found.
3   The police were going to the workroom when some human remains were found.
4   The police went to the workroom when some human remains had been found.
5   The police had been to the workroom when some human remains were found.

6 • Do you know who this man is? What was his occupation?

Work in groups of three. You each have part of a chain of events describing the crimes and eventual capture of one of Britain's most famous murderers, Doctor Crippen.

Look at your section of the chain and using complete sentences and appropriate past tenses and linkers write a paragraph describing your section of Crippen's life story.

Student A: Turn to page 163.
Student B: Turn to page 169.
Student C: Turn to page 176.

Now, as a group, join your paragraphs to make a complete story. Be ready to tell your story to the class.

7 *Discussion*

John Haigh and Doctor Crippen were both executed by hanging. If John Haigh had committed his crimes only twenty years later, his punishment would have been life imprisonment, as the death penalty was abolished in Britain in 1965. Discuss the questions below.

• What is the punishment for murder in your country?
• Do you think life imprisonment is a suitable punishment for this crime?
• Do you agree with the philosophy behind these two well known sayings?

   An eye for an eye, a tooth for a tooth.
   The punishment should fit the crime.

• Can you think of any situations where this philosophy is applied? Do you think it is effective?

Listening skills

8 *Listening and inferring facts*

A What is the function of the building in the photograph? What are the people doing? Why, do you think?

🔊 Listen to this news report about the incident and check your answers.

🔊 Now listen again and try to deduce answers to the following questions.

1 What caused the riot?
2 Where did the riot begin?
3 How many people have been killed?
4 Is the fire under control?
5 What might the police do next?

B Work in pairs.
If you were the governors of Strangeways Prison, what measures could you take to prevent a riot occurring again? Consider the topics below.

*security measures overcrowding visiting hours
exercise periods large gatherings fire precautions*

Reading skills

9 *Comparing and contrasting*

Imprisonment has frequently been used as a theme in poetry. The following extracts from two well-known poems present two very different views of imprisonment.
Read the poems quickly and then match each statement below with one of the poems.

a An innocent man feels free, even in prison.
b Prison encourages evil.
c Prison corrupts people.
d A person who feels free can never be truly imprisoned.
e Prisoners don't think about moral issues.
f Love makes people spiritually free.

🔊 Now listen to the poems and answer the questions below.

1 What are the two contrasting 'messages' of these poems?
2 Both Oscar Wilde and Richard Lovelace spent time in prison. How can you tell this from the poems? (Thinking about pronouns may help you.)
3 Which of the two poems do you agree with? Why?

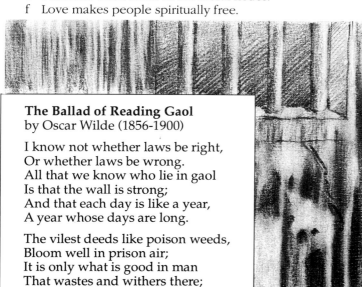

The Ballad of Reading Gaol
by Oscar Wilde (1856-1900)

I know not whether laws be right,
Or whether laws be wrong.
All that we know who lie in gaol
Is that the wall is strong;
And that each day is like a year,
A year whose days are long.

The vilest deeds like poison weeds,
Bloom well in prison air;
It is only what is good in man
That wastes and withers there;
Pale Anguish keeps the heavy gate,
And the warder is Despair.

To Althea, From Prison
by Richard Lovelace (1618-1658)

Stone walls do not a prison make
Nor iron bars a cage;
Minds innocent and quiet take
That for an hermitage;
If I have freedom in my love,
And in my soul am free;
Angels alone, that soar above,
Enjoy such liberty.

10 The problems of imprisonment have led to the consideration of alternative forms of punishment for criminals.

A   Read the article quickly and list the methods of reducing the prison population that are described.

B   Read the article again more carefully and find the answers to the following questions.

1   What has caused the government to begin a prison building programme?
2   How is it suggested in the article that the parole system actually increases the number of people in prisons?
3   What happens when a person on a suspended sentence commits a crime?
4   Why is the government in a dilemma?

Now discuss these questions.

• Are any of these alternatives to prison used in your country?
• Do you know of any other methods of punishment?
• Do you agree that certain criminals should be 're-educated' rather than 'punished'?

Writing skills

11 *Writing a summary (1)*

The article below contains approximately 550 words. Your task is to write a summary of the article in no more than 150 words.
There are five stages to writing a summary.

1   Read and understand the text.
2   Underline the important points.
3   Make a list of these points in your own words.
4   Work out a logical sequence for the listed points.
5   Write the summary linking the key points together.

By making a list of the alternatives to imprisonment in Exercise 10 above you have made a start on stage 1. Now underline the information in the article which you think is important and make a list of these points in your own words.

Compare your list with other students. Try to agree on which things are important points and which are just background information. Then go on to stages 4 and 5.

Compare your summaries in groups, checking that you have all included the important information.

PUNISHMENT
takes many forms

Jerry Hanson investigates imprisonment and its alternatives.

Once again, rising crime and the workings of the penal system are back in the news. Parliament has recently voted on capital punishment, police chiefs have voiced their concern at the growth of violent public disorder and there have been riots at several British jails.

Meanwhile, the British Home Office has been criticised over the rising prison population and overcrowding. Forced to deal with a steady increase in convictions for violent crime, it has launched an extensive prison-building programme. Providing more jails, however, merely tackles the symptoms, for the size of the prison population is affected by two factors: the number of offenders, and the sentencing policy of the courts. Thus the government has also had to consider ways to reduce the prison population through the use of non-custodial alternatives.

The most widely-used device for reducing the number of prisoners in jail is the remission and parole system. This enables prisoners who have behaved themselves to 'earn' their release before their original sentence has been completed. Some theorists believe that the over-use of this system has encouraged the British courts to impose sentences of up to a third longer than they might have previously, in order to compensate for potential early release.

The courts also have the power to impose a suspended sentence. Thus, if a suspended sentence of, for example, two years is imposed, the offender will not have to go to prison; but if he or she is convicted of another crime within these two years, then the new sentence will have the original sentence added to it. There is some evidence that the suspended sentence is used too frequently, with the result that the number of prisoners actually increases. Some reports indicate that as many as half of those given suspended sentences would not have been given a jail sentence for their first offence and are consequently sentenced twice over for their second offence.

Another option is the Community Service Order, whereby the judge can sentence a criminal to a maximum of 240 hours of community-based practical work. This serves both as a way of making amends to society and of avoiding the potentially harmful consequences of a period in prison.

The most common alternative to jail is a fine. Although appropriate for minor offences, fines are seen by the public as too lenient a punishment for those guilty of violent crime. Judges who impose fines, however swingeing they may be, are frequently the target of bitter criticism in the press, and are therefore reluctant to use this cost-effective and straightforward form of punishment.

One or two ideas have surfaced in the last few years, the most revolutionary being the use of electronic tagging. Ministers have decided to introduce a pilot scheme whereby British offenders will be forced to wear an electronic device while they are on probation, enabling their whereabouts to be monitored by police. There are also plans to extend the community service order to include help for the aged and sick.

However, all these initiatives illustrate an underlying dilemma: by building new prisons and by encouraging the courts to impose alternative punishments, the government is trying to pursue two contradictory policies at once. The problem with increasing the number of prisons is that more places tend to result in more prison sentences. Research recently published in the United States indicates that those states which embarked on prison building programmes ended up increasing their prison populations, while those which closed down a number of prisons actually reduced the number of people in jail to proportionally lower levels.

Speaking skills

12 *Discussions and informal debates*

A   In pairs, add at least two more expressions to each of the lists below.

Interrupting	Giving an opinion
Sorry, but ...	*If you ask me ...*
Can I come in here?	*I feel that ...*

Agreeing	Disagreeing
You're quite right ...	*I can't go along with that ...*
That's true ...	*You must be joking!*

Discuss your lists with another pair. Now match each expression with the most appropriate situation below.

a   a discussion with close friends
b   a formal debate or panel discussion in public
c   a meeting with colleagues at work

B   As a class, you are going to discuss and decide which types of punishment the four criminals described below should receive. The five possible methods of punishment are:

a   imprisonment.
b   community service.
c   a suspended sentence/probation.
d   capital punishment.
e   a fine.

Read each criminal's details carefully, then follow the stages described below.

Stage 1: In small groups, discuss the four criminals and decide on a suitable punishment.
Stage 2: Report your group's recommendations to the whole class.
Stage 3: As a class, discuss all the recommendations for each criminal and try to agree four sentences to recommend to judges.

1   Martin Smedley. Terrorist, aged 24. Unmarried. Helped plant a bomb which killed three scientists at a London cosmetics laboratory. Belongs to a fanatical group which believes that scientists should not use animals in experiments. No previous criminal record.

2   Rachel O'Rourke. Forger, aged 36. Married with two teenage children. Used her specialist printing knowledge to print fake £50 notes. Attempted to spend them at a department store on luxury presents for her family. Two previous prison sentences for the same offence.

3   Sam Cooper. Kidnapper, aged 19. Unmarried. Kidnapped the daughter of a wealthy businessman at knifepoint, locked her in a basement with no food for three days and demanded a million pounds from her family. He was brought up in an orphanage. One previous conviction for stealing money from a telephone box.

4   Piers D'Ortez. Confidence trickster/thief, aged 25. Unmarried. Convinced a rich old lady that he was a jewel expert, 'borrowed' her diamonds 'to have them professionally valued' and tried to catch a plane to Brazil. Good family background and private education but was expelled from school for cheating at exams. No previous criminal record.

Final task

13 *The Murder of Michael Roe*

Work in groups of three or four. You each have some information which has been sent to Sherlock Holmes. Read your information only, then discuss and solve the crime in your group.

Student A: Read the letter on this page.
Student B: Turn to page 170.
Student C/D: Turn to page 176.

Be ready to explain your solution to the class when you finish.

SCOTLAND YARD
Special Branch

Sunday 5th September, 1884

Dear Mr Holmes,

I am writing to ask you to help in an important investigation which involves a vital national secret. Naturally, you will destroy this letter after you have read it.

At present, the Admiralty is trying to develop a small light boat which will be so fast that it will be able to get close to an enemy ship, fire a torpedo at it, and escape. This boat – the torpedo boat – will give the Royal Navy a great advantage over all other navies, especially our great rivals the Imperial German Navy.

It now appears that there has been a serious failing in our security. Last Saturday night, Mr Leonard Fud, a bank clerk from Morgate in South London, visited the London Moulin Rouge club, a striptease show in Soho. When he went into the club, Mr Fud deposited his umbrella in the cloakroom. He left at about 10.30 and collected his umbrella on the way out. When Mr Fud got home at about 11.30, he noticed that the umbrella was not his; on opening it a piece of paper fell out. There were several geometric designs on it which Mr Fud did not understand, but he did understand the two words TOP SECRET printed at the top of the page.

Fortunately Mr Fud is a good citizen, and he contacted the police first thing this morning. As soon as we saw the piece of paper, we realised it was the plan for the engine of the torpedo boat. When we heard Mr Fud's story we were even more alarmed, because we knew that Captain Hans Schweiger, the German naval attache, visited the same place – the London Moulin Rouge club – last night between 10.00 and 10.30. Naturally, one of our men was following him. His report said that the Captain didn't speak to anyone in the club, and the only time he was out of our man's sight was when he went to the lavatory. Following his visit to the lavatory the Captain collected his umbrella from the cloakroom and took a cab home – still without contacting anyone and still with our agent close behind.

We have begun an immediate inquiry and the Prime Minister has been notified. It was the Prime Minister who suggested that we should contact you, Mr Holmes.

I look forward to hearing from you.

Tobias Gregson

Inspector Tobias Gregson

Introduction

1 Most people believe they can assess risks and dangers fairly accurately. Can you? The following quiz should help you find out. How reliable is your perception of risk? Work in groups of three or four, discuss the questions and try to decide on the correct answers.

Living Dangerously?

Health

1 Which is the best country to live in if you wish to avoid heart disease?
   a Britain   b Japan c USA

2 Which of the following is the major cause of stomach cancer?
   a smoking
   b being poor
   c eating too much salt

On the roads

3 Which is more dangerous?
   a driving to your local shop
   b driving on a motorway
   c driving along a country road

4 Which country has the safest roads?
   a Britain   b Holland   c Ireland

5 If you live in Britain, what is your chance of having a road accident in your lifetime?
   a 1 in 10   b 1 in 25   c 1 in 350

At home

6 Which is the most dangerous DIY* activity?
   a using an electric drill
   b using a knife
   c using a ladder

7 In Britain each year, how many people are involved in accidents in their own house or garden?
   a 3,000,000   b 950,000   c 80,000

   *Do-It-Yourself

Flying

8 Which is the most dangerous area to fly over?
   a the Middle East
   b Latin America
   c Africa

9 Statistically, if a person flies 10,000 miles a year, how many years would she/he have to fly before meeting with a fatal accident?
   a 1,000,000   b 700,000   c 99,000

At work and play

10 Which profession carries the highest risk of accidental death?
   a coal mining
   b construction
   c deep-sea fishing

11 In which sport are injuries most common?
   a rugby   b football   c boxing

12 Where are you most likely to drown?
   a in the sea
   b in a swimming pool
   c in a river

Now one person in the group turn to page 158.

Reading skills

2 Taking notes from a text

A Many people believe that flying is extremely dangerous. Read the magazine article and find the answers to questions 1 – 3 on the right.

1 How many fatal plane crashes were there in the 1980s?
2 What is the increase in flight safety mainly due to?
3 Why do stewards visit the cockpit every fifteen minutes?

FEAR OF FLYING

Do you suffer from fear of flying? If you do, you are a member of one of the world's largest clubs – millions of people across the world find flying a nerve-wracking, anxiety-provoking torment. Sufferers cope in a variety of ways: taking tranquillisers, drowning themselves in alcohol, or by the ultimate cure – never getting into a plane. This final option is one which is becoming increasingly impractical. Whether for business or pleasure, travel has become an everyday necessity and, with the current decline in sea cruises and rail services, in many instances the only realistic choice is to grit your teeth, strap yourself into that claustrophobic steel tube suspended in thin air and go flying.

The truth is that, at some time or other, almost all of us will have to fly and the only real antidote to fear is a cool, calm and thorough look at the scientific evidence before us.

In recent years, a number of statistics have been published which put the danger of flying into a more realistic perspective. Although plane crashes seem to happen with alarming frequency, we have to remember that this is balanced by the fact that the number of flights has also increased, and by a far larger factor. In the early 1950s, the chance of a fatal accident in a plane was around 18 in a million; that figure is now less than one in a million. In the 1970s, there were 270 fatal plane crashes worldwide. During the 1980s the number dropped to 232, despite the fact that there was a 30% increase in the number of flights. According to figures compiled by Condé Nast *Traveller* magazine, the world's worst accident record is held by Aeroflot. The carrier with the best record is Southwest Airlines of the United States, followed by Ansett of Australia and KLM, the Dutch airline.

The increase in the safety of flight is largely due to technical and regulatory improvements. Huge advances were made in the 1970s with the introduction of turbofan jet engines, more powerful, quieter and easier to maintain than the turbojet engines they replaced. Computer technology made it possible to develop autopilot systems, and in the 1980s these reached the stage where an entire flight, including landing, could be controlled automatically. Ground Proximity Warning Systems and Wind Shear Alert Systems were introduced on the ground and the Federal Aviation Authority established Terminal Control Areas to prevent collisions around busy airports.

Unfortunately, improvements in technology cannot be relied upon to prevent accidents. Human error is by far the largest factor in aircraft disasters. At a time when delays are commonplace, pilots frequently have to work for longer than the recommended shift. Combine this with virtually automatic control systems and you have a situation in which tired pilots, with little to do, find it difficult to stay awake. On some airlines, the stewards are advised to visit the cockpit every 15 minutes – just to check the crew are awake.

Maintenance is another major cause for concern. Sceptics fear that airlines seeking to be profitable in an increasingly competitive market may cut corners in this crucial area. Add to this the continuing threat from terrorist attacks and you can begin to sympathise with those who refuse to fly.

However, in the final analysis, one has to see the situation in a statistical perspective. As the aviation industry asserts, if you travel 10,000 miles a year, you would have to fly for a million years before meeting with a fatal accident – about as likely as being hit by lightning.

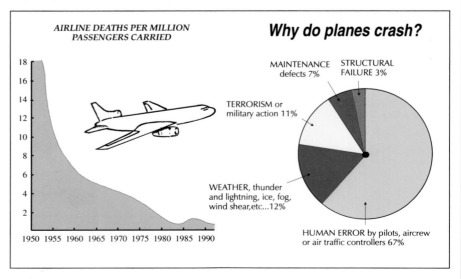

AIRLINE DEATHS PER MILLION PASSENGERS CARRIED

18
16
14
12
10
8
6
4
2

1950 1955 1960 1965 1970 1975 1980 1985 1990

Why do planes crash?

MAINTENANCE defects 7%
STRUCTURAL FAILURE 3%
TERRORISM or military action 11%
WEATHER, thunder and lightning, ice, fog, wind shear, etc...12%
HUMAN ERROR by pilots, aircrew or air traffic controllers 67%

B Now read the article more carefully and make notes under the headings given below.

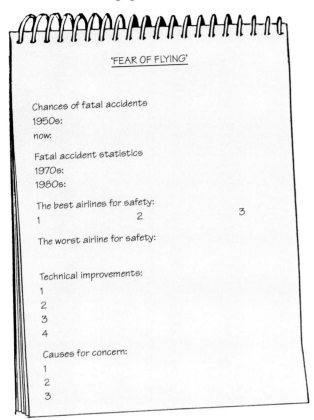

'FEAR OF FLYING'

Chances of fatal accidents
1950s:
now:

Fatal accident statistics
1970s:
1980s:

The best airlines for safety:
1   2   3

The worst airline for safety:

Technical improvements:
1
2
3
4

Causes for concern:
1
2
3

Vocabulary

3 Numbers and symbols

A Study the following extracts from the article on flying. What kind of information do they have in common?

... the chance of a fatal accident in a plane was around 18 in a million.
... there was a 30% increase in the numbers of flights.
... during the 1980s that number dropped to 232.

🔲 Statistics (numbers, proportions etc.) can be expressed in several ways. The general term for these is *figures*. Listen to Section A of the recording and match each item with the correct figure below.

125   1:25   125%
    1 in 25   ¹/25   0.125

🔲 Now listen again and match each item with its name.

fraction   number   percentage
    ratio   decimal   proportion

B 🔲 Listen to Section B and write down the figures you hear, with symbols where necessary.

Now test each other in pairs. Write a list of ten different figures including at least one of each type above. Read them to each other and write down your partner's figures. Compare your lists when you have finished.

4 Charts

A • In what visual way(s) is statistical information presented in the flying article in Exercise 2?

Two other common forms of graphic presentation are bar charts (see Section B), and pictograms (see Exercise 8, page 28).

What are the advantages of presenting information in these ways? Using the diagrams in this unit, decide which type of chart best represents the following kinds of information.

1 The percentages by nationality of foreign students who study English in Britain (e.g. 10% are Spanish, 15% are Italian, 8% are Greek etc.).
2 How the average income of British families has changed over the last 20 years.
3 The number of people injured at work in each of the last 10 years.

B Read this brief summary of the pie chart from the article in Exercise 2.

The pie chart shows the causes of plane crashes in percentages. The most common cause is human error, accounting for 67%, followed by weather at 12% and terrorism at 11%. Less common causes are maintenance defects and structural failure, accounting for 7% and 3% of crashes respectively.

Look at this bar chart of sports injuries. Write a brief summary of the information it contains.

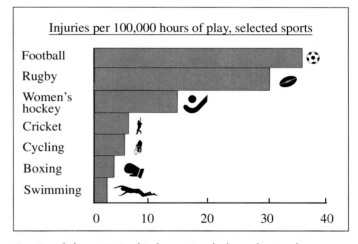

Injuries per 100,000 hours of play, selected sports

C Read the statistical information below about where people in Britain drowned in the period 1983 – 1989. Decide how this information could best be represented and make a sketch of the diagram you would use.

Location of deaths by drowning in the UK 1983 – 89		
in rivers: 34.7%	at sea: 25%	in lakes & reservoirs: 14.6%
in canals: 7.8%	in baths at home: 5.3%	in swimming pools: 5.2%
in docks: 4.9%	in ponds: 1.3%	others/unspecified: 1.2%
Source: Royal Society for the Prevention of Accidents		

Language work

5 *Substitution and ellipsis*

A   Study the two extracts below from the flying article. In Example 1, what does <u>do</u> refer back to? In Example 2, which word has been omitted from the place marked *?

1   *Do you suffer from fear of flying? If you <u>do</u>, you are a member of one of the world's largest clubs.*
2   *Sufferers cope in a variety of ways: taking tranquillisers, drowning themselves in alcohol, or by * the ultimate cure – never getting into a plane.*

The first extract is an example of substitution and the second is an example of ellipsis.
From the examples, can you suggest what is meant by *substitution* and *ellipsis*?
Why do you think substitution and ellipsis are used?

B   Study the following passage and find three examples of substitution and three examples of ellipsis. Indicate the substituted or omitted part in the same way as the examples above.

> In the early 1990s, airlines were required to introduce stricter safety regulations. Most of the larger airlines did so but some of the smaller ones were unable to follow suit for economic reasons.
>   As a result, people came to the mistaken belief that travelling on the larger airlines was safer than on the smaller. In fact, most airlines are well within the agreed international safety limits – the American and European airlines certainly are. If not, they are usually restricted to flying on domestic routes.

From the passage above, find an example of:

- substitution of a noun.
- substitution of a clause.
- omission of a noun.
- omission of a verbal form.
- omission of a clause.

C   Read the article below and underline the words and phrases which are repeated or superfluous. Rewrite the text, using substitution and ellipsis as appropriate.

- ELECTRICAL CIRCUIT
  Check your fuse box and wiring conforms with modern safety standards.

Listening skills

6 *Listening and transcoding*

The potential danger of fire is obvious, but how aware of it are you? Look at the house. How many fire risks can you see?

Now listen to a lecture given by a Fire Prevention Officer, describing six fire risks. Complete five more boxes and draw arrows to the correct places on the drawing. Label four more risks in the remaining boxes.

How safe is ... RAIL TRAVEL?

Unlike air travel, which is regulated internationally, rail travel is in many cases controlled nationally. The degree of safety of rail travel is therefore highly variable from country to country, depending on the degree of regulation and the quality of regulation in the country concerned. In Britain and the United States rail passenger deaths work out at an average of less than 10 rail passenger deaths per year. Unfortunately, the rail passenger deaths per year statistics in the less developed parts of the world are considerably higher than the rail passenger deaths per year statistics are in the western world.

In the UK over the last 25 years, there has been an average of one train accident for every million miles run. Because individual trains carry such a large number of passengers compared with the number of passengers carried in cars, buses and planes, this actually means that the degree of risk is, comparatively, one which is almost non-existent.

By far the greatest cause of railway accidents is human error, either in controlling or responding to signals. Recent improvements in the numbers of accidents are in large measure due to the introduction of automatic and computerised signalling equipment. Radio communication systems between drivers and control centres have also proved influential in reducing accidents. With the continuing development of radio communication systems and automatic signalling systems we can look forward to further reductions in what are already impressively low accident rates.

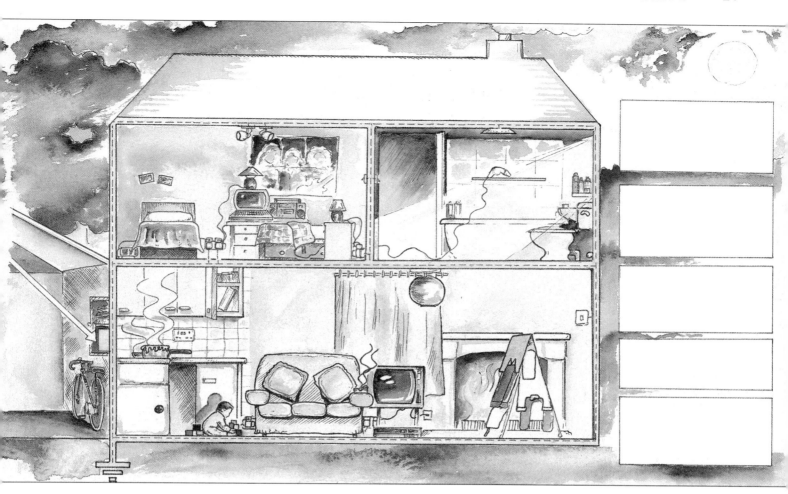

Speaking skills

7 *Advising*

A   Read the extracts from the Fire Officer's lecture below.

1   *Check that you have a functioning fuse-box, and if you're in any doubt, you really ought to get it looked at by a qualified electrician.*
2   *So always switch off and disconnect from the mains when you finish watching.*
3   *Don't put a TV in front of curtains or soft furnishings.*
4   *You should always use a fire guard in front of the fireplace …*
5   *To be honest, if you have young children I think you're better off bricking the fire up and investing in central heating.*

What language function do these examples have in common?

Study the extracts and find examples of the following.

* the imperative
* modal verbs
* idioms

What effect do the different forms have on how strong the advice seems?

Do you remember any other pieces of advice given in the talk? Listen again to check.

B   Look at the photograph of a swimming pool. In an average year about 30 people die in swimming pools in Britain.

* How many potential dangers can you spot?
* Do you know of any special laws which control public swimming pools?

Work in pairs.
Student A: Turn to page 163.
Student B: You are planning to open a new swimming pool in your home town. Although you are an experienced businessperson you don't know very much about safety regulations so you need some expert advice. Prepare a short list of questions on the following topics.

* lifeguards   * safety equipment
* diving   * water quality
* depth of water   * number of swimmers

8 The chart shows the risks of travelling on British roads.

A
- What action has been taken by governments to reduce the dangers on the road? In Britain, for example, car drivers and passengers have to wear seat belts and motorcyclists have to wear helmets.
- What are the road safety rules in your country?
- Are there any special rules for cyclists and pedestrians?
- Can you suggest any further measures which might be helpful?

B   Look at the poster and answer the questions.

- What issue is the poster concerned with?
- Which pressure group produced it?

Do you agree with any of this group's aims?

Fatalities per 100 million kms travelled	
Bus	0.03
Car	0.5
Bicycle	6.5
Walking	8

(United Kingdom Department of Transport 1991)

WHEN ARE THEY GOING TO LISTEN?

These are the facts:

- By 2025, 55 million cars will be driving on Britain's roads.
- If current trends continue, by 2025 more people will have died on our roads than were killed in the Second World War.

Five simple measures could prevent these horrific statistics becoming reality.

- The introduction of a 100 kph speed limit for all vehicles.
- Compulsory wearing of seat belts for all car and bus passengers.
- Increasing the minimum age of drivers to 21.
- Fitting all motor vehicles with anti-lock brakes.
- Transferring 50% of government investment in new roads to the rail system.

Support the fight for safer roads and better transport for all

JOIN THE TRANSPORT SAFETY CAMPAIGN

C Since this poster campaign was launched, the British government has announced a number of transport safety measures. Read the newspaper report below and note down which of the Transport Safety Campaign's suggestions the government has accepted and which it has rejected.

Government announce transport initiative

In response to mounting pressure from the public and the transport lobby the government has announced a package of new measures to promote road and rail safety. Sources close to the Prime Minister have indicated that he will personally coordinate this initiative.

Road Safety

Last year's Royal Commission into safety on the roads made a number of recommendations. These measures <u>were going to be incorporated</u> in last year's Road Expansion Act but are now to be included in a new Road Safety Bill. The Bill <u>is to be debated</u> in the spring parliamentary session and it is hoped that the legislation will be in effect by the end of the year. Under the terms of the Bill, all new vehicles will be required to have anti-lock brakes fitted. In addition, all car passengers will be required to wear seat belts, including those in back seats.

Railway Investment

Following a spate of recent rail crashes blamed on out-of-date signalling equipment the Department of Transport has revealed that a £1 billion grant has been promised to the Railways Board to finance complete computerisation of the inter-city signal network. It is hoped that a feasibility study currently under way will have been completed by the end of the year so that work can begin on the network in January. The government expect the new signalling system to be operational within 3 years.

Road Building

Despite recent speculation, the government today denied that they <u>are going to cut</u> the road building programme. Last year the government spent £16 billion on road improvements. 'Nothing is fixed and we will be monitoring the situation over the next few years,' said a spokesperson, 'and adjusting the budget on a year-to-year basis. At this stage we are not plannning a reduction in investment but our options remain open.' This <u>will be</u> a disappointment for those who have been campaigning for a switch in resources from road to rail.

TV Campaign

Next month the Department of Transport <u>is launching</u> a series of television commercials to advertise its new road safety campaign. The commercials <u>start</u> on March 22 and will be shown between children's programmes. Well-known television personalities will be appearing in the commercials, which are intended to make younger children more aware of road safety.

Ⓒ
Ⓓ

Ⓔ

Ⓕ

Ⓖ
Ⓗ

Language work

9 *Review of future forms*

A Examples of eight of the main future forms in English have been underlined in the poster and newspaper article in Exercise 8.
Find and study the underlined forms within their contexts and answer the questions below.

1 Which three examples use present tense forms?
2 Which example describes a past intention which was not carried out?
3 Which examples describe definite arrangements?
4 Which example describes an intention (not an arrangement)?
5 Which example makes a prediction about something?
6 Which examples refer to specific times in the future?

• Can you explain the differences between the uses of the forms you have given in answer to questions 1, 3 and 6?

We often use grammatical labels to describe these forms. Match each of these labels with the examples from the texts.

future simple	future continuous
present simple	present continuous
was/were going to	future perfect
(future in the past)	*be going to*
is/are to	

B Decide which of the forms you would use to perform the following tasks. Sometimes more than one form may be possible; if so, try to decide which of the forms is most useful. Write an example sentence for each task.

1 to describe your intention to become a vegetarian one day
2 to describe in an essay the government's plan to introduce a new tax next year
3 to describe the arrival time of a flight from New York
4 to predict the result of an election
5 to explain why (because of your work schedule) you can't accept a lunch invitation for next week
6 to tell someone about your holiday plans for next summer (you've already bought the tickets)
7 to explain that you plan to buy a larger car next week, before your friends arrive to stay with you the week after

C In addition to the future forms listed above, the newspaper article contains a number of verbs which can carry a future meaning in themselves, such as *planning*. Find four more verbs like this.

D   Work in pairs. Decide which of the two sentences in each item is most appropriate in each case and make a note of your reasons.

1   a   According to the timetable the new term is going to start on September 9th.
    b   According to the timetable the new term starts on September 9th.

2   a   'Jasmine is going to have a baby!' she exclaimed.
    b   'Jasmine is to have a baby!' she exclaimed.

3   a   Are you ready to go? I'll give you a lift if you like.
    b   Are you ready to go? I'm going to give you a lift.

4   a   It's almost ready. I'm finishing it in five minutes.
    b   It's almost ready. I'll have finished it in five minutes.

5   a   I'll work when you phone.
    b   I'll be working when you phone.

Now compare your choices and reasons with another pair.

Writing skills

10 *Writing a formal letter*

A   Read the letter below quickly and answer the questions.

1   Who has written the letter and who will receive it?
2   What is the letter about?
3   Is the letter formal or informal? Why?

Now read the letter more carefully and complete it by choosing the more formal of the items in brackets in each case.

B   Imagine you are Councillor Pangbourne. Write a formal letter to Mr Grenville replying to his points. Use the notes below to help you compose your letter. (Note: remember to pay attention to future forms.)

South Kerstonleigh Shopping Centre

Preliminary decisions (no action taken yet)
– new bus service for elderly between Market Street and social club

Decisions of Planning Committee (confirmed by council meeting last week)
– build new zebra crossing on Market Street
– build underpass between Market Street Estate and Mariton Road

Confirmed construction schedule

This year:
October 19 – shopping centre foundations begin
December – commence new access road

Next year:
January – March – build and complete underpass
February – install zebra crossing
May – open access roads
June 24 – shopping centre official opening ceremony

SOUTH KERSTONLEIGH RESIDENTS' ASSOCIATION
87 Carlton Avenue, Kerstonleigh, KE6 89G

Councillor R. Pangbourne
Chair of Planning Committee
Kerstonleigh District Council
The Town Hall
High Street
Kerstonleigh
KE1 9LM

Dear Councillor Pangbourne,
(1 Further to/After) a meeting of our Association (2 held/we had) yesterday, I have been (3 instructed/asked) to write to you as Chair of the Planning Committee to (4 express/tell you about) our grave (5 concerns/worries) over the proposed new shopping centre and access roads in South Kerstonleigh.
We have a number of queries regarding road safety measures for the new development. Our (6 first/primary) concern is for the local (7 schoolchildren/schoolkids). We believe that the proposals include a new road between Hunter Street and Market Street. The children (8 who go to/attending) Hunter Street School will have to cross this road to reach their playing fields. As the new road will be carrying a (9 large volume/lot) of traffic we believe this could be a serious danger to the children.
Our second concern is for our local (10 old/elderly) residents. Many of them need to get from their homes on the Market Street Estate to the social club on Mariton Road. As the proposals stand at the moment, this would involve crossing two (11 major/big) access roads. If the roads are (12 constantly/ always) busy with shoppers driving to the new shopping centre car park this would be extremely hazardous and inconvenient.
We should be grateful if you could (13 inform/tell) us of the exact timetable of the construction works and how the Council plans to deal with the safety problems we have (14 outlined/told you about).
We look forward to your (15 answer/reply).
Yours sincerely,

V Grenville

Victor Grenville
Secretary, South Kerstonleigh Residents' Association

Final task

11 *Surviving a fire*

Look at the leaflet cover.
What kind of information would you expect the leaflet to contain? Who might publish the leaflet?

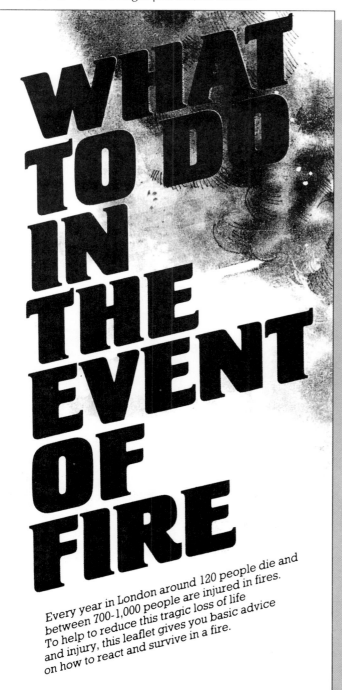

Every year in London around 120 people die and between 700-1,000 people are injured in fires. To help to reduce this tragic loss of life and injury, this leaflet gives you basic advice on how to react and survive in a fire.

A   Now look at the two sections below and, in pairs, predict what you think the guidelines are in each section. Make notes.

1   5
2   6
3   7
4   8

1   5
2   6
3   7
4   8

B   Work in groups of three. Each of you has some guidelines from the leaflet, but they are not in the correct order. Discuss your information together and work out the sequence of instructions. Write the instructions in the relevant sections of the leaflet.

Student A: Turn to page 163.
Student B: Turn to page 170.
Student C: Turn to page 177.

When you have finished, compare your version with the notes you made earlier. Then compare your version with another group.

C   What would you do if there was a fire in the room now? Does the building you are studying in have fire alarms? Where are the fire exits?
In pairs, do *one* of the following tasks.

a   Prepare a short leaflet to explain exactly what everyone should do in the event of a fire in the building.

or

b   Prepare a notice to put on the wall. The notice should contain clear, concise instructions about what to do in the event of a fire. If necessary, include a diagram of how to get to the fire exit.

Introduction

1 Do you always believe your eyes? Can you think of any occasions when your eyes have deceived you? Tell your partner.
Now try this quiz with your partner and see if you can spot the illusions.

1 Which room is bigger, A or B?
2 Which of the straight lines is longer, X or Y?
3 Which man is the tallest, A, B or C?
4 Is the Line B in front of or behind line C?
5 What can you see apart from a vase and two trees?
6 Is this a painting of a spiral?
7 Which hallway is smaller, A or B?

Now discuss your answers with another pair.
When you have agreed on your answers, turn to page 158 to check your solutions.

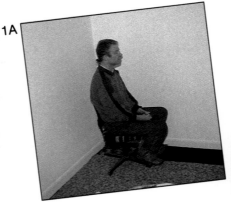

1A 1B

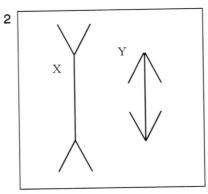

2

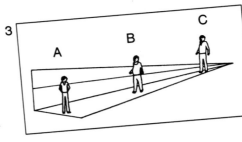

3 A B C

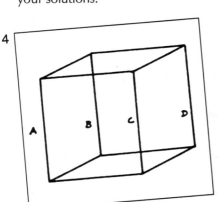

4 A B C D

5

7A

7B

Reading skills

2 *Transcribing to a chart*

As you have seen, colour can easily deceive the eye. What other effects can colour have on the observer? Read the brochure from a paint manufacturer and answer the questions below.

1 Why has do-it-yourself decorating become popular?
2 What effects can green have on an observer?
3 Which colour is best for rooms with low ceilings?
4 Which two colours make surfaces seem nearer than they are?

Now use the information in the leaflet to complete the gaps in the summary chart.

Regal Paints

P A I N T S   F O R   T H E   H O M E

Few of us can afford to pay for professional decorators to do up our house or flat. Do-It-Yourself is the solution thousands of people have discovered and by picking up this leaflet you have taken the first step towards achieving a professional finish through your own efforts – much more satisfying, and all at a fraction of the cost of professional decorators!

We have come up with a few hints and tips which we hope will fire your imagination and help you achieve that 'professionally designed' look. Read through our guide to the five colour fields, and you will find that there is a colour to match every situation. Don't be hasty – carry on looking until you find the colour range (or ranges) you prefer and then turn to our list of individual tones to select your final paint colours. And remember, splash out! It's surprising what you can get away with when you have a solid knowledge of the optical and psychological effects of colour ...

COLOUR FIELDS

REDS

Nothing is richer than a deep plum red, luxurious and inviting. Red is exciting and vibrant and because it reminds us of blood, red is often used as the symbol of danger. But watch out, red has the effect of making surfaces seem closer than they really are, so be careful not to use it in small spaces!

BLUES

Cool and tranquil, blue has been a favourite decorating colour for generations. Blue tends to be recessive, in other words it always appears further away than other colours, perhaps because it is reminiscent of the sky and sea, or a blue haze on the horizon. So, don't give up if you a have a room with low ceilings or small dimensions, blue paint will make it seem a lot larger!

GREENS

The colour of nature, soothing and restful. Ideal for an environment in which to relax and feel at harmony with your surroundings. From the dark greens of a forest glade to the light aquamarine of shallow water, greens offer a wealth of calming backgrounds and, like blues, greens are recessive, perfect for smaller spaces.

YELLOWS

From dazzling sunlight to fields of corn, nature has always used yellow as the colour of new life and fertility. Cheerful, bright and welcoming, yellow can make the darkest room look lighter than it really is. Unfortunately, being a warm colour, yellow does tend to bring surfaces closer to the observer – so it is at its most effective in fairly large or spacious rooms.

WHITES

Clean, bright and spacious, white is popular the world over for its unchallenged adaptability, from cottages to temples – it can be seen in every situation. Reminiscent of snow and ice, white can look rather cold and clinical, so be careful not to use it in rooms that get little sunlight. Optically, white has a reflective quality, absorbing the tones of surrounding colours. Make the most of this by combining subtle shades of white with rich dark colours to create exciting contrasts.

colour	optical effect	psychological effect	reason for psychological effect
			reminds us of sunlight and fields of corn
blue			
		can feel cold and clinical	
	recessive – appears distant		
		feeling of luxury vibrant/exciting	

Vocabulary

3 *Colour adjectives*

How many different colours do you think human beings can distinguish?

a 70   b 700   c 7,000   d 70,000   e 7,000,000

Some colour adjectives in the paint leaflet are used to describe a range of colours. There are, however, many more specific adjectives in English. Match these words for specific colours with the colours in the paint box on the left below.

mustard	lime green	maroon	navy blue
khaki	purple	scarlet	chocolate
aquamarine	beige	cream	violet
orange	turquoise	lemon	royal blue
peach	pink	gold	bottle green

Now, in pairs, find an example of colours which:

a complement or tone with each other (look good side by side).
b clash with each other (look bad side by side).
c are a lighter or darker shade of each other.

(Paint box samples numbered 1–20)

4 In your pairs, use the information from the paint leaflet to decide which colours you would choose to decorate the following rooms. Use colour adjectives from the previous exercise to specify the exact shades you would choose.

   a a hospital bedroom with large windows overlooking a garden

   b the north-facing living room of a Victorian house with small windows and high ceilings

   c the kitchen of a country cottage with low ceilings but with a view over a garden with a pond

   d the large bedroom of a film star in a modern penthouse apartment

Note down your decisions and discuss them with another pair. Be prepared to give reasons for your choices.

5 *Idioms of colour*

Look at the list of colours below.

   green white rose blue black grey red

Do you know any idioms in your language and in English which use these colours?
Are the associations of the colour the same or different in the languages?
Each sentence 1 – 6 contains an idiom in italics which uses the colours from the list above. Choose the correct colour(s) from the list to complete it.

1 I'm afraid there's no clear cut answer to that question, it's *a bit of a ... area.*
2 What a fantastic car! I feel quite *... with envy.*
3 Discussing politics with my father is like *showing a ... rag to a bull.*
4 I hate Monday mornings, they always make me *feel ....*
5 Jim is always so cheerful! I'm afraid he does tend to look at the world *through ...-tinted spectacles.*
6 I don't know why you're arguing about this bill. If you ask me it's completely *... and ...!*

Now match the idioms with these definitions.

a doing or mentioning something which will provoke someone into feeling annoyed ☐
b to have too optimistic a view of things ☐
c a topic which is difficult to define precisely ☐
d clear-cut, with no possibility of doubt ☐
e depressed ☐
f extremely jealous ☐

Language work

6 *Multi-word verbs*

'Paints for the Home' contains examples of the four types of multi-word verb. Some of these verbs have been put into the chart below.

TYPE 1	TYPE 2	TYPE 3	TYPE 4
intransitive phrasal verbs	transitive phrasal verbs	prepositional verbs	phrasal/ prepositional verbs
splash out	*do up*	*pay for*	*come up with*
watch out	*pick up*	*turn to*	*get away with*

A Find the verbs in the text and circle them, then answer these questions.

  • Which type has no direct object?
  • Which type has a meaning which can often be guessed from the meaning of the two parts?
  • Which two types look basically the same here?
  • Which type always has three parts?

The most important grammatical difference between some of these types of verb is the position of the direct object (a noun or a pronoun). Use the following grammatical terms to complete the labels on these two examples: *verb (x2), particle (x2), noun object, pronoun object.*

The following examples show all the possible ways of using the verbs with a direct object (in *italics*).

TYPE 2	TYPE 3	TYPE 4
doing up *a house*	turn to *the list*	come up with *hints*
doing *a house* up	turn to *it*	come up with *them*
doing *it* up		

  • What do you notice abut Type 2 (transitive phrasal verbs)?
  • What do you notice about Type 3 (prepositional verbs) and Type 4 (phrasal/prepositional verbs)?

B Using the information above, work out which of the following rules apply to each of the verb types. Then add them to the chart on the next page.

  • This type follows the same rules as Type 3 (prepositional verbs).
  • A noun object cannot be put between the verb and particle.
  • A pronoun object must not be put between the verb and particle.
  • A pronoun object can only be put between the verb and particle.
  • The meaning can usually be guessed from the meaning of the verb.

MULTI-WORD VERBS: RULES
TYPE 1 Intransitive phrasal verbs *Has no direct object.*
TYPE 2 Transitive phrasal verbs *The stress is usually on the particle.* *The meaning is not usually obvious from the parts.* ...
TYPE 3 Prepositional verbs *The stress is usually on the verb, not the particle.* ... ...
TYPE 4 Phrasal/Prepositional verbs *An adverb can be placed between the first and second particles.* ...

C Dictionaries usually indicate which type a verb is by using *something* (*sth*) or *somebody* (*sb*) as a direct noun object. Which type is each of the verbs in the following dictionary extracts?

fall down   collapse or go down freely due to loss of balance etc.
take off   (*of an aircraft*) leave the ground and rise
take sb off   ridicule by imitation; mimic
take sth out   extract, remove
take to sth   adopt as a practice or hobby; get into a habit
see through sb   not to be deceived by sb, aware of a trick
see sth through   continue and endure until something is finished

Notice that the same verb and particle combination can have more than one meaning and that the different meaning may be a different grammatical type (see *take off*).

D Some of sentences 1 – 8 contain mistakes. Referring to the grammar rules above, find the incorrect sentences and rewrite them correctly using the same words whenever possible.

1 Designers are always coming up new colours with.
2 The plane took off the runway and headed south.
3 Decorators are expensive and people are reluctant to pay them for.
4 When I saw the young girl crossing the road in front of us, I told the driver to watch her out.
5 It is difficult to get away successfully with red paint in small rooms.
6 If you want extra leaflets you can pick up them at your local DIY shop.
7 He fell down the floor and hit his head.
8 Despite the difficulties, he saw the job through to the end.

Now re-write these sentences substituting a pronoun for the words in italics.

1 Your house is very old; doing up *your house* will take a long time.
2 By picking up *these colour charts* you have taken your first step to successful decorating.
3 The index is on page 89; if you turn to *the index* you will find the reference you need.
4 Those chairs are rather valuable, I think I'll take out *my chairs* when I repaint the walls.

Listening skills

7 *Listening and taking notes*

Listen to the interview with Dr Martin Lee, a consultant psychiatrist, who compares the work of psychologists and psychiatrists and explains the role of his profession in modern medicine. Complete the notes below.

INTERVIEW WITH DR MARTIN LEE

<u>psychiatrist</u> – a fully trained doctor with additional training in psychiatry

<u>psychologist</u> – ...
<u>psychiatry</u> – the study of ...
<u>psychology</u> – ...

International Classification of Diseases (ICD)

...	...	personality disorders

<u>psychosis</u> – the person loses ...
– thoughts, feelings and behaviour grossly disorganised
– behaviour will seem ...

<u>neurosis</u> – the person remains in contact with reality
– behaviour is not ...

<u>schizophrenia</u> – a severe ...
– person may hear voices
– often have ...
– treatment: anti-psychotic drugs and provide ... support

<u>Mental health statistics</u>
– 26% of population consult ...
– ... to work are results of mental health problems
– 20% of ... is for treating mental health problems

<u>Causes of mental illness</u>
– ... vulnerability
– stress
– physical ...

Vocabulary

8 *Science and medicine*

Many English scientific and medical words are derived from Latin or ancient Greek.

A  Some of these words have special plural forms. Can you find two examples from the interview?

B In the interview Dr Lee explained how people often confuse psychology and psychiatry. Many scientific and medical words, although they are in common use, cause similar confusion. Use your dictionary to find the differences in meaning between the words in each of the following groups.

   a physics physical physician physicist
   b psychological psychiatric psychosomatic psychic
   c anaesthetic analgesic anaemia amnesia

Now use words from groups a – c to complete these sentences.

   1 Patients with mental disorders often suffer from temporary …, in which they lose their memory.
   2 In some cultures mentally ill people are believed to have … powers, for example the ability to foresee the future.
   3 Chloroform was the first effective … to be administered to patients about to undergo surgery.
   4 Albert Einstein was the twentieth century's greatest … .
   5 Aspirin and paracetamol are two of the most common forms of … .

Pronunciation

9 *Stress in longer words*

Put each of the words in the following groups into the correct column below according to its stress pattern. The first group has been done for you.

   1 physicist physician physicality
   2 psychologist psychotic psychological
   3 schizophrenia schizophrenic
   4 neurosis neurological
   5 technician technical technicality technology
   6 photography photographic photograph
   7 amnesia anaesthetic
   8 persona personality personal personify
   9 advertisement advertise
   10 economic economical
   11 intellect intellectual intelligence

● • •	• ● •	• ● • •	• • ● •	• • ● • •
physicist physician				physicality

 Check that you have six words in each column then listen to the words on the tape and check your answers.
Do you notice any patterns? (Look at the endings.)

Speaking skills

10 *Exchanging information*

Before the medical advances of the twentieth century people suffering from mental illnesses were known as lunatics or maniacs. The treatment of such people was often very harsh and arbitrary, often due to ignorance rather than cruelty. A good example of this is provided in one of English literature's greatest novels, *Jane Eyre*, written by Charlotte Bronte in 1847. The novel is written in the first person.

Read this summary of the first part of the story.

Jane Eyre is an orphan from a poor but respectable family. In order to earn a living she takes a post as a governess looking after and educating a young girl, Adele, at Thornfield Hall, a remote mansion belonging to a wealthy bachelor, Mr. Rochester. She moves into the house and strange things begin to happen …

A Work in five groups. Each group has a short extract from the novel. Read your extract together, helping each other with any vocabulary problems.

Group A: Turn to page 163.
Group B: Turn to page 171.
Group C: Turn to page 177.
Group D: Turn to page 155.
Group E: Your extract is on the next page.

It was a room without a window, with a fire burning and a lamp suspended from the ceiling by a chain. Grace Poole bent over the fire, apparently cooking something in a saucepan. In the deep shade at the far end of the room, a strange figure ran backwards and forwards. What it was, whether beast or human being, one could not tell. It grovelled on all fours and it growled like some strange wild animal but it was covered with clothing, and a quantity of dark, grizzled hair, wild as a mane, hid its head and face.

'Good-morrow, Mrs Poole!' said Mr Rochester.

'Ah! Sir, she sees you!' exclaimed Grace. 'You'd better not stay.'

'Only a few moments, Grace. You must allow me a few moments.'

'Take care then, sir! For God's sake, take care!'

The strange creature at the end of the room screamed. She parted the shaggy locks of hair from her face and stared wildly at her visitors. I recognised well that purple face – those lunatic features. This must be Mr Rochester's wife!

Mrs Poole advanced.

'Keep out of the way,' said Mr Rochester, thrusting her aside. The three gentlemen retreated simultaneously. Mr Rochester flung me behind him; the lunatic jumped up and tried to bite his cheek; they struggled. She was a big woman, almost as large as her husband, and strong. She showed virile force in the contest – more than once she almost choked him, athletic as he was. At last he mastered her arms, Grace Poole gave him a cord and he tied them behind her. With more rope he bound her to a chair. The operation was performed amidst the fiercest yells and screams. Mr Rochester then turned to the spectators. He sighed and looked at them with a sad smile. 'That is my wife,' said he. 'Is this the only marital embrace I am ever to know?'

B When you have finished studying your extract, work in new groups. Describe your extracts and work out the order in which you think they occur (the extracts are not in the correct sequence). Then decide what happens to Jane Eyre. When you have finished, complete the summary you read earlier.

When you have completed the summary, discuss these questions with your group.

1 What does Bertha Mason look like?
2 What behavioural symptoms does she demonstrate?
3 What do you think she is suffering from? (Consider the descriptions given by Dr Lee in his interview.)
4 According to Mr Rochester, what is the cause of her mental illness?
5 Do you agree with this? Are there any alternative explanations?
6 How do you think we would treat a person like Bertha Mason nowadays?

Writing skills

11 *Punctuation*

A Extract E from *Jane Eyre* contains examples of some of the main punctuation marks in English. Study the passage and then match the marks in the chart below with their names and uses, as in the example.

MARK	NAME	USE
, ①	full stop (BrE) period (AmE)	usually informal, used after a command, an exclamation or something surprising
:	semi-colon	enclose words of direct speech
–	brackets or parentheses	usually informal, indicating a break.
!	comma ①	joins the parts of compound words
;	question mark	introduces a list or further information
'	quotation marks	shows the end of a sentence
"	apostrophe	enclose additional information, dates or references
( )	hyphen	used after a direct question
.	colon	divides two independent but related sentences
-	dash	used in contractions and genitives
?	exclamation mark	separates parts of ① the same sentence

Some of these sentences contain mistakes of punctuation. Find the mistakes and correct them.

1 She asked me, if I could lend her my copy of the novel?
2 'I love you Jane, said Mr Rochester.
3 Charlotte Bronte (1816 - 1855) lived in Yorkshire.
4 Charlotte had two sister's: Anne, and Emily.
5 Charlottes only brother Branwell, was an amateur artist.

B 🖳 *Dictation*

Listen to a short extract from *Jane Eyre*. Write down what you hear, putting in punctuation where necessary. When you have finished, compare your version with another student. Try to agree on your punctuation then check your answers on page 158.

Language work

12 Meanings of particles in multi-word verbs

In many cases the particles in multi-word verbs have one or two broad areas of meaning – knowing these can help in working out the meanings of new multi-word verbs you meet.

A Look at the following sentences taken from the earlier exercises in this unit.

From Exercise 2:

... few of us can afford to pay for professional decorators to do up a house or flat.

... by picking up this leaflet you have taken the first step towards achieving a professional finish.

Don't be hasty – carry on looking until you find the colour range (or ranges) you prefer.

So, don't give up if you have a room with low ceilings ...

From Exercise 4:

Note down your decisions and discuss them with another pair.

From Exercise 6:

Using the information above, work out which of the following rules apply to each of the verb types below.

The plane took off and headed south.

He fell down and hit his head.

Despite the difficulties, he saw the job through to the end.

Those chairs are rather valuable, I think I'll take them out when I repaint the walls.

These sentences provide one example of each area of meaning connected with a particular particle. Study the particles used (they have been underlined) and complete the chart below. (The first line has been done as an example.)

particle	area of meaning	example
on	starting/continuing/ progressing	*Don't be hasty – carry on looking until you find the colour range (or ranges) you prefer.*
	– completion/finality	
	– growing/improving /increasing	
	– movement in upward direction	
	departure/distance in time and space	
	– collapse/movement downwards	
	– connected with writing	
	endurance	
	– into the open	
	– thoroughness	

B Now, looking at the context sentences 1 – 6 below and the information in the chart, write out a definition of the verbs 1 – 6.

1 put sth off
2 take sth on
3 keep sth up
4 jot sth down
5 get through sth
6 see sb out

Context sentences

1 I'm too busy to deal with that today, I'll have to put it off until next week.
2 My boss loves a challenge, she's always taking on new jobs.
3 Your essays are getting better, keep up the good work!
4 I'd better jot down that number in my notebook.
5 That test was really hard, I'm surprised I got through it.
6 I'm afraid you can't stay in here, so I'll get the security guard to see you out.

On page 154 you will find a multi-word verb chart. Put all the verbs from this exercise into the relevant sections of the chart and complete the columns following the example given. Every time you come across a new multi-word verb you should add it to the chart. This chart will also be referred to in later units.

Final task

13 Colour and personality quiz

For many years people have believed that a person's favourite colour can be an indicator of his or her personality. In his book *Mind Over Body*, Dr Vernon Coleman published a 'Personality Prism', relating choice of colour to personality traits.

A Write down five adjectives which you feel best describe your personality traits, for example: *creative, logical, fun-loving, argumentative.*

Now think of your three favourite colours. Look at the paintbox on page 33, choose the colours closest to them and note them down in order of preference.

B Look through these groups of personality traits and tick the group which you think is closest to your own personality.

1 aggressive creative intense energetic forceful
2 argumentative uncertain confused adaptable
3 wise logical knowledgeable unemotional detached
4 accurate precise consistent proud peaceful
5 calm self-assured relaxed balanced loyal
6 mysterious spiritual poetic artistic philosophical
7 shy impulsive youthful fun-loving careless

Write your favourite colours next to your group of traits.

C Get together with four or five other students and compare your answers. Together try to match each group of personality traits with one or more colours from the paintbox on page 33.

Compare your results with another group and agree on a final version. Your teacher will tell you whether you have reached the correct conclusion, according to Dr Coleman!

Introduction

1 Languages are related to each other in a number of ways. The three puzzles below will help you to discover more about the way they relate to each other.

A Look at the numbers 1 – 5 in eight different languages and say which languages are related to each other. There is a clue on page 158 if you need help.

ARABIC	CHINESE (CANTONESE)	ENGLISH	FRENCH	GERMAN	HEBREW	ROMANIAN	THAI
wahed	yaht	one	un	eins	ahat	un	nung
it(nan)	ee	two	deux	zwei	shtayim	duod	song
teleta	som	three	trois	drei	shaloshe	trais	sam
arba	say	four	quatre	vier	arba	quatter	see
hamsa	ng	five	cinq	fünf	hamesh	tschinch	nah

B The ten languages below are the languages with most speakers in the world today. Put them in order 1 – 10. There is a clue on page 158 if you need help.

- ☐ Arabic
- ☐ Bengali
- ☐ Chinese
- ☐ English
- ☐ German
- ☐ Hindi
- ☐ Japanese
- ☐ Portuguese
- ☐ Russian
- ☐ Spanish

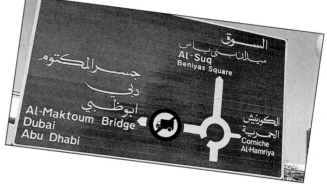

C English has always borrowed words from other languages. Below is a list of twenty of these words, which have become part of the English language by now. Where does each one come from? Choose one of the countries a – h for each word.

a France d India g Russia
b Germany e Italy h Spain
c Holland f Mexico

- ☐ *blitz*
- ☐ *bungalow*
- ☐ *café*
- ☐ *canyon*
- ☐ *dollar*
- ☐ *garage*
- ☐ *gin*
- ☐ *hurricane*
- ☐ *influenza*
- ☐ *menu*
- ☐ *poodle*
- ☐ *potato*
- ☐ *pyjamas*
- ☐ *quartz*
- ☐ *shampoo*
- ☐ *studio*
- ☐ *tomato*
- ☐ *violin*
- ☐ *vodka*
- ☐ *yacht*

The answers to these three puzzles are on page 159.

Reading skills

2 *Understanding meaning from context.*

The article on page 40 looks at the influence of English in the world today, and at how many English words and phrases are being absorbed into other languages.

A Before you read the whole text, look at paragraph 1 and work out what the words in italics mean. (It may help you to read them aloud first.) Then put the verbs below in the appropriate gaps.

buy   conduct   drink   eat   turn on   wear

B Now read the whole text quickly. Which nationalities have accepted the influence of English readily, and which have resisted it? Do you get any idea of the reasons from the text?

3 Insert each of the following phrases (removed from the text) in the appropriate places marked A – E.

1 So many French and West Germans casually and constantly mix English words with their native tongues that the resulting hybrids are called *Franglais* and *Denglisch*. ☐

2 Some experts look down on pidgins, seeing them as little more than baby talk. Others, however, argue that pidgins are full-fledged languages. ☐

3 The court language of the czars was French and the country displayed a keen interest in German until World War II. ☐

4 A discotheque in Hong Kong is a *dixie-go*, for example, and to be a 'swinger' in Ecuador is *travoltarse* (for John Travolta). ☐

5 In France the attempts to expunge Franglais are decidedly formal. The High Committee of the French Language draws up lists of 'un-French' sounds in the hope that government workers – and the general public – will avoid them. ☐

4 Answer these questions about the text.

1 In paragraph 2 the writer describes two kinds of borrowings – those where the words remain intact, and those where they change to become barely understandable. Go through the text and find five examples of each.

2 What example does Broder Carstensen give of snobbery? Why is this snobbish?

3 Why does the German father in paragraph 2 feel that his daughter does not speak German sometimes?

4 How has the word *Japlish* come about, and what does it mean?

5 What do you think is the origin of each of the three phrases from Papua New Guinea? (paragraph 6)

6 Where in Papua New Guinea is English used?

7 Can you think of any words in your language which derive from English?

8 Do you accept these or do you think that languages should be kept 'pure'?

Sprechen Sie Franglais?

(1) … *der TV* in West Germany and you might hear *der talkmaster* on *eine talkshow* (2) … *das interview* with *der autor* of *der bestseller*. Visit Japan and you could (3) … a *nekutai* in a *depato* or (4) … a *hotto doggu* and (5) … an *orenji juisi*. And in the Soviet Union, teenage children of high-ranking officials love to *veendserf*, (6) … *dzheenzi*, fly in *glidera* or smoke *mentolovky*. To them anything *importnaya* is imported.

English is mixing with and marrying other languages around the world. Sometimes the 'borrowed' words and phrases remain intact: other times they blend with local languages into new words and pronunciations barely understandable in an English-speaking country. Ⓐ Snobbery accounts for some of the borrowing. 'English has become the prestige world language,' says German linguist Broder Carstensen – primarily because of the media. 'The foreign correspondent based in Washington hears a new American political term and simply incorporates it into his report,' Carstensen says. The new word often sticks, especially with the young. 'My daughter will tell you she doesn't speak English,' says the father of a fourteen-year-old in Bonn. 'But some-times when I hear her talk, I could swear she is not talking German either.' Ⓑ

Resistance

Governments in both Bonn and Paris have tried to eliminate English words – with

mixed success. Until recently the German post office, which runs the country's telephone system, had insisted on the word *fernsprecher* when everyone else was using *telefon*. Last year the post office finally caved in and removed *fernsprecher* from all directories and phone booths. Ⓒ

> *"English is mixing with and marrying other languages around the world."*

In the Soviet Union there has been only some resistance to the onslaught of English words – perhaps because the Russians are accustomed to foreign influences. Ⓓ English currently flavours the language of popular culture, technology – even government. A Muscovite can drink a *viskey* or a *dzhin-in-tonik*, or go to a *dzhazz saission*. A scientist can work on *computeri* and a government official can prepare the *budzhyet* or even fudge a *statistika* along the way.

New verb

The Japanese readily absorb new words into their language, often giving them new forms and new meanings. A person who has a driver's license but rarely drives is a *pepaa doraibaa* (paper driver); a young man who likes to date older women is a *madamu kiraa* (madam killer). And a divorced man responsible for his children

is a *Kuraama-zoku* (from the film *Kramer versus Kramer*). There is even a verb *Makudonaru*, to eat at McDonald's. The Japanese also shorten and combine words such as *pasokon* or personal computer. 'Native English speakers often have a hard time understanding these words when Japanese try to use them in speaking English,' says Michihiko Yokohagi, author of the book *Correcting English Made in Japan*. But few Japanese have trouble understanding them. In fact, so many English words have been absorbed that the Japanese refer to them as *Japlish*.

Pidgin English – a marriage of English and a local tongue – is both colorful and phonetic. Linguists have identified over a hundred varieties of these polyglot tongues worldwide. In Papua New Guinea the phrase that means to mourn is *sori long*, to marry is *kisim ring* and to remember is *holim long ting ting*. Ⓔ In Papua New Guinea, Melanesian Pidgin is one of three official languages, and more than 750,000 of the people speak it. There is even a pidgin English newspaper complete with comic strips. 'If pidgin stopped, the churches and the government would stop too,' says Frank Mihalic, a Roman Catholic priest who put together the country's first pidgin dictionary.

This article was written in 1982. It is clear that if attempts to prevent the mixing and matching of languages hadn't worked by then, they certainly haven't become any more successful in the last decade or so. In fact, it's beginning to look as though the language which remains untouched by English will have become extinct by the year 2000.

Vocabulary

5 *Words with two or more functions*

Find forms of *official* (line 8) and *import* (line 10) in the text.

• Are they nouns, verbs or adjectives here?

Official can be a noun and an adjective. *Import* can be a noun or verb.
Decide which parts of speech each of the following can be, then enter them in the chart below.

*blend   local   report   influence   display   trouble
complete   comic   match*

noun	verb	adjective
official		official
import	import	

Add any other words you can think of which use the same form for different parts of speech.

6 *Multi-word verbs with particle* in

Look at this sentence from the text.

Last year the post office finally caved in and removed fernsprecher *from all directories and phone booths.*

What does *caved in* mean? The particle *in* with multi-word verbs often (but not always) has one of two meanings: *collapse* or *make smaller*. Which is it above?

Look up the multi-word verbs below in a dictionary and use them to complete sentences 1 – 6. Add them to your chart on page 154.

cave in   turn in   fall in   take in   give in   set in

1   The Council showed some resistance to using the language but eventually they … .
2   This dress is too big. I'm going to … it … .
3   That building is dangerous. If it … and injures someone, we will be in trouble.
4   Oh, I can't cope any more; I'm going to … and move down a class.
5   Poor man – look at his hands; arthritis has really … .
6   I'm exhausted – I'm going to … and get a good night's sleep.

Pronunciation

7 *Words with two stress patterns*

Sometimes two words look the same but are pronounced in different ways according to their part of speech, as in this example.

import   noun   **'im**port
        verb   im **'port**

📻 Look at the words below, decide what two parts of speech they can be and how their pronunciation differs. Then listen to the tape to check.

contrast   frequent   produce   suspect   desert

Work in pairs. You each have three words that can be two parts of speech. Put them into sentences to show this and read them out to your partner, giving the words the correct stress. Your partner tells you what part of speech the word is, for example:

A   My father im **'ports** Scandinavian furniture.
B   Im **'ports** – that's a verb.
A   My father's in furniture **'im**ports.
B   **'Im**ports – that's a noun.

Student A: Turn to page 164.   Student B: Turn to page 171.

Language awareness

8 *Words with multiple meanings*

Go through the text on page 40 with a partner and make sure you understand all the borrowed words and phrases. Why have they all been written in such a way?

A   • What is the meaning of the word *match* in paragraph 7? What other meanings can it have?

Match is one of many English words with a number of different meanings. Read this text.

> Sometimes we so load a word with meanings that it becomes almost absurd. *Fine*, for instance, has fourteen quite separate meanings as an adjective, six as a noun and two as an adverb. *Sound* has nearly as many, and *round* has even more, though the champion is almost certainly *set* with fifty-eight meanings as a noun, ten as an adjective and 126 as a verb.

B   Work in pairs. In ten minutes, find as many meanings as you can for the four words mentioned in the text *(fine, sound, round* and *set)*. You can use a dictionary, but you must be able to explain or exemplify every meaning you find. The pair with the most (correct!) meanings wins the game.

Language work

9 *Perfect tenses*

In English the perfective aspect is very important. There are three perfect tenses. Find at least one example of each tense from the text and write them down.

A   Now look at the time lines showing how perfect tenses are used. Decide whether each line refers to the present perfect, the past perfect or the future perfect. (There are two for one of the tenses.)

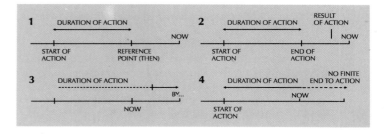

B Match the tenses with these rules.

1 The … relates an action started in the past to the present time, either because it is still continuing (or could potentially continue) or because there is an obvious result.
2 The … relates an action started in the past to another time in the past, in the ways mentioned above.
3 The … relates a future time to an action started (and possibly finished) before that time.

C Decide if each sentence 1 – 8 is correct or incorrect and put a tick or cross in the box. Correct the incorrect sentences. (Two sentences are correct in American English, but not British English. Which are they?)

1 I hadn't learnt any French before I had started that course. ☐
2 By the time my son leaves school, English will become the world language. ☐
3 If you've found the course that difficult, you'll have to leave the exam till next year. ☐
4 We learnt three tenses and about three hundred words so far in our English course. ☐
5 Give me a ring at ten – I have finished all my work by then. ☐
6 We already prepared your room before you phoned. ☐
7 Before they had realised what was happening, the car hit them. ☐
8 You can't join now – the course already started. ☐

10 Suzanne Marteau is a well-known linguist and interpreter for the United Nations. In this interview she explains how she became fluent in eight languages before she was thirty-five.

A Listen and name the languages she speaks and countries where she has worked or studied. Then complete this summary of her life.

Suzanne Marteau was born in Lausanne in 1956 to a Swiss-French father and an American mother. By the time she left school at eighteen she (1 *learn*) … four languages, although she (2 *become*) … a bit rusty in German and her Italian was only school standard. She left Switzerland in 1975 to study in Manchester, and by the time she returned to Switzerland several years later, she (3 *gain*) … a degree in Spanish and Portuguese and (4 *live*) … in Brazil for two years, where she (5 *teach*) … English. By her return she (6 *also perfect*) … her knowledge of Spanish and Portuguese. Three years later, after she (7 *spend*) … three years at a school for interpreters, she got a job at the United Nations, where she remained for another three years until she went to live in Prague with her husband, Jan. Her marriage didn't last and she then went to live in Japan. Now, at thirty-seven, she is back in Switzerland, at the UN, where she (8 *work*) … on and off since 1984; her Japanese (9 *already be*) … very useful and she (10 *interpret*) … from Japanese into French for the last two years. She has two main aims for the future: she hopes that she (11 *receive*) … a substantial promotion at the UN by the age of 40, and that by 45 she (12 *learn*) … another two or three Oriental languages.

B Look at the *Find someone who …* instructions below. Write three more instructions, covering similar periods of time. They can be about language learning or other topics.

Find someone who:
had started learning a foreign language before the age of ten.
has lived in their current house/flat all their lives.
will have turned thirty by the year 2000.

Now ask around the class. Can you find a person to fit each statement?

Listening skills

11 *Predicting, identifying and note-taking*

You are going to hear three people on the tape talking about their experiences learning a foreign language: one very traditional, one modern and one very different and unorthodox.

Which of these words do you think you will hear? Which kind of language learning experience (traditional, modern, unorthodox) would you associate them with?

speaking listening grammar functions reading translation writing tests/exams communication dictionary drills

Listen to check your predictions.

• Which speaker (Louise, Tony or Mark) describes which experience?
• Which speaker mentions the words above?
• Which methods of language learning are discussed?

Listen again if necessary and make a list of the methods. Discuss each method in groups.

Speaking skills

12 *'Fillers'*

In English a lot of phrases are used as 'fillers', to allow time for thought or to involve the listener in the way the speaker's mind is working. Look at sentences 1 – 7 from the recording you have just listened to and work out the function of each filler, using clues a – e below.

1 *Well*, I did learn Japanese on my own …
2 *I mean*, my grammar was probably appalling …
3 … I just remember learning tables in Latin … and in French, *you know*, the same.
4 … it was *in fact* direct method …
5 … I literally learnt it through learning words, and, *in fact*, it worked quite well.
6 … at the same time I felt *sort of* guilty …
7 … it was interesting because I actually felt, *you know*, the most communicative things … were really exciting and interesting.

a This adds explanation for the listener. ☐
b This is a qualifier, often used with adjectives. ☐
c This emphasises or adds surprising details. ☐
d This usually introduces or continues a sentence. ☐
e This often includes the listeners by assuming that they have certain knowledge. ☐

⌨ Use fillers to complete this dialogue, then check your answers with the tape.

A Didn't you learn one of your languages through a very interesting method?

B Mm, yes, I did. I learnt Turkish here, in London, through a, a (1) … humanistic method.

A Humanistic? What's that?

B It's, mm, (2) …, a method which is intended to be pleasant, and to give the learners total involvement and control.

A Oh, I see. (3) …, what exactly was it?

B Ah, (4) …, it's called Community Language Learning and it can only really be done with a teacher who's totally bilingual. It's, em, (5) … translation-based, (6) … oral translation, there's no written translation.

A So what happens exactly?

B (7) …, the learners all sit in a group and decide on a topic they want to talk about, usually keeping it fairly simple (8) … asking simple questions about each other. Someone asks a question, in the foreign language or in their native language if necessary, and the teacher provides any new language, but into the learner's ear; so he or she then asks the question in the group.

A But surely the other learners won't understand the question?

B No, (9) … understanding is easy. That's the funny thing. I think it's because of body language and certain expectations, (10) …, if you're talking about work, the obvious question is 'What do you do?', isn't it?

13 *Discussing a text*

A Do you agree with any of the statements below about language learning? Discuss them with a partner.

- You have to learn about the language to use it effectively.
- Everything in a language class should be conducted in the target language.
- Language learning should involve real tasks and real communication.
- People retain things better if they learn them actively and if they work things out for themselves.

B Read these five descriptions on the right of different ways of learning and teaching a language. Do the statements above apply to any of them?

C Now work in groups to discuss the following questions.

1 In your view, what are the advantages/disadvantages of each method/approach? Do you know any other methods?

2 Have you learnt a language by any of these methods/approaches? (Do you recognise any of them in this book, for example?)

3 Do you think they would all be successful for all types of people, or do you think some people may be suited to one method rather than another?

Grammar Translation

The method most commonly used in schools throughout the history of language teaching, the Grammar Translation method, concentrates on teaching students the rules of the language, on doing written exercises to practise the structure of the language and translating both into and out of the target language. It is based on giving students a thorough understanding of the way the target language works.

Direct Method

This originated in the United States during the Second World War as a means of teaching soldiers languages very quickly. It is based on total immersion – i.e. ensuring that students experience as much of the language as possible. In the Direct Method classroom, therefore, only the target language is spoken – the mother tongue is not used for comparative purposes or to conduct the lesson. The grammar of the language is not studied – the language is learnt through demonstration, repetition and drilling, often in a language laboratory. Students do not learn about the language; they learn how to use it.

Community Language Learning

Developed in the 1960s by Charles Curran, CLL takes place amongst a small monolingual group of learners who sit in a circle, talk to each other about a topic of their choice in the target language and tape-record their conversation. They then play it back, write it down and analyse it, which is where the teacher comes in. During the conversation the teacher remains outside the group, feeding in words and structures where required and helping ('counselling') rather than teaching. This method allows the learners to engage in meaningful conversation in a relaxed environment while taking complete control of the 'lesson'.

Inductive/Discovery Approach

A fairly recent approach, this leads the student into 'discovering' the language for him/herself by providing input (often 'authentic') from which the student extracts and studies relevant parts of the language, trying to formulate and understand the 'rules' for him/herself. The teacher acts as a facilitator in the process and as a check for false hypotheses. The idea behind the approach is that the learner will understand and retain more of the language if he/she has been involved in discovering it.

Communicative Approach

Probably the most common approach in English language teaching at the moment, this can be combined with other methods in order to make the learning more communicative. The idea behind it is that most students want to learn to communicate in a language, either orally or in writing and to do so they should perform communicative tasks in order to learn to use the language, rather than learning about the language. Therefore, tasks and situations are set up in the classroom which enable the students to communicate in a way that emulates real life use of language.

Mats is an elderly man, who already has quite a good command of English (mid/high intermediate). He wants to join an English group mainly for the weekly social occasion, therefore he's mainly interested in discussion. He's very nervous of speaking the language, however, and he gets very embarrassed about roleplaying. He would be quite happy just to talk about the language.

Elena is a businesswoman in her mid-thirties with very little time to spare. She is very intelligent and analytical. She already knows some English (she's about low-intermediate level) and she needs to improve her knowledge of it for social business purposes on trips to English-speaking countries.

Karel is a twelve-year-old child whose parents are moving to the USA. He is a total beginner. His parents want him to learn as much English as possible in a short time so that he won't feel totally isolated at his new school.

Fatima is a woman in her early twenties, who has some basic English. She wants to travel around Europe for a few months and she knows that she will be able to make herself understood in most situations if she improves her English. She likes talking to people and thinks that English will be able to help her to do this. She is not interested in learning about the language.

D   Above are descriptions of a few people who want to learn English. Which method would suit each of them best? (You can choose more than one method.)

Writing skills

14 *Making recommendations*

Look back to Exercise 13C, question 1, about the advantages and disadvantages of teaching methods. Now read this paragraph about Elena.

> It is likely that Elena would benefit most from a mixture of methods. As she is intelligent and analytical she would benefit from a cognitive method, such as Grammar Translation or the Discovery Approach. However, she also needs to be able to speak the language, so the disadvantages of the Grammar Translation method, i.e. the lack of communication, outweigh the advantages. While she might learn how to speak with the Direct Method, she might be frustrated by the lack of attention to the grammar. CLL could be a possibility: on the one hand it provides real communication and analysis, but on the other hand it might be too slow, and she might not be a high enough level. It seems that the best solution would be a mixture of the Discovery and Communicative Approaches, providing her with both analysis and communication.

Work in groups. Choose one or two of the people described and write a similar paragraph for each person, recommending the methods you chose in Exercise 13D. Try to use some of the underlined phrases from the model.

Final task

15 While the *method* of teaching/learning a language is very important, the *techniques* used in the classroom are equally important. The techniques are the ways in which reading, listening or vocabulary, for example, are taught.

A   Work in groups of three or four. You each have part of a questionnaire about techniques in language learning. Each one of you should read your questionnaire and answer the questions for yourself.

Student A: Turn to page 164.
Student B: Turn to page 171.
Student C/D: Turn to page 177.

B   Before you ask each other the questions on the questionnaires, practise the intonation of questions. Look at these extracts from Exercise 11.

1   *Have you had any interesting experiences in learning a language?*
2   *But what about pronunciation?*
3   *How did you know how to pronounce the words?*
4   *And how did you react to it?*
5   *... am I really learning?*

🔊 How do you think these questions will be said? Is there a rise in the intonation or not? On which words? Mark the intonation and stress on each of the questions. Then listen to the tape to check.

C   Now ask each other the questions from your questionnaires, marking each person's answer in the correct column. When you have finished, decide as a group what your needs are and how you would like to learn English. Then discuss your decisions with the class. Do you all agree?

Introduction

1 Look at the photograph in pairs.

- What is the woman doing?
- What is the dilemma?
- Should she be doing this?
- Would you do the same?

2 This quiz, *How moral are you?*, comes from a magazine.

Work in groups of three. You will each have different questions to ask.

Before you start, look at the example below and then find the words in *italics* in your questions. Write a short definition or paraphrase of each of them, using a dictionary if necessary.

flatmate   *the person who shares your flat.*

Student A: Answer the questions on the right. Then interview B and C.
Student B: Turn to pages 171 – 2.
Student C: Turn to pages 177 – 8.

Then check your answers on page 159.

There can be different types of dilemma. Decide which ones to put in these columns.

personal	professional	political
A1	B5	

What is the difference between these?
Do you agree with each other?
Which kind of dilemma is worse?

How moral are you?

A fun quiz to find out how you live your life!

1 You are tidying up at home one day and find an opened letter addressed to your flatmate. Do you:
a read the letter?
b tidy around it?
c without reading it, put it somewhere *discreet*, where no one else can find it?

2 You find a briefcase containing *top secret documents*, which could be very damaging to your government, with whose policies you disagree. Do you:
a leave it where you found it?
b give the documents to the press, for a fee?
c give the documents to the press, for no fee?
d hand the case and documents to the police?

3 You are in love with someone of a different religion. You want to get married, against the wishes of your family and community. Do you:
a change your religion to that of your partner?
b give the relationship up to please your family?
c get married in a *registry office*, but continue to practise your religion?
d explain your feelings to your family and continue to see your friend, giving your family time to accept him/her?

4 Your cat is injured in a road accident and the person who found it paid £150 for vet's care. You discover this, and your cat, a month later, by which time its *adopted* family are very fond of it. Do you:
a leave the cat with its new owner?
b explain the situation, offer to pay the £150 and ask to take him back?
c steal the cat one night without telling anyone?

Reading skills

3 *Reading for gist and detail*

A   The text below looks at another kind of dilemma. What is it?

B   Answer questions 1 – 6, referring to the text as necessary.

1   What happened to Derek Heyson and his wife in 1985?
2   When and why were Elizabeth Heyson and Jens Züring arrested?
3   What is Elizabeth's current situation?
4   What is Züring's current situation?
5   Why is he fighting extradition to the United States?
6   What does the European Court believe is a contravention of the Convention of Human Rights?

4   What would you advise the British Government to do? Would your response be different if:
   • you were an American citizen?
   • you were a British citizen?

If you were a member of the British Government and you had to vote on this issue, which way would you vote?

Count up the votes, and find out what the class decision is.

British Government in Moral Dilemma

A prisoner on Death Row uses a mirror to watch the corridor.

One fateful night in 1985, in Lynchburg, Virginia, Derek Heyson and his wife, an elderly couple, were stabbed to death in their own home. Such force had been used to carry out the brutal murder that both heads were almost severed from the bodies. Although no arrests were made, it was thought that the couple's daughter, Elizabeth, and her boyfriend, German Jens Züring, might be involved. It was several months later, however, in June 1986, that they were arrested by chance on a charge of cheque fraud in the United Kingdom. By August of that year, the United States had requested extradition of the couple to stand trial in the US for the double murder of the Heysons. Their daughter accepted extradition, returned to the States in May 1987, and confessed to being an accessory to the crime, claiming that Züring had actually committed the murders. She has since been sentenced to 90 years' imprisonment. Extradition to the US is being fought by Züring's lawyers, as Züring is hoping to be tried in the UK or Germany. Why? Because his punishment if convicted in either European country would be life imprisonment; in the States he would face the electric chair.

So, what is the dilemma? In 1972 Britain signed an extradition treaty with the United States. However, European tradition upholds the Convention of Human Rights, which, it is maintained, the United States contravenes by its treatment of prisoners facing the death penalty. Note that it is the treatment of prisoners which is the problem, not the death penalty itself. Most prisoners sentenced to capital punishment in the States wait an average six to eight years before the sentence is carried out. This delay is due to the appeals that take place after sentence has been passed – appeals intended to eradicate any trace of doubt as to the guilt of the offender. The European Court maintains that the delays are only a 'carrot you hold out while you torture people, till you kill them.' The European Court has, in fact, blocked the extradition of Jens Züring under Article 3 of the Convention of Human Rights, which states that no human being should be made to suffer inhumane or degrading treatment.

Should the British Government disobey the European Court ruling and extradite Jens Züring? Or should they break the extradition treaty of 1972 with the United States? Either way, their position is unenviable.

Vocabulary

5 Guessing meaning from context

A Find the word *upholds* in the text (line 36) and answer the following questions.

- What part of speech is it? (noun, verb, adverb etc)
- What is the general context of the word?
- Are there any clues which help you understand it?
- Can you guess its meaning?

Look at page 159 if you need some help.

B Find these words in the text, try to guess their meanings, then match them with the definitions below.

> *fateful* (para 1) *brutal* (para 1) *severed from* (para 1)
> *fraud* (para 1) *extradition* (para 1) *accessory* (para 1)
> *contravenes* (para 2) *eradicate* (para 2)
> *trace* (para 2) *ruling* (para 3) *unenviable* (para 3)

Definitions

1 the crime of gaining money or benefits by deceit or trickery
2 completely separated from
3 the deportation of an individual by one country to another where he/she will be tried in a court of law
4 very violent and harsh
5 not to be desired
6 someone who helps a criminal commit a crime
7 a tiny amount
8 get rid of completely
9 bringing death or disaster
10 goes against, comes into conflict with
11 a decision made by a court of law

6 Prefixes

A There are several words in the text that are formed with prefixes, such as those below.

> *imprisonment contravenes inhuman unenviable*

Underline the prefix in each of the above words. Now match the prefixes to the following meanings. (Two prefixes share the same meaning.)

1 the opposite or the negative of the root word
2 against, preventing something
3 in, towards, within

B All the words below start with one of the above prefixes – or look as if they do. Cross out any words which do not, in fact, contain a prefix. Use a dictionary if necessary. Then divide the words into three categories according to meanings 1–3 above.

> *immigrant inanimate contraption understand*
> *untidy contradict impatient imagine*
> *unimaginable imbibe undeniable contribute*
> *insistent universal uncertain incapable*
> *implant imperfect contraction*

C Match definitions 1 – 8 with a word from Section B.

1 drink, adopt others' ideas
2 not having any life
3 beyond our range of thought
4 certainly true, beyond question
5 not able to do something
6 someone who comes to a country to live there
7 not very neat, scruffy
8 establish something firmly or transfer something

Language work

7 The passive

A Look again at the text in Exercise 3. Find examples of each form of the passive listed below and complete the chart.

form	who / what?	form of *be*	past participle
present simple	the sentence	is	carried out
present continuous			
past simple			
present perfect			
past perfect			
modal			
infinitive			

B Complete this text with each of the verbs given in *italics* in the correct tense and the passive form.

Have you ever thought about the fact that your home could (1 *break into*)? If you live in an inner city for five years, your house is likely (2 *burgle*) at least once, according to statistics recently released. What should you do in the case of a break-in? First, if you have any suspicions that burglars are still inside your home, don't go in; phone the police from a neighbour's house immediately. If, as is more likely, you open the door to the living room and realise that you (3 *burgle*), phone the police first and then make a list of everything that (4 *take*). Try not to disturb anything – the police will ensure that a check (5 *make*) for fingerprints as soon as they arrive. While your property (6 *check*) for fingerprints, the police may want a statement, so you should be clear about all the details. Try to ascertain how the burglars got in – (7 *window / leave open*)? Or did they force a lock? This kind of detail can be important: an arrest (8 *make*) some years ago in North London after one unfortunate victim remembered that the only window that (9 *leave*) ajar was a very small bathroom window. The police realised that the break-in must (10 *carry out*) by a very small youth who knew the area, a description which corresponded to a young man at that time on probation for similar offences.

8 There are a number of reasons for using the passive voice.

A Match reasons 1 – 4 with examples a – d from the article in Exercise 3.

1 We don't know who did the action.
2 The subject of the action is known but unimportant.
3 We want to emphasise the object of the verb by putting it at the beginning of the sentence.
4 We want to describe a general feeling, not attributable to one person.

a *Derek Heyson and his wife were stabbed to death in their own home.*
b *Such force had been used to carry out the brutal murder that …*
c *Elizabeth and her boyfriend were arrested on a charge of cheque fraud.*
d *It was thought that the couple's daughter might be involved.*

B Work with a partner. Read the active sentences below and decide whether each one would be better in the passive. Make any necessary changes.

1 At the end of the trial the jury found the offender guilty.
2 Someone committed the murder with a great deal of force.
3 The United States requested extradition of the couple.
4 The British Government sent the couple back to the States.
5 Someone bought *Sunflowers* for £24 million. Van Gogh painted it.
6 The police told the crowds not to panic.
7 A cooperative formed by the staff took the company over.
8 My uncle left me several thousand dollars in his will.
9 People think that the serious crime rate is increasing.

Now change the sentences below from the passive into the active if you think they should be active.

10 She has been sentenced to 90 years' imprisonment.
11 My new house was visited by my two cousins last week.
12 This crime was not committed by the same person as the others.
13 It would have been done more quickly if you'd let me do it.
14 I was really disappointed by his actions.

9 It is quite common to use a passive to express a belief or feeling which may be held by a number of people, especially if we do not wish to indicate who holds the belief. For example:

It was thought that the couple's daughter might be involved.

Another way of expressing this is:

The couple's daughter was thought to be involved.

There is a slight grammatical difference between these two sentences. What is it?

Rewrite this short report, changing the form of the verbs in *italics* and any other words as necessary to use the structures in the examples above.

A local man, Mr Keith Gardner, was charged with fraud at Kingston Crown Court yesterday. The police (1) *allege* that he swindled an amount in excess of £20,000 from the charitable institution for which he worked. Colleagues at his office (2) *say* that he is a quiet man with few friends, but that they always (3) *considered* him an honest, hard-working member of the staff. Mr Gardner's neighbours (4) *think* that he may have taken the money in order to support his elderly mother, whom they (5) *believe* is in a home for the mentally handicapped. Apparently, people in the area (6) *have known* for some time that Mr Gardner is in financial trouble. The other local newspaper (7) *has reported* that Mr Gardner has been in fear of losing his house for the past few months, as he has been paying for his mother's care rather than the mortgage. We (8) *expect* the case to be heard in three weeks' time.

Study skills

10 *Semantic categorisation*

All the words below are to do with various aspects of crime. Look at the headings in the chart and decide which aspect of crime each word refers to. Then complete the chart.

fraud sentence capital punishment appeal stabbing murder imprisonment burglary rape mugging libel assault verdict judge convict

violent crime	non-violent crime	court/prison

Now add any other words that you can think of. Compare your chart with those of other students.

Listening skills

11 *Note-taking*

A ▣ Most people do not have to worry about dilemmas on the scale of the one described on page 46. Listen to this summary of a professional situation and take notes of the details.

B ▣ Complete the summary below, using your notes. Write as many words as necessary in each case.

While Brian was working as a (1) … at Bennett Electrics he had some problems with Marion Lynch, the new (2) … . At first she was very good and handled problems (3) … but after a while all that changed and she became (4) … , making errors such as (5) … . Brian had a problem when he was given a (6) … because Marion didn't put it through on time, and he had difficulties because he (7) … . He has now left the company and has found another job but he has since found out (8) … , which puts him in a very difficult position.

C ▣ Listen again to check your summary. What exactly is the dilemma in this situation?

12 *Multi-word verbs*

These multi-word verbs all appear in the listening.

*be out to   put oneself out   deal with   put through
come up   walk out   get away with   get on*

▣ In pairs, listen to them again in context and try to work out their meanings. First look at the particles: do any of them appear in your chart on page 154? If so, does that help you to work out the meanings?

Now match the verbs with definitions a – h and use them to complete the sentences.

Definitions
a handle, tackle
b make mistakes with no punishment
c arise
d have the intention to
e leave suddenly
f progress
g make a personal effort
h organise, effect

1 Maria seems to be … well with the new job.
2 He's very kind; he always … for his friends.
3 I was so disgusted with the play that I … .
4 A problem … with the new computer: it won't store data properly.
5 The new manager … increase productivity.
6 She's very good at … awkward clients.
7 That child's parents let him … murder!
8 You'll receive the goods shortly, but it always takes at least two weeks to … the order … .

Finally, enter these verbs in your chart on page 154.

13 *Listening to infer*

▣ Work in pairs. Listen to the dialogue between Marion Lynch's boss and a friend of Marion's. You should each make notes about the questions you are going to answer (see below).

Student A: Answer questions 1 – 5.
Student B: Answer questions 6 – 9.

1 What does Jennifer ask Steve?
2 What has happened over the last six weeks?
3 What is the major problem Jennifer mentions?
4 What does she discover about Marion's mother's death?
5 Does she believe that Steve has told her everything?
6 What does Steve say about 'the business with Brian'?
7 According to Steve, when did Marion's mother die?
8 What problems has Marion encountered recently?
9 Is Steve telling everything he knows?

Discuss the problem in your pairs. What do you think happened?

Read the report by Marion's psychiatrist on page 159.

Were you right?

Reading skills

White couple lose battle to bring up black foster child

1 A white couple failed in the Court of Appeal yesterday to win the black child that they had brought up since he was younger than a month old.

2 James and Lynne Melling, the foster parents, had remortgaged their home and spent £8,000 in a legal battle to prevent the child, now aged two, from being taken away from them.

3 The court was told that Mr Melling, aged 42, and his wife, aged 40, had 'showered the child, David, with love and affection since he was 24 days old in February 1989.' At the beginning of last year the Mellings said that they wanted to make a permanent home for the boy and bring him up with their other adopted son, Tyrone, aged nine. In November, however, Lancashire County Council told the couple that long-term carers had been found for David, who would eventually adopt him and bring him up with their two other adopted black children.

4 Matthias Kelly, counsel for Mr and Mrs Melling, told the court that the authority* had a rigid policy on placing children with families of the same cultural and ethnic background, but, he said, 'The council has paid too little attention to the deep and binding love the couple has bonded with David and he with them.'

5 Lord Justice Balcombe, one of the three judges hearing the appeal, said that there had never been any suggestion that the couple had given other than excellent care to the child. On the contrary, 'One cannot but feel sympathy for them after they raised David for the first two years of his life. They have obviously grown very fond of him and want to keep him on a permanent basis.'

6 The council said Mr and Mrs Melling knew that they were only short-term carers while a long-term solution was being sought. The judge said that it was for the court to interpret the law, and under the 1980 Child Care Act the couple would have to prove that the local authority had been so unreasonable and its decision so perverse, that no other local authority could make the same decision in similar circumstances.

7 Passing judgement, Lord Justice Balcombe said that in his view no court could come to that decision, and that the application for a judicial review must be dismissed. He could only sympathise with the couple who had 'taken on the task of giving love and care to children whose own parents did not.'

8 After the hearing, Mrs Melling said she had hoped that the interests of the child would outweigh the letter of the law. 'It's all very well these judges having sympathy for us. We have had lots of sympathy. Instead of sympathy, we want David returned to us, or, at the very least, a review of our case.

9 'It appears that, while they may agree with us emotionally, they do not want to set a precedent. Since David was taken away we have not heard a thing about him, not even a note to say how he is doing.'

* The *authority* here refers to the county council.

14 Finding evidence to support/refute a statement

A This newspaper article deals with a dilemma of a different nature. Read the article to answer questions 1 – 3.

  1 What is the difference between adoption and fostering?
  2 What kind of people are the Mellings?
  3 Why exactly did they lose the child?

B Find evidence in the text to support or refute these statements.

  1 The Mellings had brought David up well.
  2 The Mellings could easily afford the court case.
  3 The Mellings have not got any children of their own.
  4 Lancashire County Council agrees with integrating races.
  5 The judge and barristers were unsympathetic towards the Mellings.
  6 Lord Balcombe felt that the council had acted unreasonably.

C Read through the article again and list words and phrases from the article under the headings below.

the courts and the legal system	adopting children
Court of Appeal	foster parents

Compare your lists with your partner's.

Language awareness

15 *Words which are easily confused*

In the fourth paragraph of the article there are two words which look and sound very similar but which have different meanings. What are they and what do they mean?

Here are some more pairs. What is the meaning of each of the words?

principle, principal	canvass, canvas
stationary, stationery	affect, effect
serial, cereal	currant, current
precede, proceed	dessert, desert

If you are not sure of any of these, do as follows.

Student A: Turn to page 164.
Student B: Turn to page 172.

Language work

16 *Connectives of contrast (1)*

A   Look at these sentences and clauses from the article.

a   *In November, however, the county council told …* (para 3)
b   *… but, he said, 'The council has paid too little attention to the deep and binding love …'* (para 4)
c   *On the contrary, 'One cannot but feel sympathy … ,* (para 5)
d   *Instead of sympathy, we want David returned to us.* (para 8)
e   *It appears that, while they may agree with us emotionally, they do not want to set a precedent.* (para 9)

Each of the above expresses a contrast with an idea in the text that follows or precedes it. What is the contrast in each case? Underline the word or phrase (the connective) that makes the contrast. Which one of the connectors is used to introduce a clause?

Replace the connective (in *italics*) in each sentence 1 – 5 below with one from examples a – e above.

1   In the UK there are many children without parents. *Yet* it is difficult for childless couples to adopt.
2   *Although* everyone appreciates the reason for this decision, few people agree with it.
3   We were unhappy about the changes but we didn't complain. *Quite the opposite*, we decided to accept them gracefully.
4   *In place of* the settlement we wanted from the company, we were offered something totally unacceptable.
5   The authority is well-meaning. *Nevertheless*, it has disrupted a young child's life.

B   Join the two sentences in each item below with a connective from Exercise 16A. Make any other changes necessary.

1   Many childless couples in the UK desperately want to adopt a baby. Inflexible adoption regulations make this almost impossible for couples in their mid-thirties and older.
2   The regulations are intended to ensure that children go to good homes. They ensure that many stay in children's homes.
3   Couples often find it impossible to adopt in the UK. So they forget the UK and look abroad for their families.
4   This can be a solution for some. Only the wealthier couples can afford it.
5   Adopting overseas has been an option for some time. The British government is bringing in legislation to prevent it.

Writing skills

17 *Writing a summary (2)*

Read this summary of the article about the Heysons in Exercise 3. Take note of:

- which points have been taken from the article.
- how they are divided into paragraphs.
- how the sentences and paragraphs are linked.

In 1985 an elderly couple were murdered in Virginia. Their daughter and her German boyfriend were arrested in Britain some months later on an unrelated charge and the daughter was extradited to the States, where she confessed. The boyfriend, however, is fighting extradition because he wishes to be tried in Europe, where he would not face the death penalty.

The British Government faces a difficult dilemma here: on the one hand it has to return the German under the terms of its extradition treaty with the United States; on the other hand it is bound by the decision of the European Court not to extradite the man because the United States is considered to contravene the Convention of Human Rights in its treatment of prisoners facing the death penalty. Whichever way the British Government decides, it will be breaking a convention of some kind.

Now write a brief summary of the article in Exercise 14. Look back at Unit 2 (page 20) for the stages to follow in writing a summary. List the key points and compare with a partner. Then write your summary individually. Use the summary above as a rough model.

Speaking skills

18 *Expressing opinions formally*

Divide the following expressions into groups under the following three headings: giving an opinion, agreeing, disagreeing.

> *I'm afraid I can't go along with that.*
> *I'm totally in agreement with …*
> *In my opinion …*
> *If you ask me …*
> *You're right / X is quite right.*
> *I'm afraid I can't agree with …*
> *I think X is mistaken.*
> *That's absolutely right.*
> *I feel quite/very/rather strongly that …*

Try to add one or more phrases to each section. Now work in pairs. Agree or disagree with these statements about the article.

1 The Mellings were wrong to fight the decision – they are only foster parents.
2 The council's policy of placing children in appropriate ethnic backgrounds is correct.
3 More consideration should have been given to the child's feelings.

Now discuss your responses in groups.

Final task

19 *Debate*

Adoption of any available children should be open to all couples with no restrictions imposed by age, ethnic background, wealth or personality factors.

Treat the topic above as a formal debate.
Someone has to propose (support) the motion (the statement above), and another person seconds the proposer.
Someone has to oppose the motion, and another person seconds the opposer.

A The class divides into four groups: the proposer, the proposer's seconder, the opposer, and the opposer's seconder.

Proposer and seconder groups: Look at page 164.

Opposer and seconder groups: Look at page 178.

B Discuss the questions on these pages for about ten minutes and elect a spokesperson.

C The four elected spokespeople go to the front of the class. They present their arguments to the class in this order:
proposer, opposer, seconder for the proposer, seconder for the opposer.
The seconders should try to present different arguments from the proposer and opposer.
The rest of the class listens to the four speakers.
Then they can ask questions and raise other issues.

D A vote is taken to see whether or not the motion is carried. The four speakers may not vote.

Introduction

1 Which are the most popular school subjects?
The following questionnaire should help you find out.

Follow this procedure.

1 Complete Column A with your prediction of the general popularity of each subject.
2 Now complete Column B with your personal preferences.
3 Join a partner and complete Column C with his/her scores.
4 Join with another pair to complete Columns D and E.
5 Add the numbers (B – E) together across the chart to get a total for Column F.
6 Now calculate the totals as a 1 – 10 score (the highest number will be 10, the lowest number will be 1) and write the number in Column G.

	A	B	C	D	E	F	G
Subject	Prediction	You	Your partner	Rest of group		Total	Score
Art							
Biology							
Chemistry							
Foreign languages							
Geography							
History							
Literature							
Music							
Physics							
Sports							

SCORING SYSTEM: 10 = most popular   1 = least popular

How do the scores in Column G compare with your prediction? Compare your Column G scores with other groups to find out the overall popularity of subjects in the class.

2 How much do you know about the educational background of famous people?
With a partner, match these famous people with the information below:

1 This person applied to Art School in Austria but failed the entrance test.
2 This person is a qualified English teacher.
3 This person has a Master of Arts degree from Yale university.
4 This majestic person never went to school at all.
5 This person studied for a law degree in Paris.
6 This person is a qualified research chemist.

What are their names?
When you finish check your answers on page 159.

WHO NEEDS A DEGREE?

No number of letters after your name can teach you about life.

KATE SAUNDERS takes a roll call of people who, like her, have succeeded without going to university.

1 In the tightly-knit literary circles of the metropolis, people don't ask you which university you went to. They want to know how they could have possibly missed you at Oxford or Cambridge. Like 93% of the adult population, I did not go to any university at all, and this has become faintly embarrassing since I accepted the honour of helping to judge this year's Booker Prize. Certain colleagues look down their noses when they discover I have no dreaming spires in my CV. The sorry truth is that while my contemporaries were frolicking in the groves of Academe, I was playing a nurse in a TV soap, and toting a spear at the National Theatre.

2 However, I am in excellent company. My fellow graduates of the University of Life include not only entrepreneurial wizards such as Alan Sugar of Amstrad, but also politicians such as John Major and James Callaghan. In the literary field, P. D. James, the thinking person's crime novelist, best-selling romancer Jilly Cooper, and playwright Tom Stoppard have achieved eminence without university degrees.

3 The fact is, although universities are wonderful places, putting yourself through one of them is no guarantee of brilliance. And many people who have engineered their own education actually believe that they would have been less successful if they had slapped a three-year preservation order on their adolescence and gone to university.

4 The novelist Lisa St Aubin de Teran was too busy roaming the world and picking up three foreign languages in her youth to fit in going to Cambridge, as she had originally planned. 'I probably learned more, living the life I did,' she says.

5 Instead of swotting for exams, de Teran was managing a sugar plantation on a remote *hacienda* in the Venezuelan Andes. 'When I was younger I did regret not going to university,' she admits. 'It seemed such an easy way to spend three years. But I was 25 when I returned from Venezuela, and I couldn't really see myself sitting there with a lot of eighteen-year-olds.'

6 Exotic experiences are far more useful to a novelist than a degree. However, the graduate-dominated world of the media is another matter. So it's refreshing to learn that Michael Grade, head of Channel 4, never went to university. Neither did Anne Wintour, head of features at BBC Radio. 'I remember feeling self-conscious about it at first,' she says, 'but I stopped worrying about it years ago. Graduates get on by conforming and I think people without degrees tend to be more original.'

7 'It all comes back to experience of life,' declares Ann Winterton, Conservative MP for Congleton. Like Winston Churchill before her, she has no degree, having entered politics 'straight from the kitchen sink' in 1983. 'No number of letters after your name can teach you about life. I used to be rather in awe of people with qualifications. But, being self-taught allows you to do things in your own way. I think a lot of people go to university to put off the evil hour of getting stuck into a real job – it can be a soft option.'

8 I must confess, it's this soft option element which makes me wish sometimes that I had gone to university – it does sound such fun, discussing the meaning of life over midnight coffee. And there's a lot to be said for the classic liberal education which broadens the mind by filling it with a lot of delightful and rather useless knowledge. By the time you leave you may not be able to type, but you sure as hell know about Cosimo de Medici.

9 Picking up culture without a degree is rather like doing Venice without a guide book. You may not have anyone to advise you where to look for the highlights so you are forced to find them for yourself. And you will be freer to form an original opinion, uncoloured by those who wore down the stones before you.

Speaking skills

4 *Checking and clarifying information*

Study this short dialogue between two students discussing the article above.

A The author says that all her colleagues look down their noses when they find she hasn't been to university, doesn't she?

B Not exactly, she actually says that only certain of her colleagues look down their noses.

A Oh, I see.

Work in pairs and make mini-dialogues like the model.

Student A: Turn to page 164.
Student B: Turn to page 172.

3 From the results of Exercise 2 you might feel that educational qualifications are not really relevant to people's careers. The newspaper article above examines this idea.

Read the article and find three reasons which are given to support the idea that it is better not to go to university.

- Do you agree with the author's opinion?
- Can you think of any arguments against the three reasons she gives for not going to university?

Vocabulary

5 Match the words from the article 1 – 10 with their definitions a – j.

1	*tightly-knit* (para 1)	a	shy, embarrassed
2	*faintly* (para 1)	b	carrying
3	*toting* (para 1)	c	learning without formally studying
4	*brilliance* (para 3)	d	an easy or lazy alternative
5	*roaming* (para 4)	e	studying very hard
6	*picking up* (para 4)	f	slightly
7	*swotting* (para 5)	g	exceptional intelligence or creativity
8	*hacienda* (para 5)	h	travelling widely without a specific destination
9	*self-conscious* (para 6)	i	closely connected, cohesive
10	*soft option* (para 7)	j	a type of farm

Metaphors

The article contains several metaphors – words or expressions which are not used in their everyday sense but have a special figurative meaning.

With a partner, find expressions 1 – 8 in the article and study the context. Then match each expression with one of the clues below and use the clue to help you work out the meaning of the expression. One clue refers to two expressions.

1 *look down their noses* (para 1)
2 *dreaming spires* (para 1)
3 *groves of Academe* (para 1)
4 *wizards* (para 2)
5 *preservation order* (para 3)
6 *straight from the kitchen sink* (para 7)
7 *uncoloured* (para 9)
8 *wore down the stones* (para 9)

Clues

a Universities are academies of learning. Some of the older buildings have towers with pointed roofs.
b Making a lot of money from business is almost magical.
c You spend a lot of time here as an average housewife.
d Many historic buildings cannot be altered because of special laws which protect them from change.
e With the right camera lens you can make a grey sky look blue.
f So many people visit Westminster Abbey that the floor carvings have almost disappeared.
g Why do tall people always feel superior to short people?

Language work

6 *Verbs + -ing or infinitive*

A REGRET, GO ON, STOP, REMEMBER, FORGET
Which of the verbs above can you find in the extracts below? Are they followed by -ing or the infinitive?

> *When I was younger I did regret not going to university ...*
> *I remember feeling self-conscious about it at first ...*
> *I stopped worrying about it years ago.*

Now look at these sentences and answer the same two questions.

> *I regret to tell you that your application has failed.*
> *I must remember to sign the course registration forms.*
> *I stopped to buy a newspaper on my way home from college.*

Compare the examples and explain when we use the -ing form and when we use the infinitive after these verbs. (Thinking about time and direction might help you.)
Note that *go on* and *forget* follow the same rules.

B ALLOW, ADVISE, FORBID, PERMIT
Look at these extracts from the article. Ask yourself the same questions as at the beginning of Exercise 6A.

> *Being self-taught allows you to do things in your own way.*
> *You may not have anyone to advise you where to look for the highlights.*

Now look at these sentences. Ask yourself the same questions again.

> *The college only allows smoking in designated areas.*
> *The school does not advise parking on the main road.*

Compare the examples and explain when we use the -ing form and when we use the infinitive.
Note that *forbid* and *permit* follow the same rules.

C Now complete these sentences using the correct form of the verb in brackets.

1 We do not allow ... in the school corridors. (run)
2 I often regret ... music as a child. (not study)
3 The rules don't permit candidates ... a calculator in the exam. (use)
4 I stopped ... while I was pregnant. (teach)
5 Most driving schools advise ... a short course before going out on the road with friends. (take)
6 I went on ... a Master's degree after I finished my Bachelor's degree. (take)
7 Don't forget ... your dictionaries for the test tomorrow. (bring)
8 When my brother broke his leg he had to stop ... to skiing classes. (go)
9 I absolutely forbid you ... a mini-skirt again! (wear)
10 We regret ... you that you have failed the entrance test. (inform)

Reading skills

7 *Understanding anaphoric reference*

We often use reference words in written text to refer back to something and to avoid repeating information. Look at this example.

> Like 93% of the adult population, I did not go to any university at all, and <u>this</u> has become faintly embarrassing since I accepted the honour of helping to judge this year's Booker Prize.

> this = *not going to university*

Now explain what the underlined words in these two extracts refer to.

The fact is, although universities are wonderful places, putting yourself through one of <u>them</u>[1] is no guarantee of brilliance. And many people who have engineered their own education actually believe that <u>they</u>[2] would have been less successful if <u>they</u>[3] had slapped a three-year preservation order on their adolescence and gone to university.

I must confess, it's this soft option element which makes me wish sometimes that I had gone to university – <u>it</u>[4] does sound such fun, discussing the meaning of life over midnight coffee. And there's a lot to be said for the classic liberal education which broadens the mind by filling <u>it</u>[5] with a lot of delightful and rather useless knowledge. By the time you leave you may not be able to type, but you sure as hell know about Cosimo de Medici. Picking up culture without a degree is rather like doing Venice without a guide book. You may not have anyone to advise you where to look for the highlights so you are forced to find <u>them</u>[6] for yourself. And you will be freer to form an original opinion, uncoloured by those who wore down the stones before you.

Listening skills

8 *Listening and transcoding to a chart*

Many people believe that education is a basic human right. Look at this extract from the *United Nations Declaration of Human Rights*.

> *Article 26. (1).* Everyone has the right to education. Education shall be free, at least in the elementary and fundamental stages. Elementary education shall be compulsory. Technical and professional education shall be made generally available and higher education shall be equally accessible to all on the basis of merit.

All the members of the United Nations have signed this declaration. Do you think that they all provide *free* and *equally accessible* education?

In this exercise you will be able to compare the type of education provided in different countries.

Look at the chart on the right. Using the *Britain* column as a model, fill in the column headed *Your country*.

🖭   Listen to the interview with Jamie Shambaugh and complete the gaps for the column headed *The United States*.

🖭   Listen to the interview with Ken Miki and complete the gaps for the column headed *Japan*.

Now, in small groups, compare the four education systems. In your opinion, what are the advantages and disadvantages of each system?

STATE EDUCATION SYSTEMS

Age	Britain	Your Country	The United States	Japan
4			pre-school	
5				
6				
7	primary school			
8				
9				
10				
11				
12			junior high school	
13	secondary school			
14				
15				
16	secondary school/college			
17				
18				
19	college/ university		university	
20				
21				
22				
23				

Pronunciation

9 *British and American English*

A   Listen to this extract from the interview with Jamie Shambaugh.

> *Um, the age of five you enrol in kindergarten, which is the lowest level of <u>proper</u> education, and kindergarten is divided into <u>afternoon</u> and morning sessions and, um, you spend <u>half</u> the day …*

Now listen to the same words spoken by a British actor. What did you notice about the three underlined words?

From these three words can you work out the two most important differences between British and American pronunciation?

B   Listen to the models on the tape. For each group of three words you will hear first the British and then the American pronunciation.

A	B	C	D	E
half	proper	water	missile	due
after	mother	winter	fragile	tune
bath	lover	better	agile	new

Can you explain the pronunciation rule for each group?

C   Now listen to the words again. Decide whether you can hear the British or American pronunciation of each word and tick the relevant column in the chart below.

Word	British	American
1 half	☐	☐
2 after	☐	☐
3 bath	☐	☐
4 proper	☐	☐
5 mother	☐	☐
6 lover	☐	☐
7 water	☐	☐
8 winter	☐	☐
9 better	☐	☐
10 missile	☐	☐
11 fragile	☐	☐
12 agile	☐	☐
13 due	☐	☐
14 tune	☐	☐
15 new	☐	☐

Vocabulary

10 *Educational word groups*

Find the odd word out in each of these short lists and make a note of what the other three have in common.

1 high school kindergarten edifice college
2 writing co-educational reading copying
3 cursive swotting revision studying
4 boarding elementary private compulsory
5 university junior high academic primary
6 degree certificate diploma course
7 childhood pre-school adolescence infancy
8 professor undergraduate pupil student

11 In Britain the educational system is different from many other countries because of the large number of traditional private schools which still exist.

In the extracts on the right, two well-known British authors write about some of their school experiences forty years ago. Work in two large groups, each reading one extract and answering the questions below.

Group A: Read Extract A.
Group B: Read Extract B.

1 What kind of school did the author attend?
2 What do you think was the author's social background?
3 What was discipline like at the author's school?
4 What sort of character did the author have as a child?
5 How do you think his/her education has affected the author's personality?

Compare answers with another student from your group.

Now find a partner from the other group. Together compare your answers and then decide if you agree with the following statements. Use evidence from the article you have read to back up your opinions.

• A private education makes people self-confident.
• Strict discipline makes people subservient and insecure.
• A strict atmosphere is the best for effective learning.

A   JILLY COOPER

My outrageousness dates back to when I was nicknamed 'The Unholy Terror' at my boarding school. I was very very naughty – out of control. I had been terribly spoilt at home by lovely parents whom I adored. Miss Harris, our easy-going house mistress, was debagged by us. We got her out of her petticoat, poor woman. I remember one night we stuffed my pyjamas with pillows and hung them out of the window. The others rushed to Miss Harris and said, 'Jilly's so unhappy at school she's trying to commit suicide, she's hanging herself!' She ran in and tugged what she thought was me back. I remember laughing from under the bed. Of course I feel ashamed now, very guilty.

B   DEREK JAMESON

I still have nightmares about my schooldays and childhood. My education began on the streets of Hackney, East London. The setting was always a battlefield, mud and dirt, people fighting, poverty everywhere, the streets ruled by bullies and bigots. Those early years have dominated my life and that is why I laugh so much now, to take away the pain.

My first school was Detmold Road Elementary, a forbidding Victorian edifice near Hackney Marshes. The way we were taught the three Rs was to whack it into us. I remember Mr Hart had a cane hanging from one of the pegs by the side of the blackboard. His mission in life was to persuade us that knowledge was the key to success, our passport out of that bleak world. You were given ten words to learn overnight and if you didn't know how to spell them next morning he would give you a hard crack against the ear. Can you imagine that today? Complaining to your parents was impossible in those days.

Language work

12 *Gerund or infinitive phrases*

Look at this sentence from Extract B.

Complaining to your parents was impossible in those days.

This can also be written:

To complain to your parents was impossible in those days.
It was impossible to complain to your parents in those days.

Which of the three forms is usually used in formal written English only?

Rewrite the passage below using gerund phrases to replace the underlined verbs, changing the word order as necessary.

Language teaching policy
People say it is easy to learn a foreign language when one is young. To acquire a language is something we all do in our infancy without even thinking about it. Thus we believe that to study a foreign language in kindergarten is a vital first step to eventual mastery. It is ideal to start at the age of five or six.

Rewrite the passage below in a formal style using infinitive phrases to replace the underlined verbs.

Mertonleigh School
Studying at Mertonleigh is a way of experiencing a unique and stimulating environment. Learning in our quiet and contemplative surroundings is a way of taking part in a centuries-old scholarly tradition.

Writing skills

13 *Recounting an event or experience*

A In Exercise 11 Jilly Cooper recounts an event at her boarding school. Put these headings into the correct sequence to describe her account.

☐ an explanation of how she feels about it now
☐ an explanation of the background
☐ a narrative account of the event
☐ an introductory link between the past and present
☐ a description of the characters involved

B You have been asked to write a short article (250 words) about an amusing or unusual childhood experience for your school magazine.

Use the headings above to help you organise your account. You can write about something that really happened to you or you can make up a story from your imagination.

If you can't think of anything, use the picture for ideas.

Final task

14 *Decision-making*

Work in groups of three or four. You are the timetabling committee at Winterbrook High School, preparing the timetable for the fourth form (thirteen- to fourteen-year-olds).

A Look at the list of subjects below. The fourth form has thirty one-hour lessons a week. English and Mathematics are compulsory subjects in your school, as shown in the timetable below. These lessons have already been fixed and cannot be changed. This leaves 24 lessons for other subjects. Look at the list of subjects. Decide which ones are the most important for thirteen- to fourteen-year-olds and approximately how many lessons of each there should be. Make a note of your decision.

*Art Biology Chemistry Computer studies
Economics Geography History Literature
Music Physics Sports*

B Now you are going to complete the timetable.

Student A: You are responsible for the part-time teaching staff. Turn to page 164.
Student B: You are responsible for the full-time teachers and for liaison with the other timetable committees. Turn to page 172.
Student C: You are the school principal.
Because of problems with the school budget you can't afford separate teachers for every subject. Most of your teachers teach two subjects, and many of them are part-time (they also work at other schools). Look at the timetable below. Use the information from your colleagues to work out the best way of completing it and fill in the lesson boxes with the name of the subject and teacher.

WINTERBROOK HIGH SCHOOL: FOURTH YEAR TIMETABLE						
LESSONS	9 – 10	10 – 11	11 – 12	1 – 2	2 – 3	3 – 4
Monday	English Ms Gray					Maths Mr Karl
Tuesday					Maths Mr Karl	
Wednesday		English Ms Gray				
Thursday				English Ms Gray		
Friday						Maths Mr Karl

Unit 8   Round the World

Introduction

1 For centuries people have dreamed of travelling around the globe. Since the advent of intercontinental air travel this dream has become an everyday reality. *Trailfinders* is a London travel agency which specialises in round-the-world tickets. The map shows the major stopping points on their worldwide routes.

Working in small groups, try to agree on these questions.

- If you were travelling around the world,
- a which three destinations would be 'must sees'?
- b which five further destinations would be most worth seeing?
- c which three destinations would not be worth seeing?

2 Work in pairs.

Student A: Turn to page 165.
Student B: You are planning a round the world trip for which you are prepared to pay up to £1500. Choose six or seven destinations from the map, remembering that you must always travel in the same direction – either eastwards or westwards – and that your starting and finishing point will be London. Make a note of your proposed route. Your partner has the *Trailfinders* itineraries and will help you select the best route once you have explained your proposed trip.

When you have finished, compare your choice with the rest of the class. Which itinerary is the most popular?

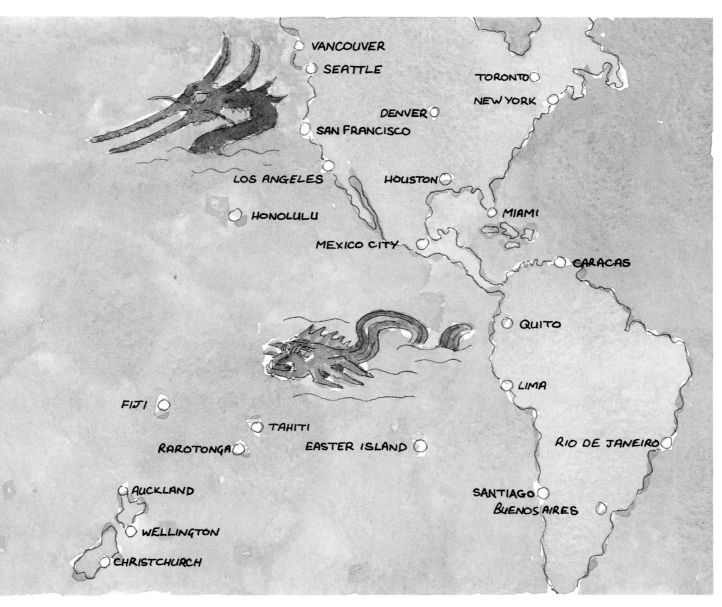

VANCOUVER
SEATTLE
TORONTO
NEW YORK
DENVER
SAN FRANCISCO
LOS ANGELES
HOUSTON
HONOLULU
MIAMI
MEXICO CITY
CARACAS
QUITO
LIMA
FIJI
TAHITI
RAROTONGA
EASTER ISLAND
RIO DE JANEIRO
AUCKLAND
SANTIAGO
BUENOS AIRES
WELLINGTON
CHRISTCHURCH

3 This is Phileas Fogg, fictional hero of Jules Verne's classic novel *Around the World in Eighty Days*. What do you know about Phileas Fogg and his round-the-world adventure?

A   Look through the flyleaf of Jules Verne's novel and answer these questions.

- Who are the three main characters in the novel?
- Why does Phileas Fogg try to go around the world in eighty days?
- What sort of problems occur on the journey?

AROUND THE WORLD IN EIGHTY DAYS

by Jules Verne

Around the World in Eighty Days is a marvellous journey of the imagination. The secret lies in the delicious nostalgia of Verne's story of globe encirclement. Readers today are just as intrigued as to how Phileas Fogg can make good his bet at the Reform Club, interrupting his punctiliously regulated life to embark on the adventure of the eighty days. In fact what would be so easy for him to accomplish in the jet age is exciting and breath-taking in his feverish boardings of steamer and train. Passepartout, who accompanies him, is one of the most engaging manservants in all literature – French to his backbone, resourceful and loyal.

Zest is added to the tale by the fact that on the day that Fogg takes up the challenge there is a bank robbery, and the assiduous detective, Fix, suspects that Fogg is the guilty party trying to escape. Fix applies for a warrant of arrest, but in order not to lose touch with his quarry he leaves before the warrant arrives; and it is a question of whether the warrant will reach Fix in time for him to detain Fogg on British territory. The three then share incredible adventures all round the world. Quixotic detours are made – to save an Indian widow from *suttee*, and again to save Passepartout from a Red Indian threat. Storms and other setbacks increase the suspense and threaten to wreck Fogg's schedule, but Verne reserves for the ending the brilliant eleventh-hour stroke which, if one has not read the story, or has forgotten it, must be kept for the reading.

B   With a partner, discuss the differences between a round-the-world trip in 1873 and nowadays. Complete the chart with your ideas.

	present day	1873
means of transport		
customs and passport regulations		
standard of comfort and hygiene		

C   Read the flyleaf of Palin's book and compare the description of his journey with your ideas in the chart. Are there any differences?

AROUND THE WORLD IN EIGHTY DAYS

In the autumn of 1988 Michael Palin set out from the Reform Club to circumnavigate the world, following the route taken by Phileas Fogg 115 years earlier. The rules were simple. He had to make the journey in eighty days and never use aircraft, only forms of transport that would have been available to Fogg.

But if the rules were simple, nothing else was. Palin's Passepartout was not a loyal French manservant but a five-person BBC film crew, there to record his every move. The golden age of sea travel with regular timetables and ocean liners was, he discovered, long since dead. State cabins and deck quoits were replaced by crowded Red Sea ferries, mattresses of date sacks on an open dhow, hospital beds on a Yugoslav freighter and bunks on eerily creaking container ships.

He discovered, too, that the days are past when a signed photo of Queen Victoria was enough to admit an Englishman anywhere. Passports, visas, customs forms, carnets delayed him at every frontier – and there were seventeen of them.

Whether seeing Venice from the back of a rubbish barge, riding around the Pyramids on a camel called Michael, drifting helplessly in the Straits of Hormuz after engine failure, being shaved by a blind barber in Bombay, attacked by a cockatoo in Hong Kong, served a snake's bladder liqueur in China or subjected to a bizarre initiation ritual as he crossed the International Date Line, Palin managed to do everything the hard way. Fogg brought back a Princess, Palin a lot of dirty laundry and a television series that stands as an unparalleled tribute to man's ability to make life difficult for himself.

This book is the story of, and the story behind, the making of the series. Based on Palin's daily diaries it is a full, frank, no-holds-barred account of a journey that turned into a great twentieth century adventure.

Laugh, cry, but for God's sake buy your own copy!

Vocabulary

4   *Travel and transport*

A   In this exercise the meanings given below are in the order in which the words occur in the texts.

Find words with these meanings from the Jules Verne flyleaf.

1   a sentimental desire or feeling for the past
2   a gentleman's personal valet or male assistant
3   a sense of stimulation or excitement
4   a person or animal which is being hunted
5   to prevent from leaving or to keep waiting
6   an Indian ritual in which a widow is burnt alive on her husband's funeral pyre

Find words with these meanings from the Michael Palin flyleaf.

7   a luxurious kind of bedroom found on large ships (two words)
8   the name used for the floor surfaces on ships
9   containers made of rough cloth
10   a long flat-bottomed boat for use on inland waters
11   a large tropical bird with a crest on its head
12   a strong sweet alcoholic drink

B   The passages contain many words connected with travelling and with personal impressions, reactions and feelings. Find words from the two texts to complete these lists.

means of transport	adjectives	nouns connected with travel
ocean liner	breath-taking	detour
dhow	brilliant	route

Study skills

5   *Adjective collocation*

Adjectives always describe or refer to a noun, although the noun can sometimes be implied rather than stated. Compare these two examples from the Jules Verne flyleaf.

adjective   noun it describes

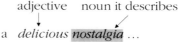

a   *delicious* **nostalgia** …

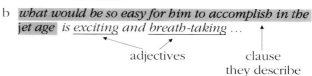

b   **what would be so easy for him to accomplish in the jet age** *is* *exciting* *and* *breath-taking* …

adjectives   clause
they describe

In Example b the adjectives describe a clause which replaces a noun. What is the implied noun that they describe?

It is important to know which noun an adjective is describing because not all adjectives can be used with all nouns. For example, which of the following three phrases are not possible in English?

a loyal manservant   a loyal journey   a loyal nostalgia

Can you make a rule about the collocation of the adjective *loyal*?

The chart below shows the types of noun with which some of the adjectives in the two flyleaves collocate.

ADJECTIVE/NOUN COLLOCATION (TYPE OF NOUN DESCRIBED)			
person	event	written account	means of transport
engaging (manservant)	breath-taking (journey)	frank (account)	crowded (ferries)

Add more examples from the flyleaves to each of the columns.

Compare your lists with a partner. Decide if any of the adjectives can be used with other types of noun and write an example of each, as shown below.

'Crowded' can be used to describe places:
I feel uncomfortable in crowded clubs.

Language work

6   Groups of nouns

A   There are three main ways that nouns can be grouped together in English. Look at the six examples taken from the flyleaf of Jules Verne's book and divide them into three types.

> *Verne's story   the adventure of the eighty days*
> *manservant   bank robbery*
> *a warrant of arrest   Fogg's schedule*

Now match each type with the correct definition below.

a   compound nouns
The first noun classifies the second; we use this type to describe common well-known things. The two nouns can be written in one of three ways: as two separate words, as two separate words joined with a hyphen, or as one word.

b   the *'s* genitive
The first noun refers to something living, a particular place or person, or something closely related to human activity.

c   the *of* structure
This structure refers to something inanimate. It cannot be used where the subject is a particular person.

B   Re-write sentences 1 – 8, where necessary using the most suitable noun form for the words in brackets, as in the example.

> According to (the book written by Palin) he travelled with a large (group of people whose profession is making films).
> *According to Palin's book he travelled with a large film crew.*

1   (The reputation made by Jules Verne) is based on the fact that he virtually invented the type of book known as (fiction which is based on the possibilities of science).
2   (The suspicion of Fix) is that Fogg is a (person who has robbed a bank).
3   (Navigation all the way around the world) is much easier nowadays because of (aircraft powered by jet engines).
4   (The journey of Palin) is made more difficult by the number of (forms required by customs) he has to fill in.
5   (Tables showing the time of departures etc.) seem to be much less reliable now than they were in (the time of Jules Verne).
6   (The task of Palin) was to use only those (forms of transport) which had been available in the nineteenth century.
7   (The purpose of the journey) undertaken by Fogg was to win a bet with his fellow (members of a club).
8   (The diary of Palin) records many of the dangers of (travel on the sea) including (failure of the engine) and storms.

Pronunciation

7   Stress in compound words

A   Underline the main stress in the following compound words.

> *manservant   housewife   bank robbery   film crew*
> *jet engine   blackbird   grandmother   pair work*

☐ Listen to the words on tape to check your answers.

B   ☐ Now listen to these two sentences and answer the questions below.

a   *She's an English teacher and she comes from Paris.*
b   *She's an English teacher and her subject is Geography.*

Which sentence contains a compound word?
What is the difference between the stress patterns of the two sentences?
Can you make a general rule about the usual position of the main stress in these compound words?

C   Work in pairs. In each of the pairs of sentences, **a** contains a compound word and **b** does not. Take it in turns to read the sentences to your partner in jumbled order. Your partner must decide whether you are reading **a** or **b**.

1   a   I saw a blackbird in the garden.
    b   I saw a black bird in the garden.

2   a   My mother enjoys cooking apples.
    b   My mother enjoys cooking apples.

3   a   Could you give me that paperback sometime?
    b   Could you give me that paper back sometime?

4   a   Have you ever seen a pair of walking shoes?
    b   Have you ever seen a pair of walking shoes?

5   a   He's a grandfather.
    b   He's a grand father.

6   a   For some reason my son loves washing machines.
    b   For some reason my son loves washing machines.

Reading skills

8 *Recognising tone and purpose*

Now that you have studied the flyleaves in detail you should be able to form an opinion abut the tone of the writing.

Look carefully at these short extracts from the texts.

> *a marvellous journey of the imagination*
> *Readers today are just as intrigued*
> *exciting and breath-taking*
> *Storms and other setbacks increase the suspense*
> *an unparalleled tribute to man's ability to make*
> *   life difficult for himself*
> *Laugh, cry, but for God's sake buy your own copy*

Which one of the following adjectives best describes the language in these extracts?

> *emotional objective enthusiastic exaggerated*
> *honest*

Why has this type of language been used?
What does this tell you about the purpose of a flyleaf?

9 Work in pairs. Look at this list of things Phileas Fogg took on his journey.

Phileas Fogg	You
a travelling bag	
two woollen shirts	
three pairs of stockings	
a macintosh	
a travelling cloak	
some stout shoes	
Bradshaw's 'Continental Railway, Steam Transit and General Guide'	
£20,000 in cash	

Together make a list of the things you would take on a present-day round-the-world trip. Everything you choose must fit into a small suitcase, so limit yourself to ten items of clothing and ten other things.

When you have finished, compare your list with Michael Palin's on page 159.
Can you suggest any reasons for the similarities and differences between the three lists?

Listening skills

10 *Listening to form judgements*

A   🔲   Terri and Simon are talking about their experiences of long-distance travel. Listen and number the places listed below according to the order in which you hear them. Two of the places are not mentioned at all.

☐ Tijuana   ☐ Moscow
☐ New Haven   ☐ New York
☐ London   ☐ Hong Kong
☐ Singapore   ☐ California

B   🔲   Now listen again and complete the notes using a few words. You do not need to write full sentences.

Simon obtained a special visa which allowed him to (1) … . Unfortunately he didn't know that this visa (2) … for three months. As a result he got into a lot of trouble at the (3) … in Tijuana. Now he thinks it's very foolish to travel without (4) … .

Terri bought her ticket to Hong Kong after she saw an advertisement in (5) … . The flight was delayed and arrived (6) … in Moscow. She couldn't get on the next flight because her ticket was only valid for (7) … . Terri had to spend three days in the hotel. She couldn't go out because she didn't (8) … .

C   Now imagine that you and your partner are considering a round-the-world trip. Use the information from Terri's and Simon's stories to decide the following.

a   what you should do before buying a cheap ticket
b   what precautions you should take with visas and customs regulations

Compare your judgements with another pair. Did you reach the same conclusions? Why/why not?

Speaking skills

11 *Paraphrasing*

Work in pairs. Three extracts have been taken from each of the two books, describing the same three points in each journey.

Student A: Your extracts are on page 165.
Student B: Your extracts are on page 172.

Look at your three extracts and identify which book each extract comes from. Then, without reading aloud, describe your extracts to your partner. Together decide which extracts match, then decide which of the following they relate to.

a Suez   d crossing the Pacific
b Bombay   e trains in America
c crossing the Atlantic   f trains in China

What clues helped you to identify the book and the situation?

Language work

12 *Inversion after negative adverbials*

Look at these examples from the extracts.

> *Rarely had he seen such a curious spectacle.*
> *Never was it more than a gale, but unfortunately it stayed obstinately in the south-east …*

What do you notice about the subjects and verbs? Why do you think the author has done this? It is possible to invert the subject and verb after the following negative adverbials.

> *rarely   never   nowhere   not since*
> *not until   never again   never before*

Rewrite sentences 1 – 5 to make them more emphatic. Use a suitable negative adverbial from the list above, as in the example.

> The detective wouldn't be able to relax until he caught Fogg.
> *Not until Fogg was caught would the detective be able to relax.*

1 There had been very few times that Palin had been so tired.
2 Passepartout had never had such an adventure before.
3 Such a journey has not been possible since the invention of the jet engine.
4 There isn't anywhere where you can escape timetables and schedules.
5 World travel will not be possible for everyone until airfares become much cheaper.

Now rewrite sentences 6 – 8 to make them *less* emphatic.

6 Rarely have I read such an exciting adventure story.
7 Nowhere would you find such colourful ceremonies.
8 Never before had Palin had such a difficult challenge.

Writing skills

13 *Physical description*

A   Below are the two descriptions of trains from the extracts in Exercise 11.

> … Amtrak Superliners, two-tiered coaches in silver, red and blue livery. Its interior, like the bullet train in Japan, but unlike the trains in China and India, owes much to aircraft design. A lightweight shell, moulded seats in open coach formation, inadequate but neatly-designed lights, fold-down tables. There are also sleeping cabins … *(Michael Palin)*

> The carriage he occupied was a sort of long omnibus carried by two four-wheel bogies, which enabled it to take sharp curves. It had no compartments; two rows of seats lined its sides, and between them was an aisle which led to the lavatories and dressing-rooms with which each carriage was provided. Throughout the length of the train the carriages were linked together by gangways so that the passengers could walk from one end of the convoy to the other. There were saloon-cars, observation-cars, dining-cars and refreshment-cars at their disposal. *(Jules Verne)*

From the two extracts find further examples of the following features of descriptive writing and add them to the chart.

DESCRIPTIVE FEATURE	EXAMPLES
comparing similar objects	*a sort of long omnibus* *owes much to aircraft* *design* …
showing the position and relationship between objects	*rows of seats* *open coach formation* …
describing colour, material, shape or construction	*moulded seats* *a lightweight shell* …
describing the function of objects	*fold-down tables* *dining-cars* …

B   Now work in pairs. Look at the photograph on page 65 of the first-class cabin of a jumbo jet.
With your partner make notes under the following headings. (You may find a dictionary helpful.)

> Interior surfaces of cabin
> Seating arrangement
> Seating material and functions
> Position of aisle etc.

Compare your notes with another pair and add any new notes to your list.

C   Transpacific Airlines has launched a competition with the prize of a free round-the-world ticket. The prize will go to the person who writes the best description of a Transpacific Airlines first-class cabin.

Use the photograph and your notes from above to write a 250-word description of the cabin.

   ***Transpacific Airlines***

WIN A ***FREE*** ROUND-THE-WORLD TICKET!

Can you write a detailed and accurate description of our luxurious first-class cabin? If so, you could win a fabulous trip of a lifetime.

Call toll free 0800 999 3000 for details and entry forms.

Final task

14 *The Round-the-World Game*

Turn to page 156 to play this game. You can find examples of test box questions on page 160.

Unit 9 You Are What You Eat

Introduction

1 What kind of reputation does British food have internationally? Here are five famous (or infamous!) British dishes.

Work in groups of five.
Each of you has the name of one of these dishes together with half of the description and half of another dish's description (but not necessarily in that order!).
Get together to see if you can match up the halves of the descriptions, match them with the names of the dishes, and then match the names to the pictures.

Student A: Turn to page 165.
Student B: Turn to page 173.
Student C: Turn to page 178.
Student D: Turn to page 155.
Student E: Turn to page 160.

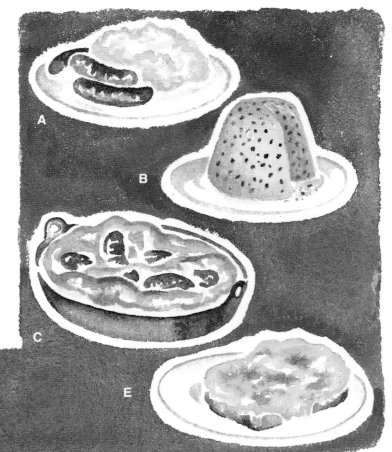

2 Pictures A – F show six eating places in London.
- What kind of food does each place serve?
- Which place would you prefer to eat at?

Answer this questionnaire and compare your responses in small groups.

Then work out your group's preferences and report back to the class.

EATING OUT

Dishes		Types of cuisine		Drinks	
Pizza	☐	Greek	☐	Coffee	☐
Fried chicken	☐	Italian	☐	Tea	☐
Hamburgers	☐	French	☐	Wine	☐
Fish and chips	☐	Indian	☐	Beer	☐
Sandwiches	☐	Chinese	☐	Fruit juice	☐
Pasta	☐	Japanese	☐	Pepsi	☐
Shellfish	☐	American	☐	Mineral water	☐

A Number each of the lists in rank order (1 – 7) to indicate your personal preferences. Write 1 beside the dish you like best.

B You are planning a romantic evening meal with your girl/boyfriend. Where would you go?

....

C You are in the centre of town waiting to see a film which starts in half an hour. Suddenly you feel very, very hungry. What would you do?

....

....

D You are planning an end of term celebration for your class at a restaurant. Where would you go?

....

A

B

C

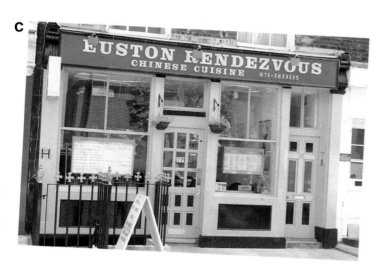

D

E

F

3 In many countries more and more restaurants offer fast food.

In pairs try to write down a definition of fast food and give two or three examples of what you mean.

🔲 Now listen to the first part of a discussion on fast food.

- What five characteristics of fast food do the speakers mention and what examples do they give?
- Do you agree with any or all of the characteristics they give?

Reading skills

4   Re-ordering jumbled paragraphs

The world's largest fast food business is McDonald's. Have you ever eaten McDonald's hamburgers? What do you think of them? The following paragraphs are from a newspaper review of a book describing the history of McDonald's. The paragraphs are in the wrong order. Read the text and number the paragraphs in the correct order.

Compare your order with other students. What clues helped you to work out the correct sequence?

A   The story traced by John Love goes back to the craze for drive-in takeaway food in California in the 1950s. Two brothers, Maurice and Dick McDonald, set up their business in 1955 selling burgers and milkshakes to movie-goers. A travelling representative named Ray Kroc spotted a potential goldmine and bought their name and their recipes. Later that same year he opened his first McDonald's restaurant in Des Plaines, near Chicago, Illinois. It was an immediate success.

B   Before his death in 1984 Ray Kroc expressed his own perceptive view of his company: 'We're not in the hamburger business, we're in showbusiness.' In fact the corporation has an annual advertising budget in excess of half a billion dollars and this may well be the true explanation for its huge success. Wherever you are in the world, and whatever your personal opinion of their product, there is no disputing that McDonald's is one of the most visible symbols of the triumph of international consumer culture, and in this book John Love has gone a long way towards illuminating that symbol.
McDonald's: Behind the Arches is published by Bantam Press at £12.95.

C   John F. Love's *McDonald's: Behind the Arches* is the first book to trace the history of one of America's greatest success stories. The ubiquitous McDonald's is the world's largest restaurant chain with over 11,500 restaurants in 52 countries, and expanding daily. Like Coca Cola and Walt Disney it is a living embodiment of the Great American Dream, and the purveyor of consumer culture to the most remote corners of our shrinking planet.

D   Love describes many of the factors which explain this phenomenal growth and success – a large part of which seems to be due to the rigorous standards imposed by Ray Kroc himself. From the beginning he had a simple philosophy – a ruthless rationalisation of production methods and complete standardisation of product, so that every French fry, every burger and every milkshake always tastes exactly the same as the one before it and the one after it. The company's motto of Q S C & V (Quality, Service, Cleanliness and Value) was backed up with regular inspections and individual restaurants were given points by the inspectors.

E   In the 1980s and '90s the chain continued to grow. By 1984 McDonald's were serving 18 million customers a day, almost equivalent to serving the combined population of Greece and Sweden. In 1990 McDonald's opened its largest restaurant with 900 seats in Pushkin Square, Moscow, making Russia the 28th working language in which the company operates.

F   From these small beginnings in 1955 the company was to grow at a steadily increasing rate – within thirteen years there were over 2,000 McDonald's in the United States. In 1967 the world got a taste of things to come with the opening of the first restaurants outside the USA in Canada and Puerto Rico. And by 1972 sales had exceeded $1 billion and a new restaurant was being opened at the rate of one per day. Britain's first McDonald's opened in Woolwich, south-east London in 1974 and within ten years there were 200 more.

5 Using the information in the text above, complete this chronological chart of McDonald's history.

1955 – *McDonald brothers sell first burgers at California drive-in movies.*
    – ...
1967 – ...
1972 – ...
1974 – ...
1984 – ...
    – ...
1990 – ...
Now – ...

Vocabulary

6 *Food and drink*

A The tasks in Exercises 1 and 2 mentioned a number of food and drink items. Copy these column headings and examples on to a piece of paper.

hot dishes	snacks	ingredients
fried chicken	sandwiches	shellfish

hot drinks	non-alcoholic drinks	alcoholic drinks
tea	Pepsi	wine

Working in pairs, add all the relevant words from the famous British dishes and the questionnaire to the correct columns and then brainstorm as many words as you can to add to each list.

B Swap your lists with another pair. Re-categorise as many of the words from the other pair's lists under these new headings, adding a few examples from your own knowledge.

starters	main courses	desserts

7 Some of the names of dishes contain participles describing the method of cooking or preparation, for example *fried chicken*.
Here is a list of these participles. Can you explain the differences between them?

fried grilled roast(ed) stir-fried steamed sautéed shredded sliced chopped charbroiled baked chilled poached boiled

In pairs, combine some of the participles above with the words below to make a list of well-known dishes or ingredients. You will probably be able to think of lots of different combinations.

potato soup egg parsley beef hamburgers cabbage onions vegetables chicken carrots fish

Listening skills

8 *Comparing*

You are now going to listen to the second part of the fast food discussion from Exercise 3.

A Here is a list of nine statements you might expect people to make in such a discussion. Listen to the tape and tick only those statements which correspond with opinions given in the discussion.

1 Fast food is very convenient.
2 Perfect Pizzas are perfect.
3 A pizza is better for you than a McDonald's.
4 McDonald's contain cholesterol and fat.
5 Chinese take-aways are healthy.
6 The occasional burger is unhealthy.
7 People think fast food is healthier than it really is.
8 McDonald's have analysed what goes into their burgers.
9 Sandwiches are better than McDonald's.

B Now listen again and compare the statements below with the tape. Which are true and which are false?

1 The person who rarely goes to places like McDonald's also
    a thinks that pizzas are a lot better than McDonald's.
    b says that fish and chips make her feel ill.
    c prefers sandwiches to McDonald's.

2 The person who is a huge fan of fast food also
    a loves pancakes.
    b thinks the healthy reputation of Chinese food is a myth.
    c says sandwiches are fresher than McDonald's.

3 The person who thinks fast food is very convenient also
    a has cravings for fish and chips.
    b thinks Chinese take-aways are healthy.
    c thinks sandwiches are the ultimate fast food.

C Write down two statements from the recording with which you agree and two with which you disagree.

Compare statements in small groups.
Try to draw up a short list of things you agree on concerning fast food to present to the class.

Language work

9 Emphatic devices

A English offers a number of ways to make statements more emphatic. Here are some examples from this unit.

From the book:

a *You are in the centre of town waiting to see a film which starts in half an hour. Suddenly you feel very, very hungry.*

b *Phenomenal growth and success – a large part of which seems to be due to the rigorous standards imposed by Ray Kroc himself.*

From the tape:

c *... when I eat the food I think, 'Oh, this is so disgusting I don't know why I came ...'*

d *... after I've had it I think 'Oh God! It was horrible ...'*

e *... I think people do probably think it's, it's even less healthy than it is ...*

f *... it's all cholesterol and fat, isn't it?*

Match each of these extracts with one of the emphatic devices below. Underline the part of the extract which provides the example.

- emphatic reflexive pronoun
- emphatic use of auxiliary verb
- exclamations
- emphatic use of *so*
- use of question tags
- repetition of intensifiers

Using the extracts as examples, can you explain exactly why and how these emphatic devices are used?

B Re-write this short dialogue using appropriate devices in the positions indicated by asterisks to make each utterance more emphatic.

JIM   I * believe that was the worst meal I've ever eaten.
ANN   That steak was * overcooked *.
JIM   And the vegetables were * really soggy.
ANN   And the bill was * far too expensive. Didn't you say Monica recommended it * ?
JIM   Yes, she said she eats here * every day.
ANN   * She must be mad!

C Now look at these three sentences. Which two sentences are emphatic?

a What makes me feel ill is fish and chips.
b Fish and chips make me feel ill.
c It's fish and chips that make me feel ill.

Which type of sentence is used if you want to emphasise the verb?

D Re-write the sentences below to emphasise the word(s) in italics.

1 Bad manners *infuriate* me.
2 My boyfriend loves *Italian* cuisine.
3 I *hate* overcooked vegetables.
4 *They* despise people who won't try new recipes.
5 I tried lots of new restaurants *during the summer holiday*.
6 She always prepares *salad* for lunch.
7 *My parents* are going to try out that new pizzeria next week.
8 People who don't leave a tip *get on his nerves*.

Pronunciation

10 Emphatic stress

In speech it is usual to use stress to emphasise the important part of a sentence.

A 🖳 Listen to versions 1 – 5 of the response below. Match each of them with one of questions a – e.

My partner opened a vegetarian restaurant yesterday.

a Whose partner opened a vegetarian restaurant yesterday?
b What kind of restaurant did your partner open yesterday?
c When did your partner open a vegetarian restaurant?
d What did your partner do yesterday?
e Who opened a vegetarian restaurant yesterday?

B Write questions a – e above in a different order. Read out the answers to a partner, using stress to show which questions you are answering. Your partner should be able to identify the order of your questions.

C 🖳 Listen to these four answers on the tape. Which of the previous questions a – e are they answering?

1 It was a vegetarian restaurant that my partner opened.
2 It was my partner who opened a vegetarian restaurant.
3 It was yesterday that my partner opened a vegetarian restaurant.
4 What my partner did was open a vegetarian restaurant.

D With a partner, make up pairs of questions and answers like the examples above but based on these sentences.

- My best friend went to Pizza Hut last night.
- Our teacher can't stand Chinese food.
- I love eating Italian food at the weekend.
- McDonald's make the best hamburgers.

Read each answer to a partner, who should listen and tell you which question you are answering.

Language work

11 Actually *and* really

A 📻 Listen to the extracts and read the tapescript below.

Extract 1

JANET   But I think that's a lot better than um,
         McDonald's the, the kind of, I don't know,
         rubbery meat burgers that they give you in
         those places I think … [Well they, yeah …] a
         nice pizza is okay …

LOUISE   I don't know, I, I think (A) <u>really</u> you probably
         find if you analysed what was in these things
         that a McDonald's was (B) <u>actually</u> better for
         you than a pizza, 'cos I mean, what's good for
         you in a pizza?

Extract 2

MARK   … yet I also have cravings and every few months
         I (C) <u>really</u> get a craving for a burger …

Extract 3

MARK   But what about things like, you know, Chinese
         take-aways? I mean, they're quite healthy
         (D) <u>really</u>.

Extract 4

LOUISE   Is that any less healthy that having a sandwich
         every day for lunch?

JANET   Well, I don't know. Earlier I was going to say to
         you if I'm out and about lunchtime and I, I
         don't (E) <u>really</u> want to go to a restaurant,
         then rather than go to McDonald's I would
         probably go into a supermarket and buy
         sandwiches which I (F) <u>actually</u> do think is
         better, yes.

Now refer to the underlined words A – F to answer
these questions.

- Which word(s) make(s) a verb stronger?
- Which word(s) introduce(s) something unexpected
  and reinforce(s) opinion?
- Which word(s) make(s) a whole sentence less
  emphatic?
- Which word(s) make(s) a verb less emphatic?
- What do you notice about the relationship between
  the position of *really* and its effect on the meaning?

B Add *actually* or *really* to these sentences in a suitable
   position to:

1 make the verbs weaker.
   a I don't think much of her cooking.
   b He doesn't feel very well.
   c That fried chicken wasn't very good.

2 show that the statements are unexpected.
   a I don't agree with that.
   b Well, I think pizzas are very unhealthy.
   c You'll find that some fruit is very fattening.

3 make the statements more emphatic.
   a I think fish and chips aren't healthy.
   b Sometimes I feel like a huge juicy burger.
   c They are overweight.

4 make the statements more hesitant.
   a It's not much of a restaurant.
   b I don't fancy a heavy meal.
   c I think shellfish is rather overpriced.

Speaking skills

12 *Expressing opinions*

A Does fast food in your country have a reputation for being
   bad for your health?
   Do you think health is the main thing people think
   about when they choose fast food?
   What other criteria do people use when choosing
   meals in restaurants?

B In the recording the speakers explained their preferences
   and compared their opinions of fast food. Look at the
   tapescript on page 181 and make a note of the phrases
   people used to introduce their opinions.

C Now work in groups of four or five. Your task is to
   complete the chart below as a group, giving each of
   the fast food dishes a star rating under each category.
   You must discuss your opinions and all *agree* on the
   same ratings. Use this key.

***** *excellent* **** *good* *** *average* ** *poor* * *bad*

dish	taste	effect on health	value for money
hamburger			
fried chicken			
pizza			
kebab			
fish and chips			
sandwiches			
baked potatoes			

D Compare your chart with other groups.
   Which dish got the most stars?

Writing skills

13 *Writing a personal letter*

You are planning to visit England this summer. You have offered to let an English friend and her family stay at your place in your home town while you are away. She has written to accept your invitation.

Write a suitable reply, giving Jane the information she needs.

Bramble Cottage
Staverston
Yorkshire

20th May

Dear ... ,

Thanks for your invitation to stay at your place this summer with the kids. I'm looking forward to it already!

As you know, I'm not exactly the world's greatest cook, so we're planning to eat out most lunchtimes and evenings. Do you think you could give us some advice on where to go? We're on quite a tight budget so cheaper places would be best. And I'd love to try out some of your famous local cuisine! The kids will be with us at lunchtime but we're hoping to find a babysitter so Steve and I can be alone in the evenings. If there's anywhere we can go that's got food and some kind of entertainment that would be great.

Give my best wishes to all the family.

Love,

Jane

Final task

14 *The Restaurant Game*

Your teacher will give you one of five roles to play. Half the class will be customers. The winner of the game is the customer who completes his/her task sheet correctly first.

Customers: Turn to page 160.
Restaurant Owner A: Turn to page 165.
Restaurant Owner B: Turn to page 173.
Restaurant Owner C: Turn to page 178.
Restaurant Owner D: Turn to page 181.

Introduction

1 This picture comes from a popular
series of advertisements on British
television.

- On the basis of the picture,
  what reasons would you give
  for the adverts' popularity?
- How do you feel about this
  image of animals as behaving
  like humans?
- Do you think that animals can talk?

We asked the question 'Do you think that animals can
communicate?' Look at some of the answers below
and decide whether you agree with each statement or
not.

1 No. They make noises but it's not
really communicating; it's just like,
well, machines making noises, I
suppose.

2 Well, I think they can probably communicate
simple things, like danger; I mean, they can
give each other warnings, or threats, but I
don't think they can really communicate any
more than that.

3 Yes. Animals have a system of communication
which is just as complex as ours. We don't
recognise it as such because it's different from
our means of communication.

Discuss the statements in pairs or groups. Decide
which one is closest to your opinion. Now listen to
Mike Down, an Education Officer at London Zoo. We
put the same question to him. Do you agree with his
opinion on whether animals can communicate?

4 I really don't know. To be honest, I
think that we really don't know enough
about animals to be able to say.

Language awareness

2 *Defining language*

If animals can communicate, can we actually say they
have language?
In pairs, write a definition of language. Use the words
below to help you.

*communication signal stimulus arbitrary
creative*

Now discuss your definitions as a class and make a
note of the best ones.

5 Of course animals communicate, especially
with us. Ju-ju, that's my little dog, can tell me
when she's happy, when she's angry, when
she's hungry, and so on. Of course they can
communicate.

3 Look at the pictures of eight animals below.
Match the pictures with the animals' names.

parrot sheep grasshopper Siamese cat
Alsatian nightingale dolphin bee

🔊 Now listen to the sounds that these animals make.
Match them to the animals.
Which of the sounds represent some kind of
communication? What are they communicating?
According to the definitions you wrote in Exercise 2,
are any of these animals using language? Which one(s),
and how?

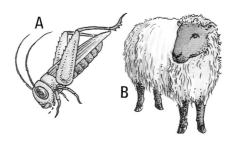

Reading skills

4 *Skimming and scanning*

A Read the texts below and on the right, from a book on
linguistics, and choose the best title from a - h for each
paragraph. Not all the titles will be needed.

Paragraph 1   a Meaningless imitation
Paragraph 2   b Paying attention to pitch
Paragraph 3   c The robin's territory signal
Paragraph 4   d Wolves' language
Paragraph 5   e Dance of the bees
              f Gestures which inform
              g Responding to situations
              h 'Pretty Polly' language

B Read the texts again quickly and complete the chart. The
first one is done for you.

animal	communication	what the system lacks
bee	dancing	flexibility

How do these systems of communication compare
with your definitions of language from Exercise 2?

1 A study of higher animals also reveals no 'language'
systems that are creative in the way that human language
is. Wolves use many facial expressions, movements of
their tails, and growls to express different degrees of
threats, anxiety, depression and submission. But that's all
they can do. And the sounds and gestures produced by
nonhuman primates, the monkeys and apes, show that their
signals are highly stereotyped and limited in terms of the
messages which they convey. Most importantly, studies of
such animal communication systems reveal that the basic
'vocabularies' produced by either sounds or facial
expressions occur primarily as emotional responses to
particular situations. They have no way of expressing the
anger they felt 'yesterday'.

2 Unlike human language, the communication dance of
the bees is confined to a single subject, or thought. It is
frozen and inflexible. For example, an experimenter
forced a bee to walk to the food source. When the bee
returned to the hive, it indicated a distance twenty-five
times further away than it actually was. The bees had no
way of communicating the special circumstances or taking
them into account in its message.

3 'Talking' birds, such as parrots and mynah birds are
capable of flawlessly enunciating words and phrases of
human language. The birds imitate what they have heard.
But when a parrot says 'Polly wants a cracker,' she may
really want a ham sandwich or drink of water or nothing
at all. A bird that has learnt to say 'hello' or 'goodbye' is
as likely to use one as the other regardless of whether
people are arriving or departing.

4 Two French scientists have studied the song of the
European robin. The song studied was that which signalled
the robin's possession of a certain territory. The scientists
found that the rival robins paid attention only to the
alternation between high-pitched and low-pitched notes,
and which came first didn't matter at all. The message
varies only to the extent of expressing how strongly the
robin feels about his possession and how much he is
prepared to defend it and start a family in that territory.

5 Most animals possess some kind of 'signalling'
communication system. Among the spiders there is a
complex system for courtship. The male spider, before he
approaches his lady love, goes through elaborate gestures
to inform her that he is indeed a spider and not a crumb or
a fly to be eaten. These gestures are invariant. One never
finds a 'creative' spider changing or adding to the
particular courtship ritual of his species.

5 The paragraph below from the same book gives one viewpoint of the differences between animal and human communication.

> **6** Descartes pointed out more than three hundred years ago that the communication systems of animals are qualitatively different from the language used by men:
>
> *It is a very remarkable fact that there are none so depraved and stupid, without even excepting idiots, that they cannot arrange different words together, forming of them a statement by which they make known their thoughts; while, on the other hand, there is no other animal, however perfect and fortunately circumstanced it may be, which can do the same.*
>
> Descartes goes on to state that one of the major differences between man and animal is that man's use of language is not just a response to external, or even internal, emotional stimuli, as are the grunts and gestures of animals. He warns against confusing human use of language with 'natural movements which betray passions and may be ... manifested by animals.'

Write a one-sentence summary of the differences between human and animal communication explained here. Do you agree?

Language work

6 *Defining relative clauses*

A Complete these extracts from the texts with a relative pronoun if necessary:

1 There is no other animal _____ can do the same. (*Text 6*)
2 ... forming of them a statement by _____ they make known their thoughts. (*Text 6*)
3 They have no way of expressing the anger _____ they felt yesterday. (*Text 1*)

Match the sentences with the following statements.

a The pronoun refers to the subject of the clause.
b The pronoun refers to the object of the clause.
c The pronoun is not necessary.

Now find another example of each of the relative clauses described above in the texts.

Find the relative clause starting with *what* (Text 3). Study it carefully. What does *what* refer to?

B Use relative clauses to make one sentence from each of the pairs of sentences below. (The first three come from the texts.) Look at the example before you begin.

> A bird learns to say hello or goodbye.
> It is as likely to use one as the other.
> *A bird that has learned to say hello or goodbye is as likely to use one as the other.*

1 A study of higher animals reveals language systems. None of these systems is creative in the way human language is.
A study ...

2 The song was studied. It signalled the robin's possession of a certain territory.
The song ...

3 The birds have heard something. They imitate it.
The birds ...

4 The scientists studied animals. The animals did not have real communication systems.
The animals ...

5 Humans communicate in a particular manner. It is highly creative and flexible.
Humans ...

6 The man tried to say something. The people around him did not understand it.
The people ...

C Complete this text with appropriate relative pronouns where necessary.

> The subject of communication in general is one (1) ... fascinates people, whether it is human beings, animals or computers in (2) ... they have a particular interest. It is strange, however, to note that the people working in this field are often those (3) ... find personal communication difficult. It is also amazing how fierce animal lovers can become when they discuss the possibility of their pets communicating: they can't bear the possibility of not being on the same wavelength as the animals (4) ... they live with. They will swear that they have dogs (5) ... can 'ask for' certain foods, or cats (6) ... are able to sympathise with their moods. I can't help wondering whether the animals in question look upon the humans (7) ... they 'communicate' with in quite the same benevolent way.

Listening skills

7 *Finding words and phrases*

A 📟 Listen to Mike Down from London Zoo again talking about the social behaviour of animals. Listen carefully for the names of the animals below. Tick the ones you hear and number them in the order in which you hear them.

- ☐ orang utan   ☐ lion   ☐ horse
- ☐ field mice   ☐ zebra   ☐ cow   ☑ ant
- ☐ piranha fish   ☐ chimpanzee   ☐ bee
- ☐ cheetah   ☐ spider   ☐ gorilla

B 📟 Now listen again and complete the chart below with the type of groups these animals form and a brief description of that group. The first one is done for you.

animal	type of group	description
lion	multimale/pride	two or three males, a dozen females, cubs – real group = females and cubs.
zebra		

C Why do you think animals form social groups? Discuss in pairs and make notes.

📟 Now listen to Mike Down talking about the advantages of social grouping. Were your answers right? What other reasons does he give?

8 In the last two extracts you heard two names for special groups of animals and two names for the young of certain animals.

A Complete these sentences.

A group of lions is called a … .
A group of wolves is called a … .
A baby lion is called a … .
A baby zebra is called a … .

📟 Listen again to check.

B Now make a chart with the names of animal groups and of their young. The animals, groups and young are given below. Use a dictionary if necessary. You will need to use some of these words more than once.

*calf cow cub dog flock foal goat goose
gosling herd kid lamb lion pack pride
pup puppy sheep school whale wolf zebra*

animal	group	young
lion	pride	cub
zebra		

Speaking skills

9 *Expanding and exemplifying*

Mike Down uses a lot of vocabulary that needs explanation. For example:

> … *an amoeba, a tiny one-celled animal* … .

A What devices does Mike use to introduce these examples or definitions? Can you think of any others?

1 … a very significant group of mammals and insects, …
2 … orang utans, for example, …
3 … gorillas live in unimale groups, …
4 … Now, chimps live in multimale groups, …
5 … Er, dogs, for example, …
6 … it helps to establish, to set up, a pecking order, …

📟 Listen again to check your answers.

B What do you think the attitude of people in your country is towards pets? What do you think of the attitude of the British towards pets? Do you think British people take their pets seriously? Work in pairs. You each have a text about pets to discuss with your partner.

Student A: Turn to pages 165 – 6.
Student B: Turn to page 173.

Vocabulary

10 *Categorisation*

Below are eighteen names of animals (including those from Exercise 3). Divide them into categories. (You can choose any categories you like, but they must be logical.)

> *dolphin human horse parrot sheep whale
> bat bee spider cat dog nightingale shark
> lion cow chimpanzee fly seal*

Compare your categories with other students'. Are they the same?

In groups of three or four, brainstorm names of animals for one minute. Now add those animals to your categories.

Language work

11 *Non-defining relative clauses*

A   Look at these two sentences.

> 1   *The song which was studied signalled the robin's possession of a certain territory.*
>
> 2   *The song, which was studied, signalled the robin's possession of a certain territory.*

In which sentence does the relative clause specify a particular song (one amongst many)?

In which sentence does the relative clause just add extra information? (A non-defining relative clause.)

Combine the following pairs of sentences to form a non-defining relative clause in each case. Study the example before you begin.

> Judy's horse went lame only two weeks after she'd bought it. It cost her a lot of money.
> *Judy's horse, which had cost her a lot of money, went lame only two weeks after she'd bought it.*

1   Cruft's dog show is the highlight of the dog breeder's year. It is held in spring every year.
2   Some people think they can understand their pets' facial expressions. They have usually lived with their pets for a long time.
3   Humans have devised a lot of complicated communication systems. All of them involve symbols of some kind.
4   Some apes have mastered certain simple ways of communicating with humans. They have been trained from birth.
5   Some higher level mammals are very social. These mammals live in groups.
6   Some animals come to rely upon the company of humans rather than their own kind. These animals are usually living in a human environment.

B   Look at the pairs of sentences below. Each pair contains a defining relative and a non-defining relative clause. What is the difference in meaning between the sentences in each pair?

1   The animals who were moved into different cages became much healthier.
    The animals, who were moved into different cages, became much healthier.

2   We bought the first cat we saw which was black and white with green eyes.
    We bought the first cat we saw, which was black and white with green eyes.

What do you notice about the commas?

Pronunciation

12 *Rhythm in relative clauses*

⊡ Listen to the sentences in the previous exercise. Look at the example. Mark the stressed words and any pauses on the sentences. What happens to the rhythm in non-defining relative clauses?

> *The 'animals who were moved into different 'cages became much 'healthier.*

⊡ Listen to these four sentences on the tape. Is the relative clause in each case defining or non-defining? Put commas in the sentences if necessary.

1   We stopped at the first hotel which had a bathroom.
2   I gave a tip to the waiter who had served our table.
3   I bought the cheapest computer which had a colour monitor.
4   He decided that the black suit which didn't have a waistcoat was the most suitable.

Work in pairs. Read the sentences in this exercise and in Exercise 11B to each other. As you listen, decide whether your partner is giving a defining or non-defining relative clause.

Student A: Turn to page 166.
Student B: Write two relative clauses from the information below, then dictate them to your partner. Check that your partner's sentences are the same as yours, especially the punctuation.

1   You bought a horse last week. You saw several, but you decided to buy the one which was trained to jump.
2   Your aunt owns a really pretty parrot. It can say two things: 'Pretty Polly' and 'Goodbye'.

Writing

13 *Sentence and paragraph construction*

Rewrite the following sentences into a text using relative clauses. Before you do this, link each pair of sentences and rewrite it, starting with the words given in italics. Then, put all the sentences together to make a fluent paragraph.

- Have you ever seen a person? That person looks like their animal. *Have you ever seen a person who ...*
- People live closely with their animals. They start to look like them. *It is said that people who ...*
- I have an elderly neighbour. She owns a little pekinese dog and takes it everywhere with her. *I have ...*
- The pekinese is a particularly ugly kind of dog. It has a very squashed face. *The pekinese, which ...*
- The old lady's face now seems wrinkled and squashed to me. It always used to seem quite attractive. *The old lady's face ...*
- I hope this is pure coincidence as I have a bulldog. A bulldog is an extremely ugly animal! *I hope ...*

Final task

14 *Words and meanings*

Look at the still from a film. Do you know what it is? If not, what do you think it is about?

In *Watership Down*, by Richard Adams, the characters are almost all rabbits and Adams has invented a kind of rabbit language to express certain concepts as they might be perceived by rabbits.

A Read the extracts below and try to work out the meaning of the invented words in *italics*. Use clues such as: is the word a noun, verb or adjective; what is the context? Look at Exercise 5 in Unit 6 again if you need help.

There are three things which the rabbit narrator does not know the word for – either in rabbit language or English. Find three descriptions in the text (the third thing is a product of the other two things).

- What three adjectives does the rabbit use to describe the first thing?
- And which three are used to describe the second thing?
- What is the effect of the third thing?
- What is each of these things and what are the men doing?

The answers are on page 160.

B Work in groups of three or four.
Many languages create words for new concepts or inventions by using existing words together in a phrase or compound noun. English does not always do this, however. Look at the examples and then at the phrases below. Do you know the usual English word for them?

a fire stick   *a gun*   a flying boat   *an aeroplane*

sight improvers   a clothes smoother
fire water   valuable paper
a sleep interrupter   wailing wood

Now try to think the other way round! Look at the example. Find a phrase that could be the name of each item below.

socks   *foot warmers*

telephone radio camera computer car aspirin
chimney   bullet train

Join another group and discuss your answers. Then think of phrases for two other items. Can the other groups guess what they are?

'What did *the Threarah* say?' asked Silver.
'I've no idea. I didn't ask him and neither did anyone else as far as I know. I went to sleep and when I woke there was no sound up above. It was evening and I decided to *silflay*. The rain had set in but I pottered around and fed for a while all the same. I couldn't see that anything was altered, except that here and there the mouth of a hole had been poked in.
'The next morning was clear and fine. Everyone was out for *silflay* as usual. I remember Nightshade told the *Threarah* that he ought to be careful not to tire himself now that he was getting on in years...'
'...I was out most of the morning and it can't have been long before *ni-Frith* when I came back through the wood. I was coming down Silent Bank – I know most rabbits preferred the Green Loose, but I nearly always went by Silent Bank. I'd got into the open part of the wood, where it comes down towards the old fence, when I noticed a

hrududu in the lane at the top of the opposite slope. It was standing at the gate by the board and a lot of men were getting out. There was a boy with them and he had a gun. They took down some big, long things – I don't know how to describe them to you – they were made of the same sort of stuff as a *hrududu* and they must have been heavy, because it took two men to carry one of them. ...'
'... Then another of the men fetched some long, thin, bending things. I haven't got words for all these men-things, but they look something like lengths of very thick bramble. Each of the men took one and put it on one of the heavy things. There was a kind of hissing noise and – and – well, I know you must find this difficult to understand, but the air began to turn bad. For some reason I got a strong scent of this stuff that came out of the bramble-things, even though I was some way off: and I couldn't see or think.'

Introduction

1 The cinema is an art form that is accessible to most people, and it is one that most people enjoy.

- Are you one of them?
- Do you follow the movie world?

Answer the questions in the quiz below to find out whether you're a film buff.

Work in groups of four.

Student A: Turn to page 166.
Student B: Turn to page 173.
Student C: Turn to page 178.
Student D: You have the questions below. Discuss the questions with Students A, B and C. If you cannot answer them, use the answers at the back (which Students A, B and C are looking at). Only one answer is correct in each case.

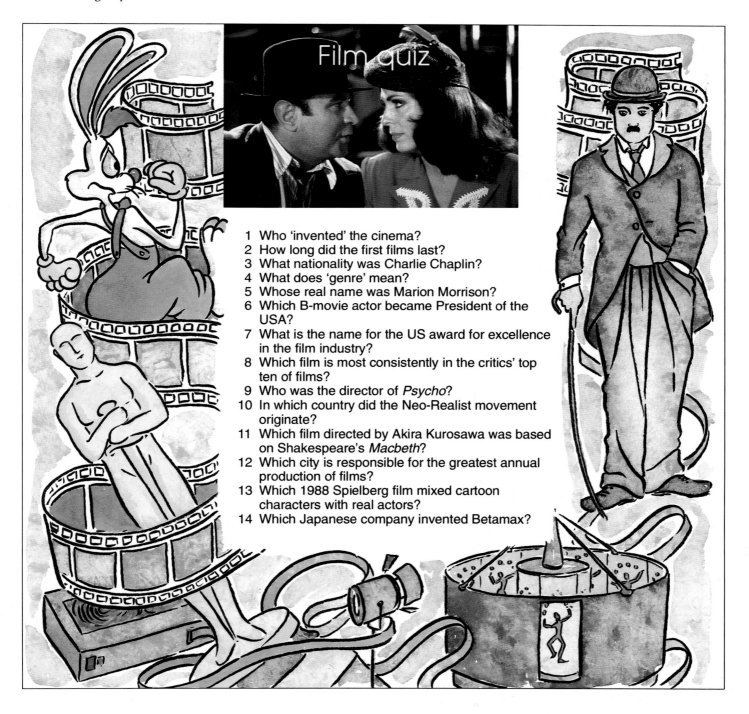

Film quiz

1 Who 'invented' the cinema?
2 How long did the first films last?
3 What nationality was Charlie Chaplin?
4 What does 'genre' mean?
5 Whose real name was Marion Morrison?
6 Which B-movie actor became President of the USA?
7 What is the name for the US award for excellence in the film industry?
8 Which film is most consistently in the critics' top ten of films?
9 Who was the director of *Psycho*?
10 In which country did the Neo-Realist movement originate?
11 Which film directed by Akira Kurosawa was based on Shakespeare's *Macbeth*?
12 Which city is responsible for the greatest annual production of films?
13 Which 1988 Spielberg film mixed cartoon characters with real actors?
14 Which Japanese company invented Betamax?

Reading skills

2 *Skimming and scanning*

A Read through the text quickly to find out the answers to the quiz. How many did you get right?

1 The origins of cinema as we know it lie in a machine patented in 1891 by Thomas Edison – the kinetoscope. This machine rotated, rapidly showing different frames, so giving the impression of a moving picture. Early films were produced solely to show off the ingeniousness of the machines that projected them, and were only one or two minutes long, but by the early 1900s films started to tell stories. During the years of the First World War, American cinema flourished and technical innovations abounded. By 1927 the use of sound on film became commercially viable and the film recognised as the first successful sound movie was released – *The Jazz Singer*.

2 It was in the late 1920s that the Hollywood golden era really began. With the advent of commercial film-making in the early 1900s various film production companies had started up in the United States in fierce competition with each other. Many of these companies became associated with stars still popular and famous today, for example, Charlie Chaplin, who, having left his native UK for the USA, became a founder in 1919 of United Artists. By the 1930s most of these studios were in financial difficulties because of the Depression. They had to make certain compromises to survive, which in part led to the development of film *genre*. A *genre* is a number of films, all containing characteristics in common, including sets and stars. Certain studios started producing a number of films from one *genre* in order to use the same sets, and to use contracted stars who were becoming popular with audiences. For example, Warner Brothers was associated with a large number of gangster films and Universal with horror films, while others were associated with melodramas or musicals. It was this studio system that typified the golden age of Hollywood, but by the 1950s it was somewhat in decline, with a stronger European film industry and the rising popularity of television hitting their box office takings.

3 One continuing feature of the studio system is that of the film star. Studios vied with each other to find and contract popular film stars as a way of increasing audience share. Some of the biggest stars of the 1930s and '40s were closely associated with particular studios, for example, Rita Hayworth with Columbia. Through the 1940s and '50s the popularity of stars such as Humphrey Bogart, Marilyn Monroe and John Wayne (who, incidentally, was christened Marion Morrison!) continued to grow. Film stars became part of people's everyday lives and some began to take an interest in other areas, for example, politics. As everyone knows, Ronald Reagan, a B-movie actor of the '40s and '50s, was voted President of the USA in 1980! Apart from the occasional presidency, the highest accolade that can be given to film stars is the famous Oscar, a little gold statuette that forms the peak of many an actor's career.

4 Of course, actors are not the only stars of the film industry. Certain film directors have achieved star status in the past, such as Orson Welles, whose innovative *Citizen Kane* is the only film to appear consistently in the critics' top tens, and Alfred Hitchcock, who really gave the thriller *genre* its name with films such as *Psycho* and *Frenzy*. Contemporary directors, while being perhaps more difficult to understand, are equally as popular, and are finding success in areas other than feature films, for example, television and pop promotional videos.

5 Not all cinema, needless to say, comes from Hollywood. Much early European cinema has, in fact, had a lasting influence on Hollywood with, for example, the low-key lighting and strange camera angles of German Expressionism being transferred to Hollywood 'film noir'. Apart from Hollywood cinema, over the last forty years or so we have seen very strong film industries emerge from many countries. In some cases these herald new movements, for example, the French New Wave and Italian Neo-Realism, in others they feature particular directors, such as Ingmar Bergman in Sweden, Akira Kurosawa in Japan (whose interpretations of *Macbeth* and *King Lear* – *Throne of Blood* and *Ran* respectively – made Shakespeare more widely accessible) and, more recently, Pedro Almodovar in Spain. In fact, while most people believe Los Angeles to be the biggest 'production village', that honour goes to Bombay, India, which has the most prolific film industry of any country in the world.

6 In many countries film-makers take their role in society more seriously than they do in Hollywood. Much European cinema, as indeed some American non-mainstream cinema, focusses on contemporary issues, such as the sociology of the inner city, violence, poverty, the psychology of marriage and racism. Possibly the most striking developments in film over the last few years, however, have been those in technology and special effects, bringing us images of space travel and strange creatures in films such as *Star Wars*, and the mixture of reality and animation in *Who Framed Roger Rabbit?* This film, of course, did little more than to carry on the tradition of the greatest cartoon film-maker of all time – Walt Disney, who was one of the most financially successful producers ever.

7 What about the future of the film industry in the 1990s and into the twenty-first century? Film-making is thriving: more money is being spent on producing films and on viewing them than ever before. However, is the ever-increasing sophistication of television and video likely to affect the popularity of cinema? With the possibility of large screen viewing in the home, and the boom in video rentals since one video standard, VHS, became fairly universal (Sony's Betamax never really took off), video and TV have become a cheaper, more convenient and more comfortable alternative to the cinema. We will have to wait and see.

B Choose the correct title (A – J) for each paragraph (1 – 7) of the text. Not all the headings will be needed.

para 1 ...   A Cinema from Other Countries
para 2 ...   B Indian Cinema
para 3 ...   C The Film Star
para 4 ...   D The Development of Early Cinema
para 5 ...   E The First Projectors
para 6 ...   F The Hollywood Studio System
para 7 ...   G The Film Editor
                H The Future of the Cinema
                I   New Developments in Film
                J   Film Directors

C The following events are all stages in the history of the film industry. Read the text again carefully and number them 1 – 6 according to their historical order.

a The first sound movie was released.   ...
b Ronald Reagan became President of the USA.   ...
c Studios experienced financial difficulties. ...
d Charlie Chaplin founded United Artists.   ...
e The Hollywood studio system was in decline.   ...
f The kinetoscope was invented.   ...

Vocabulary

3 Finding categories

A There are a large number of words and phrases in the text that refer to various aspects of the cinema. Go through the text and list them. Then divide them into categories of your choice, as in the examples below.

Category	Words and phrases
genre	*thriller, ...*
film history	*kinetoscope, ...*

B Film titles often change from language to language. Here is a list of some famous films from the USA and the UK. Do you know their titles in your language? Which *genre* do they belong to? (If you don't know the film, guess!) Then think of one more example of each *genre*.

1 *The Sound of Music*
2 *Dracula*
3 *The Silence of the Lambs*
4 *Scarface*
5 *Snow White and the Seven Dwarfs*
6 *Alien*
7 *Love Story*
8 *Ghostbusters*
9 *Raiders of the Lost Ark*
10 *Gone with the Wind*

Study skills

4 *Word formation and suffixes*

A The chart below contains a selection of nouns, verbs and adjectives. Complete it, checking with the text if necessary. Where no such word exists, the box is grey.

noun	verb	adjective
	achieve	
	commercialise	
development		
	entertain	
ingenuity		
		innovative
popularity		
	produce	

B In the chart above there are a number of common suffixes of nouns. Complete the chart below with a few more examples of these noun suffixes from the text.

Now match the suffixes with these explanations of how they are formed.

-ity	-ism	-ment	-ology	-ion
reality	racism	movement	technology	animation

1 This suffix is usually added to a complete adjective.   ...
2 This suffix is usually added to a complete verb.   ...
3 This suffix can be added to nouns or adjectives, and usually has the meaning of a movement or theory.   ...
4 This suffix can be preceded by -t or -s and is usually added to a verb, which may lose one or two letters in the formation of the noun.   ...
5 This suffix can be added to the root of a word or to a whole word, and it usually refers to an academic, philosophical or political subject area. ...

Add a minimum of three other nouns to each column.

C Use these definitions to find nouns ending in the suffixes above.

1 This -*ology* is a study of the human mind.   P _ _ _ _ O L O G Y
2 This -*ism* is a very positive outlook on life.   O _ _ _ _ I S M
3 This -*ment* is like a plan.   A _ _ _ _ _ _ M E N T
4 This -*ion* means that something has been completely got rid of.   A _ _ _ _ _ I O N
5 This -*ity* is not very common.   R _ _ I T Y

Listening skills

5 *Listening to identify attitude*

A 🖭 Listen to the film review of *The Silence of The Lambs*.

- What is the reviewer's attitude towards:
  a the film itself?
  b the director?
  c the two main actors?
  d current Hollywood treatment of horror films?
- Do you agree with her attitude towards the last topic?
- What is it that helps you identify her attitudes?

Make a list of some of the words she uses to express her attitude.

Listening for gist

B 🖭 Below is a list of the different topics that the reviewer discusses (and some topics that she doesn't discuss). Put them in the order in which you hear them by writing a number 1 – 5 in each box. Three boxes will remain empty.

details of the two main actors ☐
the reviewer's recommendation ☐
the director's previous films ☐
the plot ☐
the ending of the film ☐
an introduction to the film ☐
the feminist aspects of the film ☐
other actors in the film ☐

Writing skills

6 *Writing a film review*

A The text below is a written review of *The Silence of The Lambs*, which contains the same information as the oral review you have just heard. Complete the text with one word in each gap 1 – 10.

The Silence of The Lambs

USA Orion Pictures 1990

Director   Jonathan Demme
Actors   Jodie Foster, Anthony Hopkins

Clarice Starling, a trainee FBI agent, is assigned to the case of Buffalo Bill, a (1) ... of women. When she is instructed to visit Hannibal Lecter, another serial killer imprisoned some time before, the action really begins. Lecter, an eminent (2) ... before turning to a life of crime, eventually gives Starling some leads which result in her discovery of Buffalo Bill, but only after a number of gruelling interviews during which she is persuaded to reveal to him in an almost Faustian exchange painful details about her (3) ... . This interchange between Lecter and Starling forms the focus of the first half of the film, while the second half concentrates on the search for Buffalo Bill.

Based on a powerful novel of the same name by Thomas Harris, *The Silence of The Lambs* had the potential to become one of the most (4) ... films of the year. However, the expert and understated (5) ... of Demme, and the outstanding performances of the two lead actors, elevate the film from a mundane horror movie to a slick, tense Hitchcockian thriller in which almost everything is left to the (6) ... . The (7) ... of Foster (Starling) and Hopkins (Lecter), two well-respected actors with impeccable track records, cannot be faulted, and Hopkins' soulless steel-blue stare will go down in thriller cinema history.

The Silence of The Lambs is, interestingly and perhaps surprisingly, given its topic, receiving some attention as a (8) ... film. The reason for this is its careful examination of the thoughts and feelings of Starling, played to perfection by Foster, whose appearance of weakness and frailty (because of her sex and size) is offset by her strength of character and (9) ... to find the killer.

Viewers whose idea of a frightening film is based on extreme violence and rivers of blood may be disappointed by the implicit violence and threat in this film, but for those who appreciate the suggested terror of the (10) ... thriller, this film may prove to be the most frightening ever.

B   Answer these questions about the reviews you have
    heard and read.

   • What are the differences between spoken and
     written language?
   • Which is more formal?
   • Do we use different vocabulary in written language
     (adjectives/adverbs etc.)?
   • Do we use more or less complex grammatical
     constructions?

   Apply the questions you have just answered to the
   spoken and written reviews of the film by completing
   the chart below.

   Student A: Turn to page 181 and look at the tapescript
               of the spoken review.
   Student B: Look at the review in Exercise 6A.

aspect of language	spoken	written
the order in which information is presented		
length of sentence		
formal/informal language		
vocabulary		
grammatical constructions		

C   Look again at the review in Exercise 6A. Label the parts of
    the review which contain the following information.

   a the reviewer's opinion/recommendation
   b background information
   c direction/performances
   d the plot (story)
   e any other information

   Answer these questions about the language in the
   review.

   • Which tense(s) are used in the review?
   • Is there much use of adjectives and adverbs?
   • Is there much use of subordinate clauses?

D   🖳 Listen to the review of *Green Card*.

   • What is the plot?
   • What *genre* is it?
   • What do you hear about the director and actors?
   • What is the reviewer's opinion of the film?

   Compare your notes with your partner. Discuss what
   you would put into a written review and in what order.
   Then write the review.

Reading skills

7 *Reading for detail*

   • What do you know about Jodie Foster?
   • What kind of films does she appear in?
   • What kind of roles does she play?

   Read the interview below and find out.

'I decided early on that I wasn't going to make any dumb comedies, so my films didn't do that well …'

Jodie Foster, twenty-eight, now with a quarter of a century of experience and an Oscar behind her, shuns the filmstar image.

   'I'm an outsider,' she says. 'I'm not a member of the power structure. If someone treats me like head banana I can't work because I never lose the feeling that I'm the actress and not the person. I don't need to be somebody like Tom Cruise. I just need to work forever.'

   Most of her films have explored the darker side of life, with Foster cast as a victim. But her latest movie, *The Silence of The Lambs*, breaks the mould.

   She plays a rookie FBI agent who must interview a jailed psychopath (Anthony Hopkins) to help her track down a serial killer. When asked about the film she said that it wasn't a part she thought would win her another Oscar, but that when she'd read the script a couple of years before she'd felt compelled to do it. She explained that unlike many of her other roles, the character of Starling was that of a hero. In fact, she felt that the movie was really about the making of a female hero.

   She claims she has not had the most successful career in the world but her role as a rape victim in *The Accused* won her an Oscar and her young hooker in *Taxi Driver* gained a nomination.

   The Silence of The Lambs, a huge success in America, opens here on Friday.

Note: After this article was written, Jodie Foster won an Oscar for her role in The Silence of The Lambs.

Decide whether these sentences about the text are
true or false. Correct the false ones.

1 Jodie Foster feels that her films haven't done too well
   because none of them has been a comedy.
2 She started acting at the age of three.
3 She likes people to treat her with respect.
4 Her film roles are usually in light, superficial films.
5 She thinks her role in *The Silence of The Lambs* will
   win her an Oscar.
6 Her role is that of a victim, as in most of her movies.
7 She won an Oscar for her role in *Taxi Driver*.
8 *The Silence of The Lambs* is doing very well in the
   USA.

Language work

8 *Reported speech*

A The article about Jodie Foster contains examples of both direct and indirect speech. Sentence 1 below is in direct speech: find its indirect equivalent in the text and write it down. Sentence 2 is the reported version of some direct speech: find it and write it down.

1 'It's not a part I think will win me another Oscar, but when I read the script a couple of years ago, I just felt compelled to do it.'

2 She said that she'd decided early on that she wasn't going to make any dumb comedies, so her films hadn't done that well.

These sentences give examples of the three changes that take place in reported speech: changes in tenses, pronouns and time adverbials. Underline them. What are the usual changes within these three categories?

Student A: Write the text below in indirect speech. Vary the verbs that introduce the indirect speech. Look at the article again to help you.

Student B: Turn to page 173.

'I remember the first film I ever made, about fifteen years ago. I was very young and I was terrified, but even then I was convinced that I was going to be a star. I came to Hollywood straight after that film – I was certain that Hollywood was the place to be – but when I was living here that first time I got involved with a bad crowd and it wasn't until I left here in 1985 that success finally happened. When I came back in 1992 I knew I could cope with it. And now I've just signed a contract for two more films, but after these I'll go back home to Scotland – I'm missing it like mad!'

B Compare the two versions of the text. Can you find any times when the tense does not change?

There are two main times when we do not have to change tenses:

- after *when* (with the past simple or continuous).
- if the action/state being reported is still true at the time of reporting. For example: *She said New York is/was bigger than London.* (Both tenses are possible here.) *She said she is/was coming to my party.* (Both tenses are possible if the party has not yet taken place. If it has, only the past form is possible.)

Rewrite these sentences in reported speech, changing the tense if necessary.

1 'We saw quite a lot of films when we were living in the city.'

2 'He likes spending the whole weekend in front of the TV, watching videos.'

3 'I didn't accept that part in his new film because it was an extremely harrowing role and I felt unable to take it on.'

4 'When we arrived in Hollywood it was already the film capital of the world.'

5 'I always go to see his films because I think he's an extremely good actor.'

Listening skills

9 *Identifying speakers*

A In 1989, *Time Out*, the famous guide to what's on in London, published a list of the top hundred films, which had been compiled by asking sixty people involved with film – directors, critics etc. – to choose their top ten films. The list below is the top twenty of these films. Which of the films have you seen?

🖭 Listen to the conversation on tape and tick the films that are mentioned. What do the people on tape think about this top twenty?

1	*Citizen Kane* Welles, 1941, US	☐
2	*The Third Man* Reed, 1949, GB	☐
3	*The Night of the Hunter* Laughton, 1956, US	☐
4	*Some Like It Hot* Wilder, 1959, US	☐
5	*The Godfather* Coppola, 1971/74, US	☐
6	*Vertigo* Hitchcock, 1958, US	☐
7	*L'Atalante* Vigo, 1934, France	☐
8	*Raging Bull* Scorsese, 1980, US	☐
9	*Les Enfants du Paradis* Carne, 1945, France	☐
10	*North by Northwest* Hitchcock, 1959, US	☐
11	*Once Upon a Time in the West* Leone, 1968, Italy	☐
12	*Touch of Evil* Welles, 1958, US	☐
12	*La Regle du Jeu* Renoir, 1939, France	☐
14	*Psycho* Hitchcock, 1960, US	☐
15	*The Wizard of Oz* Fleming, 1939, US	☐
16	*Blue Velvet* Lynch, 1986, US	☐
17	*Apocolypse Now!* Coppola, 1979, US	☐
18	*A Matter of Life and Death* Powell/Pressburger, 1946, GB	☐
19	*Chinatown* Polanski, 1974, US	☐
20	*The Searchers* Ford, 1956, US	☐

B   Say whether statements 1 – 7 about the speakers are true or false, and correct the false ones. The information below will help you identify the speakers.

DIANE   first female speaker
TONY   first male speaker
JANET   the woman who forgot she had seen *Citizen Kane* (second female speaker)
MARK   the man who thinks these top twenty films are for the film business only (second male speaker)

1   Tony hasn't seen *Citizen Kane*.
2   Mark believes that people usually want entertainment from a film.
3   Tony feels that some of the films on the list are meant to be entertaining.
4   Diane believes that the top twenty should be based on attendance.
5   Janet believes that *Psycho* is quite tame.
6   Diane believes that Hitchcock is a great director.
7   Janet would recommend anyone to watch *Psycho*.

10 *Identifying function*

🔲 Statements 1 – 7 on the tape come from the conversation. Match them to these functions.

agreeing ☐   recommending ☐
asking ☐   reminding ☐
asserting ☐   suggesting ☐
explaining ☐

🔲 Listen again.

1   What was asserted?
2   What was the explanation about?
3   What was the recommendation?
4   What did one speaker remind the other of?

Pronunciation

11 *Attitudinal intonation*

A   🔲 Listen to eight short extracts from the conversation. In each one you will hear a response of some kind.

• What does each response express?
• What kind of feeling, if any, does it show?
• What function does it play in the conversation?

B   🔲 The chart below shows a convential way of 'plotting' feelings or opinions. Listen to the tape again and put crosses where you feel they should go. Can you notice any patterns in the stress or intonation?

C   🔲 As you can see, it is possible to express feeling without using any words. Listen to six ways of saying *Mmm*. Which ones express the strongest feeling? Which ones the weakest? How can you tell?

Now you try! Write five invitations for this evening, such as: *Would you like to go to the cinema this evening?* Then work in pairs.

Student A: Offer your invitations to B.
Student B: Respond with *Mmm*, but make it clear how interested you are in the invitation.
Student A: Decide which invitations B would like to accept.

Check this with B. Then swap roles.

word/phrase	strong feeling 10 – – – – 9 – – – – 8 – – – – 7 – – – –6 – – –5 – – – –4 – – – –3 – – – 2 – – –1 – – – –0 weak feeling									
1		X								
2										
3										
4										
5										
6										
7										
8										

Language work

12 *Reporting verbs*

A   In Exercise 8 you saw some reporting verbs for simple statements. But a lot of reported speech can be formed more naturally in other ways. Look at these examples from the conversation in Exercise 9.

> *But surely the whole idea of something like this is basically for the people who are interested …*
> *… in* Psycho *it's all in the imagination …*

Report these two statements, using *suggest* and *explain*, starting like this:

> *She suggested that the whole idea …*
> *She explained that in* Psycho *…*

Now report these statements from Exercise 10, using the correct introductory verb from those listed in the matching part of that exercise.

1   What do you think of the top one?
2   You've seen it … we went to see it in Germany.
3   … probably a lot of these weren't box office hits. That's true. Yeah.
4   You can't take away from Hitchcock the fact that he's one of the greatest directors that's ever lived.
5   I'd tell anyone to watch it, actually.

B   🖾 Use the verbs from Exercise 10 and those below to report the dialogue on tape. Listen in pairs and decide which introductory verbs you are going to use, then rewrite the dialogue.

> *advise   complain   promise   warn   deny   apologise*

Start like this:

> *The director asked Sam to look for Dennis. When Dennis arrived the director complained that …*

C   Complete this chart with the verbs you have used in Sections A and B.

verb + infinitive	verb + -*ing*	verb + object + infinitive	verb + *that*
refuse	suggest	ask	suggest

Final task

13 *A top ten films list*

A   Write a list of your top three or four films.

B   In groups of three or four, compare your films. Try to agree on a top ten for the group.

C   Work out the top ten for the class. Take the top film from each group and write it on the board. Give it three points. Take the second film from each group and write it in the board. Give it two points. Finally, take the third film from each group and give it one point. If any of the films on the board appear in the top tens, give them another point each time they appear. Add up the points and write up the top ten in reverse order.

Introduction

1 Can you tell a fake from the real thing?
Each of these pairs contains one genuine and one fake
object or person. Which is which?
Work with a partner and complete the chart below.

		Real	*Fake*
1	A Botticelli painting?	…	…
2	Queen Elizabeth II?	…	…
3	A medieval castle?	…	…
4	A Rolex diver's watch?	…	…

Compare your answers with other pairs, explaining
your opinions. Once you have all agreed, turn to
page 160 to find out more about the pictures.

1A

1B

2A

2B

3A

3B

4A

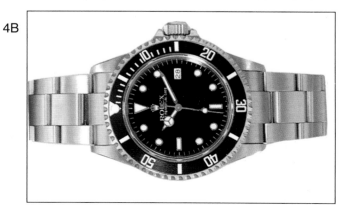
4B

2   The missing link? Or science's greatest fraud?

- What do you know about human evolution?

For many years scientists have been searching for the 'missing link', the half-man/half-ape that will finally prove man's descent from the apes. One of the most important events in this search was the discovery of Piltdown Man in England in the early twentieth century.

Read the documents and answer these questions.

1 How does Professor Smith Woodward justify his claim that the fossil remains are the missing link?
2 What alternative explanations does Sir Piers Hayworth-Drake offer?

THE DAILY REPORTER

9 December 1912

Printed in London

6d

IS THIS THE MISSING LINK?

The scientific establishment has been rocked today by an astonishing announcement from Professor Arthur Smith Woodward of the Department of Geology of the British Museum. Speaking to a packed meeting of the prestigious Royal Geological Society, Professor Woodward revealed the existence of fossil remains which could provide the 'missing link' between man and the apes.

This link, predicted by many eminent scientists since the publication of Charles Darwin's theory of evolution 40 years ago, has been the source of frenzied debate for some time. It seems that this debate may now be over, for Professor Woodward claims that his discovery proves, once and for all, that man is a direct descendant of the apes. Professor Woodward displayed a plaster reconstruction of the skull based on fossil fragments which were discovered between 1908 and last year by an amateur archaeologist, Charles Dawson, at Piltdown in Sussex.

'These fragments combine a humanoid skull with a very primitive ape-like jawbone,' explained Woodward. 'Yet the molar teeth are worn down in a way that could not be achieved by anthropoid jaw movement. The only explanation is that the worn teeth are the result of the free swinging movement of a human jaw. At last we have found a skull which shows the combination of ape and human features which must prove man's descent from the apes.'

The Professor estimates the age of the skull at 500,000 years. If this is accurate, then Piltdown Man must be the earliest human ever discovered. A fact which should revolutionise our interpretation of mankind's ancestry and its development.

THE SOCIETY OF PALAEONTOLOGY,
Grosvenor Square,
Edinburgh.

10th December, 1912

The Editor,
'The Daily Reporter',
Fleet Street,
London.

Dear Sir,

I feel I must respond to your comments regarding the so-called 'missing link' presented by Professor Smith Woodward to the Royal Geological Society on 9th December. At no point did you point out that Professor Woodward has absolutely no scientific proof for his theories. In fact, the majority of the scientific community would support my view that Professor Woodward has allowed his enthusiasm to cloud his judgement in this matter. The Piltdown remains simply cannot be made to fit in with the established pattern of the fossil evidence which I and my colleagues have amassed over the last thirty years both in this country and abroad.

The fact that the skull and jawbone were discovered at the same site could be mere coincidence. And either or both of them might be quite modern in date. The worn molar teeth might not be the result of human jaw movement but of natural deformation. In fact, Professor Woodward may be the innocent victim of a monstrous fraud.

I trust that this letter explains the very dubious nature of the claims made in your newspaper. Its publication will therefore serve to refute the somewhat sensationalist and one-sided view presented in your report.

I remain,
Yours faithfully,
P Hayworth Drake
Sir Piers Hayworth-Drake FRS PhD
Hon. President

Study skills

3 *Analysing and gap-filling*

A Find and underline these words in the two texts on the left and decide whether each word is a noun, verb or adjective.

Newspaper report
establishment geology prestigious fossil predicted eminent evolution frenzied descendant anthropoid descent interpretation ancestry

Letter
proof enthusiasm cloud evidence amassed coincidence sensationalist

B Now look at the summaries below. From the context, decide whether each missing word is a noun, verb or adjective.

Professor Arthur Smith Woodward
Professor Smith Woodward is an (1) … scientist who has been researching man's (2) … by studying the evidence of (3) … remains. He is a supporter of the theory of (4) … and believes that his discovery illustrates the dual existence of human and (5) … features which must have existed at some stage of man's (6) … from the apes.

Sir Piers Hayworth-Drake
Hayworth-Drake is honorary president of the (7) … Society of Palaeontology in Edinburgh. He questions Professor Smith Woodward's scientific (8) … in the matter of the Piltdown remains. Over the years his colleagues have (9) … a large quantity of data regarding human fossils. From this perspective he doubts whether Smith Woodward has sufficient (10) … for his theories; he believes a more likely (11) … is that the Piltdown discoveries are the result of (12) … or possibly even fraud.

C Now use suitable words from the lists in A to fill the gaps in the summaries. Use your decisions about the type of word needed for each gap to help you decide which words are suitable. Note that not all the words will be needed and words should be used once only.

Reading skills

4 *Identifying degrees of certainty/probability*

A Study the statements below. Refer back to the newspaper report or letter and note down whether the statements are impossible, possible, probable or certain according to the relevant text. Then copy down the verb phrase which indicates the degree of certainty. The first one has been done as an example.

Newspaper report
1 Piltdown Man is the missing link.
   Possible. Verb form: 'could provide'
2 The worn molar teeth are the result of anthropoid jaw movements.
3 These features prove man's descent from the apes.
4 Piltdown man is the earliest human ever discovered.
5 This fact will revolutionise our interpretation of man's ancestry.

Hayworth-Drake's letter
6 Most scientists will support Hayworth-Drake's point of view.
7 The remains fit in with the established pattern of the fossil evidence.
8 The discovery of the skull and jawbone together is coincidence.
9 The skull and jawbone are modern.
10 The worn teeth are the result of human jaw movement.
11 Woodward is the victim of a fraud.
12 This letter refutes the one-sided newspaper report.

B Check your answers with a partner and then discuss the questions below.

- Which of the scientific arguments do you think is most convincing?
- Can you suggest how Professor Smith Woodward may have been the victim of a fraud?
- Who do you think may have committed the fraud? And how exactly could he/she have done it?

Turn to page 161 to find out what actually happened.

Language work

5 *Modal verbs of probability/certainty*

A Copy the modal verbs forms you noted in Exercise 4A into the correct position in the chart below. The first two have been done for you.

The chart indicates the modal verbs which are used to show degrees of present and future probability.

Impossible	Possible	Probable	Certain
could not be	could provide		

- What do you notice about the modal verbs we use as the negative forms of *must* and *could*?
- Do you think it is possible to put *could, may* and *might* into some kind of rank order? If so, what is it?

B   Re-write the underlined sections in the article below using modal verbs to replace all the expressions of probability and certainty. You may have to adjust the word order in some cases.

SELF-PORTRAITS UNLIKELY TO BE BY HAND OF VAN GOGH

Martin Bailey examines recent findings on the life of Holland's most tormented artist

Startling evidence has been produced to show that <u>three 'self-portraits' up to now accepted as being painted by Vincent Van Gogh are possibly fakes.</u>

Dutch-born art historian Walter Feilchenfeldt last week told an international symposium at the Van Gogh museum that, after the first systematic investigation into the artist's self-portraits he had concluded that <u>'Three of them are impossible to guarantee as genuine.'</u>

All three paintings are currently on public show. The most famous is at the Metropolitan Museum in New York, another at the Wadsworth Atheneum in Hartford, Connecticut, and the third at Norway's National Gallery in Oslo. <u>There are rumours that there is a 50% chance that the pictures will now be withdrawn from public display.</u>

Feilchenfeldt explained that all Van Gogh's self-portraits were given to friends or left to his family at his death. <u>Any picture which is not traceable to one of these sources is certainly considered dubious.</u>

In addition to the problems of provenance, Feilchenfeldt has questioned the stylistic evidence. Regarding the portrait in New York he claims that <u>the majority of art historians are almost certain to support his view that the brushstrokes are haphazard.</u>

Not all of his research is negative, however. One positive result is confirmation that <u>the self-portrait in London's Courtauld Gallery is definitely genuine</u>, as it is listed as having been purchased from Jo Bonger, the widow of Vincent's brother Theo.

Speaking skills

6 *Persuading and convincing*

A   Read the short dialogue about this painting and then answer the questions below.

A I think this Vermeer's a fake.
B Really? Why?
A Well, look at the man's legs. Don't you think they look rather clumsy?
B I suppose so, but that doesn't mean it's a fake. I mean, look at the other details – they're very skillfully painted, aren't they?
A Maybe, but don't you agree the figures look rather lifeless?
B Perhaps you're right.

- Do *you* think this painting is a fake?
- What are the speakers trying to do?
- What phrases and devices do they use to achieve this?

B   Work in pairs. Convince each other of your point of view. You can add your own reasons to those given.

Picture 1: The Loch Ness Monster

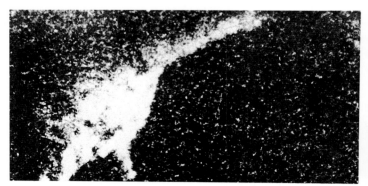

Student A: You think this picture is a fake. Turn to page 166 for your reasons.
Student B: You think this picture is genuine. Turn to page 174 for your reasons.

Picture 2: An ancient Greek statue of a discus thrower

Student A: You think this sculpture is genuine. Turn to page 166 for your reasons.
Student B: You think this sculpture is a fake. Turn to page 174 for your reasons.

Listening skills

7 *Checking and clarifying information*

A One of the greatest frauds of modern times was the case of the Hitler diaries. Read through this summary of the main events in this story and check that you understand what happened.

The story of the Hitler diaries

1945 Adolf Hitler sends a plane containing a mysterious locked trunk to Berlin. It is shot down somewhere.

... Heidemann visits Fritz Stiefel, a collector of Nazi memorabilia, and sees a Hitler diary.

1980 Heidemann sets out for West Germany to search for the site of something and eventually discovers a number of crashed planes in a village.

1981 (January) Heidemann 'discovers' Kujau and hears his story about his fictional father.

1981 (January) Heidemann starts seventeen regular visits to Kujau, swapping suitcases for each instalment of the diaries.

... Some experts in the United States and Sweden confirm the handwriting as being unquestionably that of Adolf Hitler.

1983 (April) World-renowned forger Hugh Trevor-Roper confirms the authority of the diaries.

1983 (April) *Stern* has collected the full set of diaries and begins some sort of negotiations for the German syndication rights with the world's leading publishing companies.

1983 Forensic test results are published, exposing the diaries as clever and brilliant fakes.

... Kujau and Heidemann on trial somewhere are sentenced to over fourteen years for fraud.

B 🖾 There are thirteen mistakes in the information in the summary. Listen to the extract from a radio book review programme and make any corrections that are necessary.

C 🖾 Some of the information in the summary is rather vague (e.g. *somewhere, some sort of*) and some of the information is missing (e.g. dates).
Listen again and add this specific information to the summary.
When you have finished, double-check the information with a partner.

Vocabulary

8 *Words with negative connotations*

The radio broadcast contains many adjectives, adverbs and nouns which stress the negative attitude of the speaker to the subject she is describing. Read the tapescript on page 182 and find as many words as possible to add to the lists below.

features of modern international publishing	features of the fraud	the forged diaries	Gerd Heideman	Conrad Kujau
credulity	deception	worthless	ambitious	small-time

Now put words from the lists into the correct columns in this chart and fill any gaps which remain.

noun	adjective	adverb
	deceptive	
notoriety		
	greedy	
		amateurishly
blatancy		blatantly
	gullible	
	farcical	
ineptitude		
		unscrupulously

Pronunciation

9 Assimilation

A 🔊 Listen carefully to these three extracts from the radio programme. What do you notice about the underlined sounds?

  a *that plane never arrived ...*
  b *obsessive secrecy and cut-throat competition ...*
  c *... his exorbitant conditions ...*

B 🔊 This phenomenon is known as assimilation. Listen to each of the items below and underline the sound which changes or disappears.

  1 I believe he's on that plane.
  2 We had to work under extremely strict conditions.
  3 He's rather a fat person.
  4 I prefer very hot curries.
  5 Only five pounds! That was a good buy.
  6 She's got a bad cold.
  7 Jim's the head gardener.
  8 That was a very sad ballad.
  9 What a beautiful old carpet.
  10 There's a famous Vermeer in the Red Gallery.

  🔊 Now listen and repeat the sentences.

C Can you make any rules about when /t/ and /d/ change? What did you notice about items 6 and 9? How are they different from the others?

Writing skills

10 Narrative accounts

A • What is the main difference between the way the sequence of events in the Hitler diary fraud is presented in the radio review and in the notes in Exercise 7A?
  • What are the advantages of putting events in chronological order?

It is usual to use a chronological sequence when describing a story which happened in the past. What other techniques can we use to help the reader understand what happened? Think about:

a use of tenses.
b use of linking words.
c use of time references.

B Complete this narrative account, making it as clear as possible. Use all the techniques you have just discussed.

The story of the Hitler diaries fraud

The story of the Hitler diaries fraud began in 1945 when Adolf Hitler sent a mysterious trunk of personal documents on a plane to Salzburg. The plane crashed in a remote forest near the village of Boernersdorf.

Twenty-five years later Gerd Heidemann, a journalist on Stern magazine, met Fritz Steifel and saw a 'Hitler diary' in his collection of Nazi memorabilia ...

Language work

11 Modal perfects

A Look at these two sentences from the radio broadcast.

Adolf Hitler, who <u>must have been trying</u> to save his personal documents for posterity, sent a plane ... from Berlin to a safe haven in Salzburg.

It describes in minute detail the tangled web of deception, intrigue and farce which gave rise to what <u>may have been</u> the greatest fraud of the century.

What are the two differences between the underlined phrases?

Match the statements below with these modal perfect verbs.

  *can't have ...   might have ...   may have ...
  must have ...*

  1 All the evidence indicates that Heidemann was very gullible.
  2 Kujau was certainly not very intelligent.
  3 There was a slight chance that the fraud would have worked.
  4 There was a good chance that the graves in Boernersdorf were genuine.

B Look at this old photograph. Discuss the questions, using modal verb forms in your answers.

  • When do you think it was taken?
  • Who took it?
  • Who or what are the creatures in it?
  • What are they doing?
  • Is it genuine or not?

C Use modal perfect forms with the verbs in italics to complete this passage about the photograph.

The Cottingley Fairy Photographs

We all know that fairies don't exist. If they can't exist now then presumably they (1 *exist*) in the past either. Yet in 1917 a photograph appeared which seemed to prove the opposite.

When Frances Griffiths and her cousin Elsie were late for tea one day in 1917, their mother asked them what they had been doing. They claimed they had been playing with fairies at the bottom of the garden. The girls (2 *be*) lying. Nonetheless, they told their mother they would prove their story by taking a photograph next time they played with the fairies. We know they (3 *play*) with fairies, yet a few days later the girls produced a photograph which seemed to confirm their story. Somehow they (4 *fake*) the picture but at the time nobody could work out how it had been done. They (5 *combine*) two negatives, they (6 *make*) models and hung them with wires in front of the lens, or they (7 *paint*) the fairies onto a sheet of glass – the technique frequently used in modern film-making. Whatever they did (8 *be*) very ingenious because many scientists examined the negatives and found nothing. Even Sir Arthur Conan Doyle, creator of Sherlock Holmes, was convinced they were genuine.

For over fifty years the mystery was unsolved. Then in 1983, when Frances and Elsie were both very old women, they decided to tell the truth. They had simply cut some figures out of a book of fairy stories and supported them on hat pins in front of the camera. Like all the greatest hoaxes, it was its simplicity which had made it so convincing.

Vocabulary

12 *Idioms of reality and illusion*

What is the meaning of this sentence from the radio broadcast?

> *How was it that the management of Stern … never smelt a rat?*

There are many English idioms which convey the meaning that things are not always as they seem. Match idioms a – l below with explanations 1 – 12 in the next column.

a   a wolf in sheep's clothing
b   mutton dressed as lamb
c   to take someone for a ride
d   to let the cat out of the bag
e   to make a mountain out of a molehill
f   to pull the wool over someone's eyes
g   an open secret
h   a blessing in disguise
i   a storm in a teacup
j   to pay lip-service
k   not to count one's chickens before they're hatched
l   a red herring

1   something which appears bad but will have a good effect
2   to pretend to accept or obey while in fact questioning or ignoring
3   to reveal something which is supposed to be a secret
4   to treat something unimportant as something very important
5   something which appears relevant but is in fact not so
6   not to count on events until they actually happen
7   someone who appears harmless but is in fact dangerous
8   something which is supposed to be a secret but in fact everyone knows about it
9   to hide the truth from someone
10 someone who tries to appear younger and more attractive than they are
11 to successfully mislead someone for personal motives or gain
12 a problem or conflict that is thought to be serious but proves not to be

Use an appropriate idiom to make a sentence about each of the following.

- the fact that Kujau knew about the plane crash near Boernersdorf
- Stern's hopes of selling syndication rights to the diaries
- Kujau's ability to convince Heidemann

Final Task

13 *The Strange Case of the Mulahabad Diamonds Fraud*

Work in groups of three or four. You are all Sherlock Holmes, but you each have a different letter to read. Read your own letter only, and then get together to discuss and solve the mystery.

This list of people involved in the case may help you.

Corporal Tom Cabmoll   Dr Ignatius Brown
Sir Hugh Drummond   John Tosh
Colonel Tosh (John Tosh's father)

Student A: Your letter is on page 167.
Student B: Your letter is on page 174.
Student C/D: Your letter is on page 179.

Be ready to explain your solution to the class.

Unit 13   Weather or Not

Introduction

1 The headlines below all describe unusual weather conditions in a number of places from 1987 to 1990. Match the headlines to the places a – h.

a   southern part of England
b   Alpine regions in France, Switzerland, Austria and Italy
c   Toulouse area of southern France
d   Canary Islands
e   Tigre and Eritrea regions of Ethiopia
f   eastern Australia
g   south-west England
h   Touggourt, in the northern Sahara, Algeria

Check your answers and find out more about these freak weather conditions on page 161.

4 Severe flooding creates inland sea bigger than Britain!
(April 1990)

5 ELDERLY VICTIMS OF SUNSTROKE DIE IN TEMPERATURES OVER 40° C
(July 1990)

6 MOTORWAYS MELT IN MIDSUMMER MADNESS!
(August 1990)

1 WORST HURRICANE SINCE 1703 RAVAGES SOUTH AND HOME COUNTIES
(October 1987)

2 Island snow astonishes 'getaway' tourists
(February 1989)

7 DESERT TOWN SWAMPED BY RAIN – USUAL ANNUAL TOTAL FALLS IN UNDER 72 HOURS!
(August 1990)

3 MILDEST WINTER FOR YEARS THREATENS TOURIST TRADE
(Winter 1989 – 90)

8 African drought and famine worse through long hot summers
(Summer 1990)

2 The photographs on this page all depict freak weather conditions or their aftermath. Can you name the weather phenomenon in each case? Can you think of any others?

- Have you ever experienced any freak (or severe) weather conditions? What were they?

- What caused them? Were they natural phenomena or could their cause be attributed to ecological problems such as global warming, the hole in the ozone layer or the greenhouse effect?

B

D

Reading skills

3   Predicting and interpreting attitude

A   Picture A in Exercise 2 shows the aftermath of a severe storm which took place in the southern part of Britain in October 1987. Four years later, some advertisements published by the British government caused a great deal of controversy.

1   Look at the title of the text below. What do you think it is about?
2   Why do you think the adverts caused a controversy? Read the first paragraph and find out.
3   Look at the underlined quotes in the text. Who do you think said/wrote them? The government? The government's advertising agency? Scientists?
4   What do you think the government actually claimed?

Read the whole text and find out.

B   Decide whether these statements are true or false and find evidence in the text to support them (if they are true) or contradict them (if they are false).

1   Scientists support the assertions made by the government in the advertisements.
2   In the advertisements the government tried to link weather conditions with global warming, and tried to place the responsibility on the general public.
3   The government has based its claim on scientific evidence.
4   The experts in the field are against any kind of advertising by the government.
5   The account manager in the advertising agency defends the advertisements.

C   Do you have any idea from the language in the text of what the writer's attitude might be? Is he:

a   in favour of the government's position?
b   sceptical towards the government's statements?
c   sceptical towards the scientists' statements?

Global warming ads wrong, say scientists

by Sean Ryan

Advertiments for a government energy-saving campaign, the biggest attempt yet to alert Britain to the dangers of global warming, have been exposed as inaccurate and sensational by international climate experts.

Scientists said the campaign, which links the greenhouse effect to extreme weather conditions such as the 1987 storm, amounted to unscientific scare tactics that could undermine efforts to tackle environmental pollution.

Advertising watchdogs will this week consider whether the government is misleading people with its newspaper advertisements. The first, published last week, uses photographs of the 1987 storm under the headline: 'Global Warming. We have been warned.' Another to be published this week under the slogan: 'Global Warming. How much of the responsibility rests at your door?' depicts an electric kettle whose steam is rising into a sky filled with lightning and thunder.

Meteorologists said yesterday that any rise in temperatures could make the weather calmer rather than stormier.

The Meteorological Office, which compiled the most detailed report yet on the greenhouse effect for the United Nations last year, predicted a 1°C rise in temperatures by 2025 and said storms driven to Britain across the Atlantic could weaken as a result. Asked about the storms in 1987 and 1990, Dr David Bennets, its research coordinator, said: 'We would regard them as natural events and there is no evidence whatsoever to say that they aren't.'

The small print in the advertisements concedes that scientists are 'not yet able to say if the great storm of 1987 and the "hurricanes" of 1990 are among the first signs of global warming.' The second advertisement warns that carbon dioxide and other greenhouse gases would 'throw the world's climate out of balance' and asserts: 'If left unchecked, global warming is likely to change existing weather patterns across the world.'

Brian Hoskins, Professor of Meteorology at Reading University and one of Britain's leading experts on storms, said he was disappointed that advertisements with a positive message about energy conservation had overstated the case. 'There is no way you could say that a particular storm was caused by the greenhouse effect,' he said.

Yesterday, Collett, Dickenson and Pearce, the advertising agency responsible for the three-year campaign, admitted that the claims were based on 'flimsy' evidence. Chris Denny, the account manager, said scientists did not know what changes in climate to expect. Photographs of the destruction after the 1987 storm, called 'a hurricane' in the advertisement, were chosen because they were vivid and memorable, he said. 'Inevitably advertising picks on dramatic images and simplifies things in order to get people's attention.'

Last week, the Department of Energy referred queries to the Environment Department, which was responsible for supervising the advertising copywriters. A spokeswoman denied that the claims were misleading. 'The great storm illustrates our vulnerability to extreme weather conditions which could be one result of global warming.'

Vocabulary

4   *Positive and negative bias*

A   Read the text again and find all the words and phrases that describe the government's campaign, the adverts and photos, such as *inaccurate, unscientific, scare tactics*. Underline them all and list them. From your list, find words which mean the following.

1   giving the wrong impression
2   exaggerated the argument
3   wrong
4   not based on fact
5   actions designed to alarm
6   easy to remember

B   • Which words or phrases are positive? Which are negative?
   • What is the balance between positive and negative?
   • Does this tell you anything about the writer's attitude?

Language work

5   *Predicting the future*

A   The text contains a number of predictions about the future and the possible consequences of the greenhouse effect.

Complete these three sentences with expressions and verbs from the text.

1   Any rise in temperatures … the weather calmer.
2   If left unchecked, global warming … existing weather patterns.
3   The second advertisement warns that greenhouse gases … the world's climate out of balance.

   • Which one of these structures is used most often in the text?
   • Why do you think this is?
   • Which one is used to express quite a strong possibility? Why is it used here?

B   Can you think of other ways of predicting the future? Make a list of them. Then, in groups, discuss the following questions.

   • Do you think the world will run out of oil/the human race will disappear/scientists will discover the origin of the universe?
   • Do you think we will ever know life forms from another planet?
   • Do you think there will ever be a united Europe?
   • Do you think you (or anyone in your class) will ever be famous/appear on TV/become rich/travel to the moon/go to prison/compete in the Olympics?

Listening skills

6   *Understanding cause and effect links*

A   🔊 Anne Lawson, from the Meteorological Office, is talking on a radio programme about the possible climate changes that might take place if predictions about the possible rise in temperature are true. Look at these photographs and predict what she might say about the subjects depicted

Ⓐ

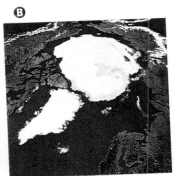
Ⓑ

Ⓒ

B   Complete the following chart with details from the tape.

cause		possible effect
1 increase in greenhouse gases	➤	change in weather patterns
2 rise in temperature	➤	calmer weather
3 ice caps …	➤	rise in …
4 …	➤	[1] … of vulnerable areas [2] submerge …
5 … by 2090	➤	total shift in …
6 change in … in …	➤	change in …

C   Listen to the tape again and complete the chart below with as many new words or phrases as you can. Can you add any more from the text on page 98?

environment	weather	geographical features
global warming	storm	ice caps

Work in pairs to find out more about the phrases in the chart. Explain them in your own words.

Student A: Turn to page 166.
Student B: Turn to page 170.

Speaking skills

7 *Speculating*

A Anne Lawson uses a number of ways to express speculation about the future. Did she use any that you discussed in Exercise 5A?
Look at these less usual ways of expressing a prediction and decide which are more possible and which are less possible.

1 *We predict there will be a rise of 1°C …*
2 *It's conceivable that some areas could be submerged …*
3 *… areas susceptible to flooding are likely to suffer …*
4 *Britain might well start to enjoy a Mediterranean climate.*
5 *We would have to contend with insects, pests and diseases …*

B Work in groups. Go back to your predictions in Exercise 5B. If appropriate, use some of the expressions above to make new predictions. Then look at the chart in Exercise 6B, and make predictions using the expressions above.

Vocabulary

8 *Multi-word verbs*

Look at this extract from the dialogue.

… the resulting deforestation, that is, cutting down the trees, is thought to contribute to global warming …

What do you think is the meaning of the particle *down* here? Look at your chart on page 154 if necessary.

Complete sentences 1 – 8 with the appropriate form of the verbs below. Use a dictionary if necessary. Does the particle mean the same in each case?

break bring burn close pour pull put wind

1 The rain has been … down all day.
2 All the buildings in the area were … down to make way for the new development.
3 The house was … down in last night's fire.
4 The rebel forces … the government down in the revolution.
5 It's very difficult to be polite to him – he … me down every time we speak.
6 I'm afraid I can't come to the party as my car has … down again.
7 Business got so bad in the recession that half the shops … down for good.
8 I find it difficult to relax when I first go on holiday – it always takes a day or two to … down completely.

Add the verbs to your chart on page 154.

Reading skills

9 *Following cause and effect links*

A These quotes all come either from a book on the possible effects of global warming, or from the dialogue. Which ones have some connection with each other? In pairs, group the quotes according to connections you may find, then compare with another group.

> **1** It has been calculated that if the emission of greenhouse gases continues at the present rate, the increase in temperature will be enough to cause a rise in sea level … of between 24 and 38 cm by 2030.

> **2** If the loss of even the scant annual rainfall of Cape Verde were to become a long-term feature, it is doubtful whether careful farming practices … could save a way of life.

> **3** Should there be a considerable rise in sea level, many of these islands would be in grave danger.

> **4** If drastic measures are not taken to reduce greenhouse gas emissions over the next couple of decades, it is likely that many Arctic species and the indigenous peoples which rely on them will not survive the 21st century.

> **5** Nineteen people were killed and the total would undoubtedly have been heavier if the gale had happened in daytime.

> **6** … if the Arctic ice cap were to melt completely by 2090 … the entire weather pattern of the Northern Hemisphere would change.

> **7** If much of Britain were to experience a Mediterranean type of climate, as most greenhouse theories forecast, there would be radical changes both in the British climate itself and in the agriculture that would be possible in the country.

> **8** If one assumes a growing greenhouse effect of global warming, … the Arctic ice cap could have melted by 2090.

> **9** If global warming has been at work, we would expect the weather to be getting progressively hotter and drier in the summer.

> **10** The rate at which most observers claim it is melting is rapid, and if that suggested rate were to be maintained, the ice around the North Pole would have disappeared within a century.

> **11** If the temperatures in the South of England increase by relatively little, it is possible that the mosquito could establish itself in areas such as the Fens …

B   Many of the quotes in Exercise 9A contain cause and effect links. Read the quotes again and complete the chart with the effects.

cause	effect
global warming	
emission of greenhouse gases	
melting of ice caps	
rise in sea level	
climate change in Britain	

Work in groups to put the cause and effect chains into simple *If* … sentences, such as:

If the atmosphere continues to get warmer, many climates will/may/might get …

Can you see any cause and effect chains starting in the right-hand column and ending in the left-hand column?

Language work

10 *Revision of conditionals*

A   Find examples of the following from quotes 1 – 7. Write them down.

- first conditional
- second conditional
- third conditional
- conditional using a modal in the main clause
- conditional with inversion instead of the *if*-clause

B   Use the correct conditional to complete these sentences.

1   If we continue to use chemicals irresponsibly, …
2   If the storm of 1987 had happened during the day, more people …
3   Should the authorities decide to install a recycling plant, …
4   We could spend more time sunbathing if …
5   If some countries don't agree to changes in their fishing practices, …
6   If I hadn't seen the tidal wave with my own eyes, I …

11 *Mixed conditionals*

A   Look at quotes 8 – 11. These are all examples of mixed conditionals, that is, conditional sentences which mix clauses from two different conditional types, for example:

If ICI had not discovered an alternative to poisonous CFC gases, Europe would not now be able to ban CFCs.

This expresses a past cause with a present effect.

Complete the chart for quotes 8 – 11. The example has been done for you.

	if-clause: verb	main clause: verb
e.g.	Past perfect (3rd conditional): 'had not discovered'	would (2nd conditional): 'would not be able'
8		
9		
10		
11		

Think about the times and tenses of the causes (*if* clauses) and their effects (main clauses). What is the relationship in each case? Why have the conditionals been mixed? How does the writer show that he is not certain of some effects?

B   According to the examples of conditionals given in the quotes, say whether these 'rules' are true or not.

1   Modal verbs can be used in the main clause of conditional sentences.
2   Modal verbs can be used in the *if*-clause of conditional sentences.
3   The *if*-clause of a second conditional sentence can be replaced by *should* in initial position.
4   It is possible to have a 1st conditional *if*-clause and a 3rd conditional main clause.
5   It is possible to have a 3rd conditional *if*-clause and a 1st conditional main clause.

12 *Further practice of conditionals*

A   Each pair of sentences below is identical except for the use of two different conditionals. Try to work out the difference in meaning between the sentences.

1   a   If he arrives on time, will you ask him to wait?
     b   If he arrived on time, would you ask him to wait?

2   a   If I had enough money, I'd buy a new car.
     b   If I had had enough money, I'd have bought a new car.

3   a   If you hadn't taken the job, you wouldn't be living in the city now.
     b   If you hadn't taken the job, you wouldn't have been living in the city.

4   a   If I didn't like her, I wouldn't have invited her.
     b   If I hadn't liked her, I wouldn't have invited her.

5   a   If the rate of increase continues, this city could have become the crime capital of the world by 2005.
     b   If the rate of increase had continued, this city could have become the crime capital of the world by 2005.

B   Complete these opinions with verbs in the appropriate forms. (Items 3 and 4 contain mixed conditionals.)

1   People … much happier if they … worry about money.
2   If the steam train …, there … an industrial revolution.
3   If the death penalty … in the United Kingdom in 1965, it … a safer place today.
4   If consumers continue to demand good quality wooden furniture, the rainforests … by the early years of the next century.

Do you agree with these opinions? Discuss them in small groups.

C   Now write conditional sentences about yourself. Describe:

1   something you regret doing in the past and its result.
2   how something you are doing now might affect your future.
3   something you might do in the future and its possible consequences.
4   something you didn't do in the past and what the situation would be now, had you done it.

Discuss your sentences in groups.

D   Use information from this unit so far to discuss the possible consequences of the topics below. In pairs, try to make 'consequence chains' as in the example below. Some ideas are given to help you.

If global warming gets any worse, the ice caps could melt.
If the ice caps melted, the sea level would rise.
If the sea level rose, many low-lying countries would be flooded.
If many low-lying countries were flooded, food production might suffer.

•   *global warming* : climate change ➔ threat to traditional crops ➔ farming practices ➔ destruction of Third World economy
•   *hole in the ozone layer* : stronger ultra-violet rays ➔ skin cancer ➔ need for more protection ➔ effect on tourism
•   *eliminating animal species* : balance of nature upset ➔ death of other species ➔ increase of pests ➔ effect on crops
•   *use of hard wood* : destruction of rainforests ➔ changes in world's atmosphere ➔ not enough oxygen ➔ danger of suffocation
•   *effective medicine* : fewer early deaths from illness ➔ rise in world population ➔ food shortages ➔ millions dying of starvation
•   *unemployment* : too much free time ➔ frustration ➔ criminal activity

Now compare your consequence chains with other pairs.

Pronunciation

13 *Sentence stress*

☐ Look at these sentences from the dialogue. Decide where you think the main stresses should be in each of them. Then listen to the tape to check.

1   *And if your predictions are conservative? If they are conservative, then there'll certainly be more developments.*
2   *Should there be a considerable rise in sea level, many of these islands would clearly be in grave danger.*
3   *… if the Arctic ice cap were to melt completely by 2090, the entire weather pattern of the northern hemisphere would change.*

The main sentence stresses are usually on the important words in the sentence, i.e. the nouns and the verbs that carry meaning. Can you find any exceptions to this in the sentences above? Why are they different?

☐ Read the conversation below with a partner. Decide where the stresses should go, then listen to check and to mark them on. Finally, read it again, paying attention to the stress.

A   Do you believe that sunbathing is really bad for you?
B   Yes, I do. I've always been very careful about sunbathing, but now I won't go into the sun without a strong sun cream on.
A   Don't you think you're being a bit, well, excessive?
B   No! You've read about the hole in the ozone layer, haven't you?
A   Well of course, but …
B   So you have to accept that more of the sun's rays are getting through?
A   Yes. But I suppose I've never taken it really seriously. I've been sunbathing through the summer for years now, and nothing's happened to me.
B   Nothing's happened *yet*, you mean!

14 Work in groups. What are your feelings about the issues discussed so far in this unit? Is there anything you do personally, or that you could do, to help the environment? Think about the following:

•   recycling paper/glass/aluminium
•   using lead-free petrol
•   avoiding the use of aerosols
•   buying environmentally friendly products
•   supporting environmental pressure groups
•   economising on the use of energy

Is there anything else you can think of?

Writing skills

15 *Hypothesising; expressing cause and effect*

A When we use conditionals we are hypothesising about cause and effect relationships, that is we are discussing the possible effects of a certain cause.

cause	effect
higher temperature in the summer	higher sales of ice cream

We can express this as a simple cause and effect.

- *Because of / Owing to / Due to the higher summer temperatures, ice cream sales have increased.*
- *Summer temperatures have become higher. Therefore / As a result / Consequently, ice cream sales have increased.*
- *(As) Summer temperatures here become higher, so ice cream sales have increased.*

However, if we are not sure that this will happen, we use a conditional.

> *If temperatures in the summer get higher, then ice cream sales will / might / could increase.*

Look at cause and effect relationships 1 – 5 below. Make one simple cause and effect sentence for each and one hypothetical sentence for each. Remember to vary the conditionals, depending on whether the events are past or present, and how certain you are of the effects.

	cause	effect
1	drop in winter temperatures	higher sales of double glazing
2	less snow than before	closure of ski resorts
3	more money on defence	less money on research
4	growing awareness of nutrition	fewer health problems
5	fewer jobs available to people	more leisure time

B You are going to plan and write an essay on the possibility of permanent climate change because of global warming. Go back over the information you have been given in this unit about climate change (e.g. the newspaper article, the chart in Exercise 6B, the quotes in Exercise 9) and make notes of your own on this subject. Then organise your notes and write the essay. Use this framework:

- Introduction to the topic
- Effects of global warming so far (using cause and effect sentences)
- Predictions for future effects (using cause and effect sentences / conditionals)
- Your personal predictions
- Conclusion

Final task

16 *If only ...*

A This picture comes from a book called *The Alteration* by Kingsley Amis. The book is a thriller based in present-day Britain, but a very different Britain from the one we know, because a certain event in the past did not happen. Use these clues from the plot to speculate on what might/might not have happened.

- The Pope is an Englishman.
- Latin is the language of the church.
- Wealthy families have priests living with them.
- America (New England) is considered a land of heathens.

B 🔲 Listen to the short dialogues on tape. Each is about something strange. Work out from each dialogue what is strange and what happened/did not happen to bring about this situation. Then speculate further on the consequences of the event/situation in the dialogue, as in this example.

In 1, the videophone has been invented and is in current use. If the videophone had really been invented, we wouldn't need to leave our homes/offices for meetings but we would always have to look our best ...

C Work in two teams, A and B. Write short dialogues like the ones on tape, based on the pictures below (Team B) or on page 161 (Team A). Think of two or three situations which may or may not have happened and write dialogues which contain clues. Read your dialogues to the other team. Can they guess what happened? Then, as a whole class, speculate further about the possible consequences of the situations.

Introduction

1 What is your idea of physical beauty?
Would you describe any of these people as beautiful?
Is it true that 'beauty is in the eye of the beholder' or do we have a uniform concept of physical perfection?

A recent magazine questionnaire tried to answer the latter question. Complete the questionnaire by filling in the first line with your personal opinion.
Now fill the other lines by questioning four or five other students. Look at the results to find the physiques, eyes, face and hair types which are most popular in your group. Compare your results with other groups to find the overall preferences of the class.

WHAT IS THE PERFECT PHYSICAL SPECIMEN?

OPTIONS:
Physique: ectomorph, endomorph, mesomorph
Eyes: blue, green, brown
Face: oval, round, square
Hair: brown, black, red, blonde

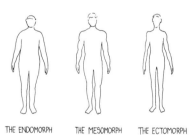

THE ENDOMORPH   THE MESOMORPH   THE ECTOMORPH

NAME	MALE				FEMALE			
	Physique	*Face*	*Eyes*	*Hair*	*Physique*	*Face*	*Eyes*	*Hair*
RESULT								

2 Few people are born with a 'perfect' body. Cosmetic surgery gives people the chance to improve on nature and in the United States teenagers and men are becoming the latest patients to seek medical 'remodelling'.

In pairs, look at the list of parts of the body on the right. Choose the three which you think are the most popular for cosmetic operations for teenagers and put them in order of popularity.

a thighs
b nose
c ears
d chest
e hair
f eyes
g lips
h muscles
i waist
j chin
k cheeks
l facial skin

Now read the newspaper article on the next page and check your rank order.

AMERICAN TEENS AND BODYBUILDERS SEEK COSMETIC IMPROVEMENTS

The Californian obsession with physical perfection is no longer confined to middle-aged women. Across the United States teenagers are going under the knife, financed and encouraged by doting parents who believe bodily perfection to be a more desirable birthday present than a stereo or a car. And in Beverley Hills surgeons have developed a technique by which men no longer have to spend hours in gyms to achieve bulging muscles.

Tiffany White, a schoolgirl aged seventeen from suburban Los Angeles, never liked her chubby cheeks. 'A lot of people said I looked like Bette Midler and that really bothered me,' she said. In the old days she would have had to lump it. But this year she joined thousands of other American teenagers in opting for surgery and had the fat vacuumed out and her nose remodelled while she was at it. Once the domain of the rich

and vain, *aesthetic surgery*, as the practitioners prefer to call it, is doing wonders for adolescent self-esteem and making millions for doctors, at the same time prompting qualms among professional bodies.

'Teenagers have become a big market for plastic surgery,' said Dr Martin Sullivan, an Illinois surgeon who says between eight and ten teenagers consult him every month. Some surgeons estimate that teenagers account for 25 per cent of their business. According to the latest figures, last year 117,000 teenagers under eighteen had rhinoplasty (or 'nose-jobs'). Almost as many had ear-pinning, followed by chin augmentation and then dermabrasion – a sort of sandpapering technique which removes acne scars from the skin. A small but increasing number of Asian teenagers are having blepharoplasty, an eyelid operation which produces a more rounded

Caucasian look. The use of silicone muscle to correct deformities has been widespread for some time, but plastic surgeons now report that 20 per cent of their clients are males seeking decorative muscles. In Beverley Hills Dr Mel Bircoll has turned more than fifty puny thoraxes into brawny specimens using a technique which inserts two or three lumps of silicone into the chest through a small nick in the armpit. Aside from chest muscles, surgeons report that the next most popular operation is to the cheeks and jaw. 'People want the square-featured Schwarzenegger look,' said Dr Darryl Hodgkinson. While many surgeons do not believe artificial muscles for males will ever catch on in a big way, they are optimistic about the growth prospects for teenage cosmetic surgery. They argue that surgery can help cure the insecurity and self-consciousness that comes from a lack of self-esteem.

- Would you yourself consider undergoing cosmetic surgery?
- Which part of your body would you like improved?

Vocabulary

3 *Parts of the body*

A number of parts of the body are mentioned in the text and in Exercise 2. Look at this illustration of the human body and use words from the list below to complete the labels. Not all the words will be needed.

Adam's Apple	shoulder blade
forehead	thigh
wrist	ribs
ankle	earlobe
toe	armpit
crown	hip
knuckle	collarbone
elbow	eyelid
cheekbone	nostril
calf	biceps
navel	jawbone
forearm	palm

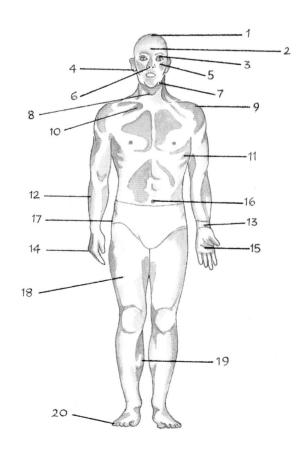

4   Categorising

A   The human body is made up of a number of components which can be grouped according to various criteria. Copy the word map on to a piece of paper.

Now, working with a partner, use the words below to complete the boxes in the word map.

calves	*muscles*	*joints*
shoulder	*bones*	*heart*
liver	*organs*	*knee*
skull	*soft tissues*	

```
┌─────────────────────────────────────────────┐
│         COMPONENTS OF THE HUMAN BODY          │
│                                               │
│    ┌──────────────┐      ┌──────────────┐     │
│    │ HARD TISSUES │      │              │     │
│    └──────────────┘      └──────────────┘     │
│    ┌────┐  ┌────┐      ┌────┐  ┌────┐          │
│    │    │  │    │      │    │  │    │          │
│    └────┘  └────┘      └────┘  └────┘          │
│  ┌──┐┌──────┐┌──┐  ┌──┐┌──────┐┌────────┐      │
│  │  ││ RIBS ││  │  │  ││      ││ BICEPS │      │
│  └──┘└──────┘└──┘  └──┘└──────┘└────────┘      │
└─────────────────────────────────────────────┘
```

B   Now add at least ten more boxes to the map, using words from your own knowledge.

Language work

5   Forms of comparison

A   How could you compare the physical appearance of the famous people in these photographs? Note down four or five ways you might compare them:

B   Work in groups of three. You each have information about the people in the photographs. The people are only identified by the letters A – F. Your task is to share the information and work out which photograph each letter identifies.

Student A: Turn to page 166.
Student B: Turn to page 175.
Student C: Turn to page 180.

C   The photographs were identified by making comparisons. From the comparisons given, find at least one more example of each form listed below. Then add your own sentences from Section A under the appropriate headings.

MAKING COMPARISONS

Metaphor	*A sings like a bird.*
Simile	*A is as thin as a rake.*
Comparative adjective	*A is darker than the others.*
Comparative adverb	*D has been married more often than the others.*
Superlative adjective	*Of this group, E is the least famous.*
Superlative adverb	*B ranks the highest.*
Expressing similarity	*B is as tall as F.*

D   Look at the four photographs in Exercise 1 on page 104 and give each photograph a secret code letter. Don't show anyone!
Using the phrases in the chart as models, write at least one sentence of each type about the photographs, using your code letters instead of names.
Show your sentences to a partner and see if he/she can match your code letters with the correct photographs.

Speaking skills

6   Describing people

A   In this unit you have seen a number of ways of describing people's appearance. We often need to describe people in order to identify or distinguish them from others. Read the short dialogue below.

LIZ   I bumped into Jan Hartley yesterday.
ANN   Jan Hartley?
LIZ   Yes, you remember – that woman from our aerobics class.
ANN   The tall one with a big nose?
LIZ   No, that was Melanie. Jan's the one with dark wavy hair, you remember – quite short, overweight, rather Mediterranean-looking.
ANN   Mm, not really.
LIZ   Early thirties, always wore a green leotard.
ANN   Oh yes, her!

Now, working in pairs, brainstorm as many words as you can which are used to describe people. Try to organise your words into categories e.g. *Height, Age.* Start with the words in the dialogue.

B Look at the three men in the pictures.
One of these men, Mr Barker, used to be a teacher at your school. You bumped into him yesterday. Decide which man he is and describe him to your partner without saying whether he is A, B or C. (Do not mention the background or surroundings.) Your partner must guess which man is Mr Barker.

A　　**B**　　**C**

C *Game*
Take a small piece of paper, put your name at the top and then write a short description of another member of your class without mentioning his/her name, age or nationality. Use the impersonal pronoun *they* rather than *he* or *she* in your description. Pass the papers around the class. Each time you receive a piece of paper write down the name of the person you think it describes, sign it and pass it on.
When your own piece of paper comes back to you, read out the description and the names which have been written underneath. You may be surprised by the results!

Listening

7 Our physical appearance is determined by a combination of the genes inherited from our parents and the environment and conditions in which we grow up.
With a partner, note down one or two ways in which the following factors influence our physical appearance.

a nutrition and diet
b health care – availability and quality of doctors, dentists, hospitals etc.
c climate
d economic and social background
e any other factors you think are important

🔊 Now listen to the extract from a radio programme called *Pause For Thought* and answer questions 1 – 5.

1 What do the low doors in medieval castles illustrate?
2 What was the effect of a lack of calcium?
3 What has happened to the Japanese recently?
4 Why did pale skin have social importance in earlier times?
5 What does the condition of Elizabeth I's teeth show us?

Did any of the speaker's points match yours?
Do you agree that the environment is the main influence on our appearance?

Language work

8 *Comparison and contrast markers (2)*

A In the radio extract the speaker used the following discourse markers to show comparison or contrast.

conversely   similarly   whereas
on the other hand   in the same way

Here is a list of the points which are linked by these markers.

1 In sixteenth-century England the queen had rotten teeth.
2 Europeans in the middle ages were shorter.
3 A dark skin indicates the ability to travel.
4 In modern societies the average height has increased.
5 People in poor countries need less dental treatment.
6 A pale skin indicates inability to afford holidays.
7 The poorest peasants had good teeth.
8 The Japanese have begun to increase in height.

🔊 Now listen again and match the markers with the points they link. Note them down as follows:

2 – conversely – 4

B Here is some information on how cultural habits can influence our health and appearance.

1 Excessive sunbathing can cause skin cancer.
2 In some traditional societies women developed deformed feet and legs because of the habit of tightly binding feet in childhood.
3 In the middle ages people often suffered from malnutrition and were therefore very slim.
4 In modern society women often suffer from foot and leg ailments due to the habit of wearing very high heels.
5 In the USA some wealthy women have collagen injected into their lips to make them appear fuller.
6 Exposure to the sun stimulates the production of vitamin A and can make us appear more healthy.
7 In some African tribes women wear circular metal plates in their lips and earlobes to make them unnaturally large.
8 Nowadays people eat too much and often suffer from obesity.

Divide these points into pairs by linking two which you think are connected.

Now write four sentences. Each of the sentences should contain two points, linked with a suitable marker from the list in Section A above.

Reading skills

9 *Matching headings*

A • How, in medical terms, do we inherit characteristics?
   • What do you know about DNA?

The construction of the genes which we inherit from our parents and which determine our physical appearance was discovered by James Watson and Francis Crick in 1953. They discovered DNA, deoxyribonucleic acid, the molecule containing a chemical code which determines every aspect of our bodies. Since this discovery scientists have made further progress and are now at the stage where it is theoretically possible to remove, alter, improve and even create human genes. Recent developments have led people to speculate about the effect of genetic engineering on medicine and human life.

Now read the newspaper article on the next page and match the headings a – l with paragraphs 1 – 12.

a Bone Growth	e Pancreas	i Revolution
b Superbabies	f Arthritis	J Healing Wounds
c Understanding Disease	g Drugs	k Lung Cancer
d Diabetes	h Strokes	l Heart Attack Prevention

B The article mentions several diseases and medical conditions. Find the names of the four well-known conditions for which the following are definitions.

1 A disease in which sugar and starchy foods cannot be properly absorbed by the body.
2 A painful disease in which the muscles and joints become stiff and inflamed.
3 A sudden and violent malfunction of the brain resulting in a loss of feeling and/or the power to move certain parts of the body.
4 A sudden attack causing violent and irregular beating of the heart or its ceasing to function.

From your own knowledge, say which of these conditions:

a mainly affects elderly people.
b mainly affects people who are overweight and do little exercise.
c is treated by regular injections of insulin.
d can result in complete paralysis of one side of the body.

10 *Understanding methods of defining/explaining*

A How many ways of explaining or defining specialist words, or jargon, can you think of?
Look at these examples from the beginning of the article. The word or phrase which provides the explanation or definition is underlined. Draw a circle around the word or term it refers to.

> *Pancreatic cancer is likely to be treated with magic bullets in ten years. These are <u>antibodies which recognise the cancer cells and carry radioactive drugs to them</u>.*
> *Insulin-like factor (IGF), <u>an ingredient which makes bones start to grow again</u> ....*

There are five more ways of explaining and defining in the rest of the text. Find the examples and write them out, circling and underlining as previously.

B • Why do you think the journalist decided to explain or define the terms in these ways?

Here is an alternative way of explaining a technical term.

> *Magic bullets may be defined as antibodies which recognise cancer cells and carry radioactive drugs to them.*

What are the reasons for using the methods of defining and explaining contained in the text rather than this alternative method?

Study skills

11 *Dictionary work*

Read this short passage and underline any words and phrases which you feel need explanation or definition. Some of these have already been underlined. Look up the words in a dictionary (some of them appear in the article on the right) and then rewrite the passage where necessary. Do not copy the dictionary definitions but use the most suitable methods of explaining or defining as outlined above. The first sentence has been done as an example.

DNA AND ITS USES

<u>DNA</u> is the basic genetic material present in most <u>animate</u> organisms. <u>Molecules</u> of DNA are found in a cell's <u>chromosomes</u>. Chromosomes occur in pairs: one from the mother and one from the father. The number of chromosomes differs from species to species: a normal human cell has 46.

DNA is made up of genes, <u>linear</u> sections of a DNA molecule which contain the instructions for the development of particular characteristics that living things inherit from their <u>forbears</u>, such as eye colour. DNA molecules contain the genetic instructions needed for cells to organise and function. DNA is a large molecule made up of two separate strands wrapped around each other to form a <u>double-helix</u>.

In 1985 Professor Alec Jeffreys discovered that the DNA of every living thing has its own <u>unique genetic pattern</u>. This 'fingerprint' can be determined and used to identify criminals from biological materials left at the scene of a crime or to settle <u>paternity</u> disputes conclusively.

DNA and its uses
DNA (deoxyribonucleic acid) is the basic genetic material present in most animate or living organisms...

BABY BORN TO LIVE TO 120

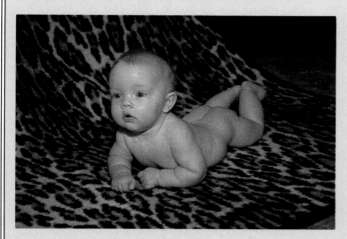

1 ...
Proteins like epidural growth factors, made by biotechnology, will increase the speed at which burns, wounds and ulcers can heal. The proteins are already being marketed in Japan.

2 ...
Pancreatic cancer is likely to be treated with magic bullets in ten years. These are antibodies which recognise the cancer cells and carry radioactive drugs to them but not to the surrounding cells.

3 ...
Interferon, undergoing trials as a rheumatoid arthritis treatment, appears to reduce inflammation and pain. Other drugs are being tested.

4 ...
Insulin-like factor (IGF), an ingredient which make bones start to grow again, will be available in 20 years to revolutionise bone disease treatment. It is currently being tested on animals.

5 ...
TPA is one of the success stories of biotechnology. It quickly dissolves blood clots and stops heart attacks. Already saving lives, it does not stay in the body long, but studies suggest there could be longer-lasting versions.

6 ...
Atrial natriuretic peptide, a newly discovered hormone, may help reduce risk of strokes. It may also be effective in other blood-related disorders.

7 ...
All cancers may be helped by magic bullets – antibodies which carry drugs to cancer cells – and by proteins which stimulate growth of white cells. It is hoped that lung cancer may be stopped by chemically engineered drugs within 20 years.

8 ...
Biotechnology has made it possible to use human insulin to treat diabetes, so reducing the risk of infection. Pigs used to be the donors. Could work for other auto-immune diseases, such as AIDS, multiple sclerosis and muscular dystrophy.

BRAVE NEW WORLD OF GENETIC ENGINEERING BRINGS HOPE OF HEALTH AND LONGEVITY FOR TOMORROW'S GENERATION
By Danae Brook

9 ...
Our babies may live to be more than 100. Perhaps 120. That is the gift of technology to the human race. Advances in medical science, in a field called biotechnology, mean superbabies may soon be a reality. Genes can actually be identified in the womb. Tomorrow we may alter them, although the prospect is so daunting the Government has set up a special steering committee to advise on 'genetic therapy'. Genetic engineering is changing life. For people under 50 the implications are extraordinary.

10 ...
Scientists can actually take human strands of DNA (the chemical that stores information and controls all growth in our bodies) and correct any flaws they contain. Within 50 – 100 years it may be common practice. Patients are transformed by the artful science of genetic engineering, with which the scientist can 'clone' or copy the DNA strands, and put them back in the body, new, improved, and healthy.

'This could reverse the effect of virtually every disease the human body suffers,' according to Dr Brian Richards, research scientist with the pharmaceutical company, British Bio-Technology. It will revolutionise the future.

11 ...
Developing drugs which copy nature by genetic engineering is now the strongest weapon in science's armoury against killer diseases says Professor Sir David Weatherall, who is a specialist in genetic diseases and adviser to the Government on the ethics of what is now called genetic therapy, the possibility of one human being physically altering another.

'Genetic therapy means correcting inherited defects in the womb, to make up for the absence of normal genes. We are not actually doing this yet ... but we will be.'

The research and development on the drugs used in genetic engineering has been in existence for fifteen years. New drugs and vaccines are being created every day to beat hitherto fatal illnesses. There are around 50 genetically engineered drugs already on the market, treating diseases from open wounds and the common cold to leukaemia.

12 ...
Bio-technology is allowing us to understand the genetic basis of disease. Scientists can now decide what needs to be extracted from a strand of DNA by using a special chemical protein called an enzyme, which acts like a pair of scissors and snips off the unwanted DNA particles. New nucleotides or particles then rush in to correct and repair the damage. The repaired strands are then cloned in a lab and put into the body where they replace the flawed pieces of DNA.

'We can do it in theory, but it may be many years before we do actually do it,' cautions Dr June Grindley of British Bio-technology.

Writing

12 *Writing an expository essay*

An expository essay is one in which factual information is presented and explained.

Using the information in the newspaper article and listening exercise, write a short expository essay following the outline below. The first and last sentences have been written for you.

GENETIC ENGINEERING – MEDICINE'S NEW FRONTIER

OUTLINE

Paragraph 1:   introduction
explanation of – biotechnology
– genetic engineering
– genetic therapy

Paragraph 2:   applications of genetically engineered drugs to disease:
e.g. 'magic bullets' – cancer
human insulin – diabetes
IGF – bone disease
Interferon – arthritis

Paragraph 3:   how scientists alter genes with enzymes
how this can correct 'flaws'
how this might affect longevity

Paragraph 4:   contrast with influence of environmental factors:
e.g. nutrition, diet, health care
conclusion

FIRST SENTENCE
In the last few decades a new branch of science, genetic engineering, has opened up new possibilities for medicine and health.

FINAL SENTENCE
Although biotechnology has succeeded in producing new and effective drugs, the possibility of interfering with human genes is still the subject of ethical debate, and it may be many years before the techniques which are now theoretically possible become an everyday reality.

Listening skills

13 *Listening for enjoyment*

A   The ability of science to understand and manipulate genes has stirred the imagination of many writers. One of the most successful works based on the possibilities of genetic engineering is *The Boys from Brazil*, written by the American novelist Ira Levin in 1976, and subsequently made into an award-winning film with Gregory Peck and Laurence Olivier.

🖭 You will hear an actor reading an extract from the novel. Before you listen, read the summary of what happens in the earlier chapters.

The Boys from Brazil

One night in 1974, eight men meet in a restaurant to discuss a plan to kill 94 men on particular dates over the next two and a half years. Their conversation is overheard by a young American, Barry Koehler, who manages to relate part of it to Yakov Liebermann, the famous Nazi-hunter, before Koehler is brutally murdered by the conspirators.

Liebermann is unable to follow up the mystery until he starts receiving reports of a number of men meeting with fatal 'accidents' on the exact dates he was given by Koehler. On investigating the deaths he discovers that all the victims were exactly the same age, with wives twenty-five years younger, and identical 13-year-old sons, all of whom were adopted.

Liebermann realises that Josef Mengele, a Nazi geneticist during the Second World War, is involved, and he unwittingly comes face to face with him at the isolated home of Henry Wheelock, one of the 94 men, whom Mengele has just murdered …

B   After you have listened, discuss these questions.

1   What do you think happens next? Do the dogs attack Mengele or Liebermann?
2   What do you think is the explanation for the deaths of the 94 men?
3   Mengele says 'I want you to know exactly what's coming in twenty years or so.' What do you think this means?
4   How do you think the novel ends?

Here are three possible endings:

a   The dogs kill Mengele. Liebermann survives and manages to kill all the 94 boys.
b   The dogs kill Liebermann. Mengele survives and completes his plan. A new Hitler appears.
c   Mengele is killed by the dogs. Liebermann survives but is unable to stop the 94 boys growing up and fulfilling their destiny.

Discuss which ending, or combination of endings, is best. When you have finished your teacher will tell you the actual ending of the novel.

Final task

14 *The human body of the future*

A   It has taken millions of years for the human body to achieve its present shape, and although the process of evolution is continuing it is far too slow to keep up with the changes in the circumstances of modern life. This drawing shows how some scientists believe the human body would look if it had adapted itself to the modern world.

With a partner, study this list of influential factors in modern life and decide what the impact of these might be on the evolution of the human body. (The first has been done as an example.)

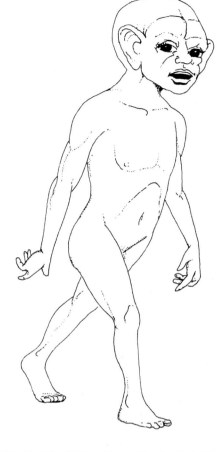

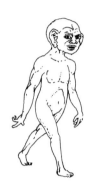

THE HUMAN BODY OF THE FUTURE?	
ENVIRONMENTAL INFLUENCES	PHYSIOLOGICAL CHANGES
1 Most humans no longer do hard manual work.	*We could be shorter and less muscular.*
2 We use mechanical means of transport most of the time.	
3 Men and women do the same work.	
4 There is no danger of the human race dying out – in fact the world is over-populated.	
5 We wear clothes to keep us warm.	
6 We travel a lot and live in many different climates.	
7 We have to do a lot of reading and working with detailed material.	
8 We operate complicated machines with our hands and feet.	
9 We do not need to respond quickly to physical danger or crises.	
10 Most of our food is processed and does not require biting.	

Can you think of any other factors which could influence the development of the human body?

B   Now compare your conclusions with another pair. When you have agreed on your conclusions, check if they match the scientific suggestions on page 161.

C   Together decide on which changes are most likely to take place. Discuss how you think they would affect the following aspects of our lives.

   a   health
   b   longevity
   c   male/female relationships

Introduction

1   What do you know about the way children learn language? Look at this cartoon.

- What does this cartoon say about children's language?
- What does it say about adults' expectations?
- What does it say about the way adults talk to young children?
- What do you think?

2   Children learn their language in a very systematic way. Work in pairs. Below are ten 'utterances' made by English children at different stages of development (in approximately chronological order). Decide what the baby is trying to say in each instance, and which linguistic rule he is 'breaking'.

Student A: Turn to page 166.
Student B: Turn to page 175.

Work together to check that your answers are correct.

- Do you know the stages that children go through in your language when they are learning?
- Are they similar to the stages illustrated?

Reading skills

3 Inferring attitude and tone

A Do you think English spelling is difficult? What makes it difficult? How did you learn it? How would you teach it to children?

The article below is about the Initial Teaching Alphabet (ITA), a simplified system of teaching English children to read and write. How do you think it might have simplified the language? Read the text to find out.

MEDIA BYGONES:
The Initial Teaching Alphabet

by Victor Lewis-Smith and Paul Sparks

The Initial Teaching Alphabet (ITA) was formulated in the sixties by a few unorthodox educational linguists. Hastily developed and badly researched but heralded as a universal panacea, the ITA blighted the lives of thousands of credulous schoolchildren.

Adults have always enjoyed lying on a grand scale to impressionable infants, telling them that there <u>is</u> a Santa Claus, that it <u>was</u> the tooth fairy that left the sixpence under the pillow, and that their pet doggie <u>hasn't</u> been put down but has gone to a farm in Wales. So it was with the ITA – the cruellest deception in education ever to be practised on the young. 'OK kids, spend four years learning this 45-letter alphabet which looks like a cross between upside-down Serbo-Croat and Greek, then forget it all, and you can learn the conventional alphabet … it will be much easier that way … honest it will'. And so for a decade Sir James Pitman and his crazed evangelical lackeys peddled their pernicious *nue speling*, instructing teachers 'not to worry whether children spell *focks* or *foks* because in any case you will eventually tell them that it is really spelt fox'.

The results were, of course, catastrophic (*kataestrofik*). But our warm-hearted society found a few safe niches where the lexicologically crippled could be usefully and gainfully employed. Where? Who knows? Perhaps the proof-reading department at the *Guardian*, as *Teletext* page-setters or even as *edaetur ov the koraespondunt*. In short, the ITA was a *bluddee ridikulus wayst of tyme*.

B Answer these questions.

1 What is the attitude of the two writers towards the ITA? How do you know?
2 What can you infer about the alphabet itself?
3 How do the writers feel about the creators of the alphabet?
4 What is implied about proof-readers at the *Guardian* and *Teletext* page setters?
5 Is the tone of the article serious? What clues are there to indicate its tone?
6 What does the second paragraph tell us about British parents' attitudes towards children?

C Match the following words from the text with their definitions.

1 *unorthodox*   5 *to put down*
2 *to herald*   6 *lackey*
3 *panacea*   7 *pernicious*
4 *to blight*   8 *niche*

a person who follows someone's orders/ideas unquestioningly
b ideal remedy for everything
c highly destructive, very harmful
d not conventional
e appropriate, secure position
f to announce and acclaim publicly
g to spoil
h to kill an animal humanely for medical reasons

D Look at the two essays written by children using the ITA. What do they say in correctly spelt English? From these, can you deduce any rules for the spelling of ITA? For example, how have the children been taught to spell the sound /aɪ /, as in eye?

Language work

4 Participle clauses

A Look at this sentence from the text. *Telling* is a present participle. What is its subject? (What does it refer to?) Is it active or passive?

Adults have always enjoyed lying on a grand scale to impressionable infants, telling them that there is a Santa Claus …

Now look at these other participle clauses.

1 The child ran into the house, tripping over the doorstep.
2 These three story books, published last week by Walker Books, will be a must for every bookshelf.
3 Stuck firmly on the wall behind the sofa, the child's drawings form the central focus of the sitting room.
4 Children of all ages are unable to group such concepts, having as yet undeveloped powers of logic.

Look at the sentences and discuss how you choose the form of the participle. What makes the time clear in each participle clause?

• Which are active?   • Which are passive?
• Which refer to the present?   • Which refer to the past?

B   Combine each pair of sentences to make one sentence using a participle clause. Decide where to put the participle clause, as in the example.

> The ITA was very unsuccessful. The ITA was designed to help children to read.
> *The ITA, designed to help children to read, was very unsuccessful.*

1   She stayed at the school for ten years. She hated every minute of it.
2   The London Book Fair is a huge trade fair. It is held once a year in the city.
3   Aidan Burrow's new book will be loved by children everywhere. It was voted 'Book of the Year' in 1992.
4   These books are all also worth reading. They were nominated for the same prize.
5   John is often sent out of his class. He is a rather disruptive child.
6   The school I attended was very well-respected. It got excellent exam results every year.

5   The definite article

A   Look at these phrases from the text and match them to the rules governing the definite article (below). Not all the rules can be matched with a phrase from the text.

1   *The* Initial Teaching Alphabet was formulated
2   under *the* pillow
3   *the* cruellest deception
4   ever to be practised on *the* young
5   in education
6   *the* proof-reading department at The Guardian

The definite article is used:

a   before a noun of which there is only one: *the Roman alphabet*
b   when a noun is mentioned for the second time
c   when a noun is defined by its locality: *She's in the classroom*
d   when a noun is defined by a phrase which follows it
e   before an adjective to specify a group: *the very old*
f   before superlatives
g   when an abstract noun is made concrete: *the fear of dying*

It is not used:

h   before abstract nouns: *fear*
i   before institutions, e.g. *church*, except when referring to the building rather than the institution

Now match these three sentences with the other rules.

7   Garfield School was renowned for *the* religious education it gave to children.
8   What time do the children go to *school*?
9   I had my English oral exam yesterday. I just fell apart, so there doesn't seem much point in taking the rest of *the* exam now.

B   In most lines of the following text there is a mistake concerning the definite article. Correct the mistake by crossing out an unnecessary article or inserting an omitted article. If there is no error in the line, tick the end of the line. The first four lines are done for you.

Of course, one of the best ways for children to learn ✔
how to spell is by introducing children to ~~the~~ books at a
very young age. Initially, young children can learn
ᴀ alphabet by reading some very simple alphabet- and   *the ʌ*
letter-based books, for example, type of book which
presents a simple story focussing on one letter of the
alphabet. The books can usually be read either at school,
in classroom, with the help of teacher, or at home, with
the help of one or both parents. While very young need
this help from adults, older children should be
encouraged to select their own reading material,
especially if there is a good library in the school they
attend, and to read at times which suit them. In this age
of watching TV for the pleasure, rather than the reading
for pleasure, it is often useful to give children a purpose
for reading. In fact, some of most widely read books
these days do exactly that. The reading is a pleasure as
well as an educational tool, and it is part of our
responsibility as adults and parents to educate children
to appreciate pleasure of reading.

Listening skills

6   Understanding anecdotes

A   🖭 Jill Murphy is a writer of children's books. Some of her books are on the National Curriculum reading list for children. She is talking here about writing children's books. Listen and note down the things that she says she must think about when writing for children.

B   🖭 Listen again. This time, listen particularly for the two anecdotes (personal stories) Jill tells to illustrate her points. Try to make notes and retell them in groups.

C   The following text is a paraphrase of Jill's second anecdote. Complete the gaps with one or more words.

Jill Murphy feels that it is a mistake to (1) … when writing for children. She illustrates this with the example of a little girl she met when she had been working in a (2) …, who had (3) … of her putting a vase of flowers on a table. The drawing was very childlike because, while it contained all the correct elements, it was (4) …. The next time Jill drew something for the children, she decided to (5) … the girl's drawing style. The reaction of the little girl was totally (6) … – she was not at all pleased. Jill felt she had (7) … from this: it showed her that while children have to compromise when speaking, reading or drawing because they lack the (8) … to behave like adults, they dislike adults trying to be like them because they (9) … patronising.

Writing skills

7 Comparing and contrasting (3)

A In the interview Jill compares children's and adults' use of language. Look at this sentence contrasting the use of one particular adjective.

> I would say that *wicked* means that somebody was absolutely dreadful … whereas a child would say 'Oh, that's wicked!' and mean … they're really brilliant.

Which word here provides the contrast? Look back at the work you did in Unit 14. How many other words or phrases can you think of to make the contrast here? How many ways can you think of to compare the following two sentences?

> Adults like to be challenged by the language in a book. Children like to be challenged by the language, too.

B Use the connectives you know, or the ones below, to join the pairs of sentences 1–5.

> Comparison: *It's the same for …*
> *It's also equally true of …*
> *By the same token …*
>
> Contrast: *While …*
> *On the contrary, …*

1 Children learn their language by listening to it.
   Most adults learn a foreign language by learning rules.

2 Children like trying out new sounds.
   Adults feel inhibited and embarrassed.

3 Children formulate their own rules and try them out.
   Adults do the same sometimes when learning a foreign language.

4 Children do not know they are doing this.
   Adults are very aware that they are doing it.

5 Children learn more quickly if they enjoy themselves.
   Adults also learn more quickly if they enjoy it.

Reading skills

8 Analysing written style

A The text below comes from a book by Roald Dahl, a very famous writer of English children's books. Look at the illustration and the title of the extract below. What do you think the text will be about? Do you think it will be a serious or a humorous story? Read the story to see if you were right.

B Think about the style of this story. Bear in mind who the readers are as you answer the questions.

1 Does the story show any of the features peculiar to children's books mentioned by Jill Murphy in the listening?

2 Is the style easy or difficult to read? Think about the length of sentences, direct/indirect speech/ conjunctions/main clauses and subordinate clauses. Is there anything else you notice about the grammar?

3 Is the vocabulary pertinent to the readers? Can you find any examples of words that might not be used in adult books?

4 What about the story itself? Would you find this in a book for adults? Why/why not?

The Glass Eye

You can play a lot of tricks with a glass eye because you can take it out and you can pop it back in again any time you like. You can bet your life Mrs Twit knew all the tricks. One morning she took out her glass eye and dropped it into Mr Twit's mug of beer when he wasn't looking.

Mr Twit sat there drinking the beer slowly. The froth made a white ring on the hairs around his mouth. He wiped the white froth onto his sleeve and wiped his sleeve on his trousers. 'You're plotting something,' Mrs Twit said, keeping her back turned so he wouldn't see that she had taken out her glass eye. 'Whenever you go all quiet like that I know very well you're plotting something.'

Mrs Twit was right. Mr Twit was plotting away like mad. He was trying to think up a really nasty trick he could play on his wife that day.

'You'd better be careful,' Mrs Twit said, 'because when I see you starting to plot, I watch you like a wombat.'

'Oh, do shut up, you old hag,' Mr Twit said. He went on drinking his beer, and his evil mind kept working away on the latest horrid trick he was going to play on the old woman. Suddenly, as Mr Twit tipped the last drop of beer down his throat, he caught sight of Mrs Twit's awful glass eye staring up at him from the bottom of the mug. It made him jump. 'I told you I was watching you,' cackled Mrs Twit. 'I've got eyes everywhere so you'd better be careful.'

Writing skills

9 *Writing a comparative essay*

The quotes and facts below give you an idea of the attitude of the British towards their children.

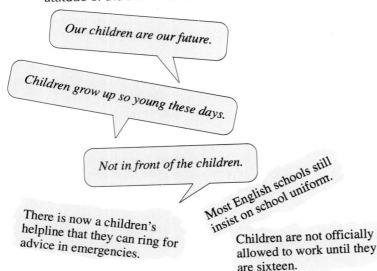

Our children are our future.

Children grow up so young these days.

Not in front of the children.

Most English schools still insist on school uniform.

There is now a children's helpline that they can ring for advice in emergencies.

Children are not officially allowed to work until they are sixteen.

Many wealthy families in Britain send their children to boarding school.

Children can be tried in a special court of law from the age of ten.

Children are not allowed in pubs (except in special family rooms).

Although children start school at five, there is little state provision for them

What does this tell you about attitudes in Britain? How does this compare with your country? Make notes as you are discussing this.

10 You are living in the UK and have been asked to write an article for a local school about the difference between attitudes to children in your country and in the UK. Follow the guidelines below.

Organising the article
Using your notes from the discussion, divide the ideas into two columns: the UK and your country, and into topics, for example, education, discipline etc. Write the attitudes in the correct column. Then decide how many topics are covered and how many paragraphs are necessary.

Joining sentences
Find ideas in the two columns which complement and contrast with each other. Decide which connectives you are going to use to join them.

Write an article of approximately 250 words.

Pronunciation

11 *Sound – spelling correspondences (1)*

- What is difficult about English spelling?
- What kind of words do you find confusing to spell? Why?

One of the main difficulties is the fact that there is no simple sound-symbol relationship in English. For example, how many ways can the sound /ɑ:/ (as in *car*) be spelt?

/i:/	/ɪ/	/e/	/æ/	/ɑ:/	/ɒ/	/ɔ:/	/ʌ/	/ɜ:/	/ʊ/	/u:/
sleep	slip	slept	slap	sharp	shop	short	shut	shirt	shook	shoot

A ☐ This chart shows the eleven full vowel sounds of English (the weak /ə/ is not included). Practise each one after the tape.

B ☐ Copy the chart above. Say each of the following words aloud and write them down in the appropriate column. Then check by listening to the tape. You now have a record of the most common spelling of these vowels.

> bath blood bought build church cities clerk
> cough could heard heart journey key laugh
> lawn leaf lose many palm plait police pretty
> private put read (past) rude salt sausage
> seize serve son symbol taught these thief
> watch wolf worse you young

C Work in pairs

Student A: Turn to page 168.
Student B: Look at the chart of words below. Say these words to Student A, in random order, for him/her to write in a similar chart. Be careful to pronounce the vowels clearly. Student A will then give you some words to put in your chart.

/i:/	/ɪ/	/e/	/æ/	/ɑ:/	/ɒ/	/ɔ:/	/ʌ/	/ɜ:/	/ʊ/	/u:/
been	bin	Ben	ban	barn	bomb	born	bun	burn	book	boon
heat	hit	head	hat	heart	hot	haughty	hut	hurt	hook	hoot
keep	kip	kept	cap	carp	cop	court	cup	curt	could	coot

Final task

12 *Writing a children's story*

Work in groups of three or four. You are going to write a children's story. The outline of a traditional African folk tale is included below to help you. Follow these steps:

1   Read the beginning of the story. How do you think it might continue?
2   Look at the pictures below. They show you the rest of the story. Discuss them and make sure you all agree on the development and ending of the story.
3   List the events in the story. Decide how many paragraphs are necessary and what should go into each one.
4   Look back at Exercises 6 and 8 and note the features of children's writing you need to incorporate.
5   Each student in the group should take a number of paragraphs and write their part of the story, following on from the introduction.
6   Compare your paragraphs; make sure they work together and write the whole story.

THE OSTRICH AND THE HEDGEHOG

One beautiful summer's morning, a hedgehog set off for a walk across the sandy desert. He was going to see how far the barley had grown in a nearby barley field. The hedgehog had watched the barley grow from the first tiny, green shoots. Now the stalks were so tall that they towered above his head, and the barley would soon be ready for harvesting.

'There's no finer sight than a field of golden barley in the desert,' the hedgehog said contentedly.

As he stood on the edge of the field admiring the view, a great, gawky ostrich came striding along. Now, ostriches cannot fly, so they have to walk or run everywhere on their strong legs. But they can certainly run very fast. The hedgehog looked up at the ostrich and called out 'Good morning,' in a cheery voice.

But the ostrich merely looked down his nose at the hedgehog and said in a superior voice, 'I am not in the habit of talking to stumpy-legged creatures like you.'

'My legs may be stumpy,' replied the hedgehog, bristling indignantly, 'but I can run faster on them than any other animal for miles around.'

'Humph!' scoffed the ostrich. 'No one can run faster than I can, with my strong, long legs.'

On your marks, get set, GO!

Are you coming, then?

You've arrived at last?

Then let's have a race after lunch, up and down the rows of barley.

What took you so long?

I'm going to race the ostrich and you're going to help me!

So you've made it at last?

Introduction

1 In Britain there are many mail-order book clubs which sell books at discount prices to their members. As a way of promoting this service the clubs often advertise special deals for new members. Look at the advertisement and decide which five books you would choose.

The chart below lists a number of books from the advertisement and a number of descriptions. Match the books with the descriptions and then decide which type is your personal favourite.

BOOK	DESCRIPTION
Mary Queen of Scots	reference book
Pirates of the Asteroids	cookery book
Hutchinson Factfinder	classic novel
The Looking-Glass War	historical biography
Top One Hundred Italian Dishes	travel guide
Tess of the D'Urbervilles	humorous novel
New England	science fiction
It Shouldn't Happen to a Vet	thriller

Now compare your choices in groups and work out:

a the most popular five books from the advertisement.

b the most popular type of book from the chart above.

Reading skills

2 *Recognising literary styles and genres*

A Here are four short extracts. Each extract is taken from one of the books in the advertisement and chart.

Study the extracts and match each of them with the correct description from the chart.

Start with any 5 from only 50p each

BOOK CLUB

Ⓐ

He looked up the slope and caught sight of the observation tower against the line of black trees on the horizon. There was no light on the tower.

He unbuckled his rucksack, stood up, holding it under his arm like a child. Taking the suitcase in his other hand he began walking cautiously up the rise, keeping the trodden path to his left, his eyes fixed upon the skeleton outline of the tower. Suddenly it rose before him like the dark bones of a monster.

Then he saw the sentry, like the silhouette in the range, not ten yards from him, back turned, standing on the old path, his rifle slung over his shoulder, his bulky body swaying from left to right as he stamped his feet on the sodden ground to keep them from freezing. Lester could smell tobacco – it was past him in a second – and coffee warm like a blanket. He put down the rucksack and suitcase and moved instinctively towards him. The sentry was quite a young man under his greatcoat; Lester was surprised how young. He killed him hurriedly, one blow, as a fleeing man might shoot into a crowd …

B

The daughter and only surviving child of King James, who now succeeded to the throne of Scotland, had been born at the palace of Linlithgow, West Lothian on 8th December. She was baptized Mary, by tradition in the Church of St. Michael, at the gates of the palace, although one rumour stated that she had been named Elizabeth, which if true would have led in later years to two rival Queen Elizabeths on the thrones of England and Scotland[23]. A certain confusion surrounds the date of her birth, as indeed it surrounds the date of her father's death, due to the perilous political situation in Scotland at the time.

C

There had not been such a winter for years. It came on in stealthy and measured glides, like the moves of a chess-player. One morning the few lonely trees and the thorns of the hedgerows appeared as if they had put off a vegetable for an animal integument. Every twig was covered with a white nap as of fur grown from the rind during the night, giving it four times its usual stoutness; the whole bush or tree forming a staring sketch in white lines on the mournful gray of the sky and horizon. Cobwebs revealed their presence on sheds and walls where none had ever been observed till brought out into visibility by the crystallizing atmosphere, hanging like loops of white worsted from salient points of the out-houses, posts, and gates.

D

The shadowy figure in the recess leading to the moon's surface worked with sure quickness. The sealed controls of the air-lock gave under the needle beam of a micro-heatgun. The shielding metal disc swung open. Busy, black-gloved fingers flew for a moment. Then the disc was replaced and fused tightly back by a wider and cooler beam from the same heatgun. The figure entered the lock and the door closed behind him. Before he opened the surface door that faced out into the vacuum, he unrolled the pliant plastic he carried under his arm. He scrambled into it, the material covering him wholly and clinging to him, broken only by a strip of clear silicone plastic across his eyes. A small cylinder of liquid oxygen was clamped to a short hose that lead to the headpiece and was hooked on to the belt. It was a semi-space-suit, not designed for the quick trip across an airless surface, not guaranteed to be serviceable for stretches of more than half an hour.

B Here is a list of qualities you might find in the four types of book you have identified. Decide which three qualities best match each of the four types of book.

a use of footnotes (numbers in the text which refer to notes later in the book)
b use of scientific terms
c frequent use of metaphors
d use of short sentences
e historical references
f use of long sentences
g an attempt to be factually accurate
h fast-moving action
i use of words invented by the author
j careful description
k some archaic (out of date) vocabulary
l sense of excitement, danger or tension

Are there any qualities which several types of book share?

C From the texts on the left, find two examples of each of the following features.

- archaic words
- scientific terms
- metaphors
- invented words

D Do books written in your language share these features? Do you think any of them are easier or more difficult to read than others? Do you find the same in your language?

3 The English writer J.R.R. Tolkien believed that successful writing *makes a Secondary World which your mind can enter.* In a good book even a short extract can give the reader a taste of this *Secondary World.* Each of the four extracts on the left is from a book by a well-known author. Choose the extract you prefer and read it again carefully, then, using your imagination, make some notes about the *Secondary World* it creates. Consider the following.

- the time (*When?*)
- the place (*Where?*)
- the characters (*Who?*)
- the story (*What?*)

When you have finished your notes, get together with the other students who chose the same extract and compare your ideas. Compare the 'clues' in the extract which helped you imagine the *Secondary World.*

4 How often do you read? How many books do you read in a year? Where do you read?

The British claim to be avid readers, and publishing is one of Britain's major industries. But how accurate is our picture of the British as a nation of book lovers? Read the newspaper article below and answer questions 1 – 4.

1 How many books does the average Briton read in a year?
2 What is the *discrepancy* revealed in the article?
3 Which recent bestseller is an example of a book which is bought but not read?
4 Why is it difficult to keep up with modern trends in literature?

READERLESS BOOKS?

1 Britain is sinking under a deluge of books. With 65,000 new titles published last year and unit sales in the hundreds of millions it seems as if our appetite for printed matter is becoming more and more voracious year by year. Bookshops now have a market worth in excess of £1.2 billion, and that doesn't include the numerous book clubs and the public libraries.

2 Yet amidst this boom in book production a nagging question has arisen – who is actually reading all these books? Recent surveys have revealed that the average Briton purchases 7.3 books a year and reads 9.2; but 40% of people never buy books, and of book buyers, 1 in 10 never reads a book. Clearly a discrepancy exists, so how has it come about? Pundits point to several factors, for instance the 'gift book' phenomenon and the 'me too' mentality.

3 It appears that a large number of people have discovered that books make the ideal birthday or Christmas gift – they are relatively cheap, easy to find, and are culturally and socially acceptable to all levels and sectors of society. Understandably, few recipients of such gifts feel obliged actually to read the books they have been given, especially when they would much rather have had the latest computer game or executive accessory.

4 Similarly, the value of books as symbols of 'culture' and literacy have led to a spate of keeping up with the Joneses. The phenomenal success of Stephen Hawking's *A Brief History of Time* is a case in point. After its many years at the top of the British and American bestseller charts I have yet to meet anyone who has either finished it or understood it. It is simply a cultural accessory which every self-respecting 'educated' person has to have on their shelf.

5 For those who do actually read the books they buy there is a plethora of choices. Anyone who would like to keep up with the latest developments in literature would need to spend 24 hours a day, 365 days a year reading, simply to get through all those books the Sunday supplements consider 'important' or 'significant'. From magic realism to neo-Gothic, there is a whole kaleidoscope of new literary movements to digest and evaluate. And with the recent trend of novels exceeding 500 pages, many far from clearly written, one can only wonder at the impossibility of anything but a cursory overview from even hardened readers.

- In your own words, how would you explain:
  a *the 'gift book' phenomenon?*
  b *the 'me too' mentality?*
- Do you agree that these two factors explain why people buy more books than they read?

5 Work in small groups. Discuss the relative importance of the reasons given below for buying books (not text books or books you are told to buy by your teacher etc.). Together put the reasons into two rank orders of importance you all agree on:

a for you as a group.
b for the general public in your country.

a	b	reasons for buying books
☐	☐	to impress your friends
☐	☐	to give you something to do on a journey or holiday
☐	☐	for the pleasure of reading them yourself
☐	☐	because you think it's important for your general knowledge
☐	☐	because you like to keep up with what's happening in literature
☐	☐	to help you with a hobby or special interest
☐	☐	because you need it for study purposes
☐	☐	to give as gifts to friends and relations
☐	☐	because somebody recommended it
☐	☐	because you read a good review or saw an advertisement

Vocabulary

6 *Gap filling*

Using a suitable word taken from the newspaper article, complete the gaps in these sentences. The words needed are in the same order as in the text.

From paragraph 1:
1 Helen can never get enough books. Her desire to read is … .
2 There are … bookshops in London. In fact, there are so many one could visit a different one every day of the year.

From paragraph 2:
3 There is a … between these reference books. Mine says Shakespeare was a playwright and yours says he was a poet.

From paragraph 3:
4 Literary awards satisfy nobody. The … of prizes are rarely grateful and those who lose are simply jealous.

From paragraph 4:
5 A sure way to make money is to write an international … .

From paragraph 5:
6 That book is full of facts and figures. I'm finding it hard to … all the information.
7 You haven't explained yourself very fully. Your explanation is rather … .
8 If you read too many thrillers you become rather … to the violence they portray.

Turn to page 161 if you need help.

Language work

7 Sentence adverbials and adverbs

A Look at the two pairs of extracts from *Readerless Books?* Can you explain the difference between the underlined words within each pair? What is the importance of their position in each sentence?

1 a *Clearly a discrepancy exists, so how has it come about?*
  b *And with the recent trend of novels exceeding 500 pages, many far from clearly written, ...*

2 a *Yet amidst this boom in book production a nagging question has arisen.*
  b *I have yet to meet anyone who has either finished it or understood it.*

B Several words can serve this dual function of adverb and sentence adverbial in English. Find two more examples of sentence adverbials in the newspaper article. Then write a sentence using each of the words as an ordinary adverb.

C Match each of the words in the following list with its meaning when used as a sentence adverbial.

personally	*certainly*	*frankly*
superficially	*admittedly*	*incidentally*
naturally	*apparently*	*ideally*

a what follows is the perfect situation
b the following is how things appear on the surface
c the following is my personal opinion or experience
d what follows cannot be disputed
e what follows is my true opinion, although it may be shocking
f what follows probably contradicts what I have just said
g the following is what anyone would expect, it is not surprising
h the following is some information which is not directly connected with the previous information
i the following is something I believe to be true, but I don't have first-hand evidence of this

D Now write out each of these sentences twice. First use the word in italics as a sentence adverbial, and then use the word in italics as an ordinary adverb.

1 I don't think he can express himself.   *honestly*
2 The exercise hasn't been explained.   *clearly*
3 She is a gifted writer.   *naturally*
4 I haven't seen him read a serious book.   *yet*
5 I don't think he will apologise.   *personally*
6 She finds it impossible to write.   *frankly*

Listening skills

8 Listening and summarising

A Look at the covers of the two novels. Can you guess what they are about?

▣ Listen to an interview with Jon Elkon, the author of the two novels, and number these subjects in the order in which you hear them discussed.

☐ what makes a bestseller
☐ political issues
☐ the computer novel
☐ faction
☐ what a novel is
☐ escapism
☐ where characters come from

B ▣ Now listen again and write a one-sentence summary of how Jon Elkon does the following. The first one has been done as an example.

1 defines the novel
  Elkon defines the novel as 'a new lie'.
2 explains the meaning of faction
3 explains where his characters come from
4 describes the most important factor in a bestseller
5 describes the plot of a typical bestseller
6 sees the novel developing in the future
7 justifies his belief that the traditional book will survive
8 sees the role of politics in a novelist's work

C In pairs or small groups, decide if you agree with these statements. Give reasons for your opinions, using examples of books you have read.

a Everybody loves to tell stories. It's a way of relaxing and entertaining people.
b People will always read novels because they are like a close friend; you're alone with the fantasy and that's a very special thing.
c Bestsellers always follow the same formula and are just a form of escapism.
d The novelist has a duty to investigate political and social issues.

Writing skills

9 *Editing and error correction*

A The final stage in written work is editing and correcting. Do you think this is important? Why/Why not? Find the errors in these short extracts from students' essays and correct them.

> **1** Shakespeare wrote hamlet when he was living in the London.

> **2** The poetry are my faverite form of literatures.

> **3** I read that book the reason is it was recomended by my teacher.

> **4** Critics agree that this book is: a load of rubbish.

> **5** Charles Dickens was born in 1812 and he wrote Pickwick Papers in 1836 and then he wrote Oliver Twist then he wrote Nicholas Nickleby then he wrote Great Expectations and some other books and then he died in 1870.

> **6** Macbeth is a trajic whereas Twelfth Night is a comic.

B The sentences illustrate several common errors. With a partner, decide which type/s of error each sentence illustrates and match it/them to the categories in the checklist below. Write in any types of error you notice which are not already included in the checklist.

Are there any other common errors which you can think of to add to the checklist?

C This is a student's summary of the interview with Jon Elkon. Using the checklist, find the errors then re-write the summary.

> John Elkon has wrote two novels and he is working on a third novel. He comes from the south Africa and he describes that the novel is 'a new lie', and contrasts fiction with 'faction' that are based on people who are really existing. The characters in Elkons novels are loosely based of the real people, but they are changed to fit in with the book:
>
> For instance, they might be having different colour hair or different ideas, for examples.
>
> According to Elkon best selling novels are writing to the formula, a most important part of which it is empathy, so that the reader is knowing how the character will be feel in certain situation. They love escapism and the most of successful bestsellers are the ones which allow people escaping to a place they really want to escape to it. Successful novels often fulfills people fantasies. For example typic plot one in which a female character lose the man of her dreams and then regains him and then ends up rich. Elkon predicts in the near future that we are going see the computer novel.
>
> The computer novel will appear on a computers' screen and with sounds and with possibly pictures also. But he believes the traditionally book will always to have a market because of it has a special relationship the reader. When you read a book you are alone with the author of it and with the fantasy and there will always be persons who want to do that.
>
> John Elkon doesn't believe it that some novelists have a duty to investigate social or investigate politics issues. He does not think novelists are force to change by society. Politics always come into a novel because that is a part of life, but novelist shouldn't never preach.

EDITING/CORRECTING CHECKLIST

a **Layout and appropriacy**
- Has the writer used the correct layout (e.g. the position of addresses in a formal letter)?
- Is the level of formality correct (e.g. avoiding colloquial expressions in essays)?
- …

b **Paragraphs**
- Does each paragraph have a clear theme?
- …

c **Punctuation**
- Have capital letters been used correctly?
- …

d **Linkers**
- Have cause and effect relationships been clearly indicated?
- Have *and, or* and *but* been used too often?
- …

e **Grammar**
- Do all the verbs agree with their subjects?
- Have definite and indefinite articles been used correctly?
- …

f **Vocabulary**
- Has the writer avoided too much repetition of the same word?
- Have all the words been spelt correctly?
- …

Language work

10 *Forms of adjectives and adverbs*

A   Study the three extracts from reviews of Jon Elkon's novels and answer the questions which follow.

   a   Elkon displays a *high* standard of comic invention.
   b   The plot has some *highly* imaginative twists.
   c   Elkon has aimed *high* in his latest work.

   1   What part/s of speech are the words in italics?
   2   What is the difference in meaning and use?
   3   What is the usual form of an adverb?
   4   a   Is each of the following words an adjective, an adverb or can it be both?
       slowly lovely pretty early fast
     b   Write a short context sentence for each of the words to explain your answer.

B   Choose the most suitable word from each pair of words in italics to complete the sentences. Use a dictionary if you are not sure.

   1   He was a *high/highly* gifted writer with a *high/highly* regard for standards of literary excellence.
   2   In Britain, membership of a public library is *free/freely* and they are *wide/widely* distributed throughout the country.
   3   If you belong to a book club you are able to order books *direct/directly* from the suppliers.
   4   She answered *most/mostly* of the comprehension questions but unfortunately her answers were *most/mostly* wrong.
   5   He was an ambitious writer but his efforts usually fell *short/shortly* of his ambitions.
   6   For many authors success only comes *late/lately* in life.
   7   The Romantic poets liked to live *close/closely* to the landscapes which inspired them.
   8   It is very annoying to be *wrong/wrongly* accused of plagiarism.
   9   My students are doing *fine/finely*, thank you.
   10 Charles Dickens has been *just/justly* praised for the power of his story-telling.

Pronunciation

11 *Rhythm and stress in poetry*

A   One of the most enjoyable forms of literature for many people is poetry.

   • Do you enjoy poetry written in your own language?
   • What are the main differences between poetry and other forms of writing?

Read the famous 19th century English poem on the right and answer these questions.

   1   What story does the poem tell?
   2   What do we know about the appearance of the woman it describes?
   3   What is the usual spelling of *ne'er* in line 8?
   4   Can you point out any special 'poetic' language, for example, metaphors or personification?

She is not fair to outward view

1	She is not fair to outward view	A	8 syllables
	As many maidens be;	B	6 syllables
	Her loveliness I never knew	A	8 syllables
	Until she smiled on me.	B	6 syllables
5	O then I saw her eye was bright,		
	A well of love, a spring of light.		

But now her looks are coy and cold,
   To mine they ne'er reply,
And yet I cease not to behold
10   The love-light in her eye:
Her very frowns are fairer far
   Than smiles of other maidens are.

H. Coleridge

B   Poetry is designed to be read aloud and is usually spoken with a more regular and emphatic stress pattern than everyday English. Look at the poem again and make a note of the rhyming sequence using the letters A, B, C etc. to show which final syllables rhyme. Then note down how many syllables there are in each line. The first four lines have been done for you.

What do you notice about the construction of the poem? Can you now predict how the lines should be spoken – for example which syllables should be stressed?

Turn to page 161 if you need help.

C   💻 Now listen to an actor reading the poem. Did you guess the stress pattern correctly?

💻 Practise reading the poem to a partner until you are able to reproduce the rhythm and stress pattern accurately.

Speaking skills

12 Reciting poetry

A Reading poetry aloud can help improve your fluency and sense of sentence rhythm in English, and it can be a lot of fun. Try reading the first verse of this humorous poem by T.S. Eliot, concentrating on the very regular stress patterns.

What do you notice about the rhyming sequence?

The sequence is known as rhyming couplets. The whole poem is written like this.

B Now you are going to work out the rest of the poem. Work in groups of three or four. Between you you have all the missing lines.

Student A: Turn to page 168.
Student B: Turn to page 175.
Student C/D: Look at the poem below and fill in the missing lines by asking your partners to read their lines aloud.

C When you have finished, turn to page 162 to check your answers then practise reading the poem aloud.

MACAVITY: THE MYSTERY CAT

by T.S. Eliot

Macavity's a Mystery Cat: He's called the Hidden Paw –
For he's the master criminal who can defy the law.
He's the bafflement of Scotland Yard, the Flying Squad's
                                          despair:
For when they reach the scene of crime – *Macavity's not there!*

Macavity, Macavity, there's no one like Macavity,
1 ....
His powers of levitation would make a fakir stare,
And when you reach the scene of crime – *Macavity's not there!*
You may seek him in the basement, you may look up in the
                                          air –
But I tell you once and once again, *Macavity's not there!*

Macavity's a ginger cat, he's very tall and thin;
2 ....
His brow is deeply lined with thought, his head is highly
                                          domed;
3 ....
He sways his head from side to side, with movements like a
                                          snake;
4 ....

Macavity, Macavity, there's no one like Macavity,
For he's a fiend in feline shape, a monster of depravity.
5 ....
But when a crime's discovered, then *Macavity's not there!*

He's outwardly respectable. (They say he cheats at cards.)
6 ....
And when the larder's looted, or the jewel-case is rifled,
7 ....
Or the greenhouse glass is broken, and the trellis past repair –
Ay, there's the wonder of the thing! *Macavity's not there!*

And when the Foreign Office find a Treaty's gone astray,
8 ....
There may be a scrap of paper in the hall or on the stair –
But it's useless to investigate – *Macavity's not there!*
9 ....
'It must have been Macavity!' – but he's a mile away.
10 ....
Or engaged in doing complicated long division sums.

Macavity, Macavity, there's no one like Macavity,
There never was a Cat of such deceitfulness and suavity.
He always has an alibi, and one or two to spare:
At whatever time the deed took place – *MACAVITY WASN'T*
                                          THERE!
11 ....
(I might mention Mungojerrie, I might mention Griddlebone)
Are nothing more than agents for the Cat who all the time
12 ....

Final task

13 The Literature Game

Divide into two teams: Noughts and Crosses. The aim of the game is to be the first team to complete a line (horizontally, vertically or diagonally) across the board by choosing boxes and correctly answering the question your teacher gives you.

Introduction

1 Above are some popular British magazines.

- What kind of information do you think you would find in them?
- What sort of popular magazines do you have in your country?
- Do you read any magazines like these?
- How do you keep your knowledge of popular culture up to date?

These magazines help people to keep up with popular culture. You are now going to test YOUR knowledge of popular culture, past and present.

Work in groups of four.
Each of you has five sets of details and six names. (One incorrect name has been added to each list.) Compare your information to find the name which matches each description.
Solve the quiz as quickly as you can.

Student A: Turn to page 168.
Student B: Turn to page 175.
Student C: Turn to page 180.
Student D: Turn to page 155.

2 Where do you think this photograph comes from? Would you describe this man as 'fashionable'? Why? Why not?

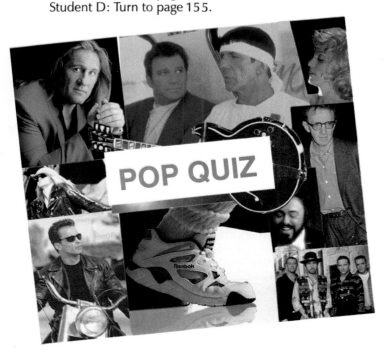

Where can you read about the latest fashions?
Why is fashion such a popular topic, do you think?
Look at this short fashion article and complete the
chart on the right.

	WOMEN		MEN	
	in fashion	out of fashion	in fashion	out of fashion
shapes				box jacket
colours		primary colours		

Autumn Hints from Paris

This autumn the accent is on earthy colours, checked
patterns and natural fabrics. In Paris the autumn couture
collections have reflected a renewed interest in the
environment, with a return to the traditional 'country' look
and a rejection of the strong primary colours and sleek,
sophisticated power-dressing of the yuppie era.

Gianfranco Ferre, previous winner of couture's most
prestigious award, The Golden Thimble, has come up with
nostalgic tight-waisted pastel silk suits. Karl Lagerfield,
designing for Chanel, displayed a range of brown and
mustard Victorian tweed riding outfits, formal yet
comfortable. For women generally, the boxy
shoulder-padded shape was definitely out, replaced by a
more curvaceous line.

Menswear displays the 'country' theme even more
prominently. Every collection contained several
traditional dark wool suits, often combined with boldly
striped shirts. But the box jacket is out, replaced by a more
figure-hugging shape and narrower shoulders,
complemented by large 1950s pointed lapels. Last year's
blues and greys are gone and ochre and fawn are this
autumn's shades, with old-fashioned Scottish plaids much
in evidence.

- How fashion-conscious are you?
- Do you read fashion articles and advertisements?
- Can you give a brief summary of what clothes are
  fashionable in your country at the moment?
- What influences your personal choice of clothes,
  hairstyles etc?

Reading skills

3 *Identifying supporting statements*

A
- How much does popular culture (including the
  fashion business) influence your daily life?
- Is it a positive or a negative influence?

Read the essay below about the influence of fashion.
Underline and number the statements, examples or
illustrations which support the following points made
by the writer.

1 Individuality is an illusion.
2 Fashion is a kind of dictatorship.
3 Teenagers are victims of fashion.
4 Our belief that we have a free choice when we buy
   things is an illusion.
5 The main purpose of popular culture is to make us
   buy things.

Fashion or Individuality

In the days before the collapse of Communism it was said that
the thing which most differentiated the free world from the
totalitarian regimes was its respect for the individual and
his/her right to be different. Pundits gleefully contrasted the
anonymous grey-clad masses of the Soviet Union and China
with the brightly dressed citizens of the West with their pop
music, political freedom and liberated morality.

Nowadays people are wondering whether this much-vaunted
individuality might be an illusion. Looking at a representative
sample in any street I can see a uniform just as anonymous as
the green jacket of the Chinese peasants; it is the uniform of
fashion. Yes, fashion has become the dictatorship of the
Western World. Young people have coined the phrase 'fashion
victim' for anyone who slavishly follows the latest trends
regardless of their practicality or purpose. But are we not all
fashion victims? A huge industry has evolved telling us what
to wear, who to listen to, where to shop, what to eat, when to
laugh, perhaps even how to think.

Teenagers are the most willing victims of all. Go to any club
in Britain or the United States and you will see an army of blue
jeans, trainers, sweat shirts and baseball caps. Ask teenagers
what music they listen to or which TV shows or movies they
watch and you will hear much the same short list of whatever
is 'in' that month. Yet each and every one of them believes that
he or she is a true individual. When we buy a new pair of jeans
we think we are exercising an individual choice, but we are
subconsciously aware that this year straight legs are in and
flares out, this year black is fashionable but yellow is not; and
so our choice is not free at all, because nobody wants to look
ridiculous by wearing something which is 'out-of-fashion'.

Fashion, music, TV, newspapers, movies. All these forms of
popular culture have one thing in common – the message that
to be fashionable we must buy things. A record by a new group,
a new style of jacket, a new video, a new magazine. Every time
something goes out of fashion and something new comes in it
is time to get out the credit cards and cheque book. The
individuality we think we are expressing through our choice of
clothes, music and entertainment is in reality a way of
conforming to the fashions which are dictated to us by the small
group of people who control the media and manufacturing
companies. Being fashionable means getting poorer while they
become rich.

B In pairs, look at the list of the writer's points again and decide whether you agree or disagree with them.
For the points you agree with, think of one or two further supporting statements, examples or illustrations which the writer could have used.
If you disagree with any of the points, decide what arguments you could use to support YOUR views.

Vocabulary

4 *Fashion: fabrics, patterns and colours*

A Complete these word maps using words from the fashion article in Exercise 2.

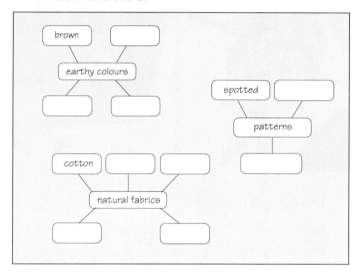

Can you add any more words to the maps?

Now use some of the words to write a description of the clothes in the picture on page 125.

B Find the words or phrases in the essay which mean the following.

1 authoritarian governments (*para 1*)
2 experts on a particular subject (*para 1*)
3 dressed in grey (*para 1*)
4 often boasted about (*para 2*)
5 invented an expression (*para 2*)
6 without considering (*para 2*)
7 soft shoes worn both for running and sports and with casual clothes (*para 3*)
8 a style of trousers with legs which get wider towards the bottom (*para 3*)
9 strange, foolish, deserving of laughter or mockery (*para 3*)
10 accepting and following a pattern of behaviour (*para 4*)

Language work

5 *Order of adjectives*

A Study the extracts from the article in Exercise 2.

> *nostalgic, tight-waisted, pastel silk suits*
> *a range of brown and mustard Victorian tweed riding outfits*
> *several traditional dark wool suits*
> *complemented by large 1950s pointed lapels*
> *old-fashioned Scottish plaids*

Complete the list below with words from the extracts.

1 Quantity or determiner: *a range   several*
2 Origin/nationality: *Victorian*
3 Opinion:
4 Colour:
5 Material:
6 Size:
7 Shape:
8 Age:
9 Defining adjective/noun:
10 Noun:

Compare the types of adjective in the list above with their positions in the extracts. Then complete A – G in the chart at the bottom of this page.

Now use the chart to write a fuller description of the suit in the picture in Exercise 2. Use all these words.

tweed dark brown elegant English suit a new

B Compare these sentences.

a The boutique stocks two beautiful, small, white French silk wedding dresses.
b The boutique stocks two beautiful, small French wedding dresses in white silk.
c The boutique stocks two beautiful, small, white silk wedding dresses from France.

Which example seems most natural to you?

Put the words in items 1 – 3 into the theoretically correct order (like example a). Then rewrite them to make them sound more natural (like example b or c).

1 inexpensive / jeans / a range of / dark blue / tight-fitting / American / cotton
2 large / polyester / bedspreads / some / grey / unattractive / old
3 motorbike / Stephen's / black / new / Japanese / expensive / Yamaha

C Describe an item of clothing worn by a member of your class, but don't say who is wearing it. Your classmates guess who the owner is from your description.

	ORDER OF ADJECTIVES							defining adjective/ compound noun
quantity/ determiner	A	B	C	D	E	F	G	

6   Impersonal/Introductory it

A   Study the extract below from the essay in Exercise 3.

In the days before the collapse of Communism it was said that the thing which most differentiated the free world from the totalitarian regimes was its respect for the individual and his/her right to be different.

- What is the exact meaning of the first underlined phrase?
- Why has the passive been used?
- What is the difference between the use of *it* in the first and second underlined items?

B   Use an introductory *it* construction to replace the words in italics.

1   *People often say* that you should wear what suits you and not what is fashionable.
2   *A philosopher has said* that culture is food for the mind.
3   *The government announced* yesterday that the fashion industry will be getting a large subsidy next year.
4   *Some people have claimed* that movies are the major art form of the twentieth century.
5   *Some writers argue* that pop music is the best form of self-expression for young people.

Now write sentences using introductory *it* constructions, about views in your country on the following subjects.

1   pop music   2   teenage fashion   3   videos

C   What is unusual about these two sentences?

- *That fashion is an effective way to express one's individuality is a commonly-held belief.*
- *To follow fashion slavishly can be extremely expensive.*

Rewrite the sentences above using an introductory *it* construction to express them in a more usual way.

Now do the same with the sentences below.

1   To watch movies is more entertaining than to read books.
2   That fashion is a conspiracy by big business is the article's conclusion.
3   That pop music is an important influence on young people is an inescapable fact.
4   To understand the mass media is of crucial importance in today's society.
5   That more people watch a single episode of *Dallas* than have ever seen a Shakespeare play is a sad fact of modern life.

Listening skills

7   *Predicting and checking information*

In the essay, the writer argued that young people all listen to the same sort of music. Recently a British radio station and newspaper conducted a survey to find the favourite five hundred pop songs. Below is the list of the top ten songs from the survey in *alphabetical* order.

- How many do you recognise?
- If you do not know any, can you guess what kind of songs they might be from their titles?
- What sort of songs do young people in your country listen to? Are they similar to the songs listed here do you think?

Working in pairs and using your own knowledge of pop music, number the songs in the order of popularity in which you think they appear in the survey.

Song title	Artist	Date
☐ *Against All Odds*	Phil Collins	_____
☐ *Bohemian Rhapsody*	Queen	_____
☐ *Careless Whisper*	George Michael	_____
☐ *(Everything I do) I do it for you*	Bryan Adams	_____
☐ *One of these nights*	Eagles	_____
☐ *Stairway to Heaven*	Led Zeppelin	_____
☐ *The Boys of Summer*	Don Henley	_____
☐ *True*	Spandau Ballet	_____
☐ *Unchained Melody*	Righteous Brothers	_____
☐ *Wonderful Tonight*	Eric Clapton	_____

▱ Now listen to the radio announcement on the tape. Number the songs 1 – 10 according to what you hear and add in the dates of release.

Check your answers with a partner.

Writing skills

8   *Writing a song review*

A   Read the review on the right of the number one song from the top ten songs on the previous page. Circle and label the parts of the review which cover the aspects in the following list.

 a overall opinion b background information
 c production   d lyrics
 e structure of the song f special features

 Which aspects are used as the introduction and the conclusion of the review?

B   Compare this review with the film review in Unit 11, page 84. What are the similarities and differences?

C   Using labels a – f in section A as headings, make notes about your favourite song. (It doesn't have to be well-known or an English or American song.) If you choose the same song as another student you can make notes together.

 Following the sequence in the review in this unit, and using the notes you have made, write a review of the song you have chosen.

BRYAN ADAMS
(Everything I do) I do it for you (single)

Originally written as the theme song for the film 'Robin Hood, Prince of Thieves', *(Everything I do) I do it for you* was recorded by Bryan Adams in 1991. It was an immediate success and became the best-selling single in the British charts for a record-breaking sixteen weeks, longer than any other song since the chart began. Although the lyrics are simple and similar to many other love songs, the song has a powerful emotional impact because of its extremely strong melody and the haunting quality of Bryan Adams' singing. The song has a classic structure with three verses and a chorus which is repeated after each verse. The production is extremely clever as the song gradually builds up from a slow and quiet beginning, getting louder and faster with the introduction of more instruments, as Bryan Adams' voice gets higher and more strained. As a clever touch, at the end the instruments die away and the last line is sung slowly and quietly, fading into silence.

Although it is a traditional ballad with little new to offer in lyrics or instrumentation, it is a masterpiece of its kind: melodic, emotionally sung and beautifully produced.

Speaking skills

9   Telling jokes

One of the most important parts of popular culture is humour. Humour comes in a variety of shapes and guises: *newspaper cartoons, comedy TV shows, humorous novels* or *everyday jokes.*

A   Look at the two cartoons below.
Do you find them funny? Can you explain why?

'Darned good shoes. I've had them fifteen years without a single repair.'

'I did it without even trying.'

B   Look at the two pictures below which illustrate jokes. What do you think the joke could be in each case?

C Listen to the seven jokes on the tape and match two of the jokes with the pictures.

Now listen again and decide:

1 which two jokes use puns (words which have more than one meaning).
2 which two jokes use stereotypes of particular professions.

Write down the words/phrases which are puns and explain what you think the stereotypes of accountants and psychiatrists are.

D Below are two more jokes which use puns. Can you explain how the puns work? Remember that there are a lot of homophones in English – words which are pronounced the same but spelt differently.

A *What do you call a man that's been buried in mud for two thousand years?*
B *Pete.*

A *What do you call a man with a spade stuck in his head?*
B *Doug.*

Do you make puns in your language? Describe one or two examples to the class.

Here is a cartoon that uses a stereotype about the British character. Can you explain what it is?

'We're desperately short of planes, of course, but there's a wonderful spirit among the chaps.'

• What stereotypes do people use to make jokes in your country?

Apart from stereotypes and puns, humour is often based on satire, sarcasm, irony and strange unexpected logic.

• Can you explain what these types of humour are?
• Are any of the jokes you have just heard based on these?

10 One of the most common types of joke based on English puns is called the 'knock knock' joke. Listen to this example on the tape.

A *Knock, knock.* – B *Who's there?*
A *May.* – B *May who?*
A *May I come in?*

• How does the joke work? What makes it funny?

'Knock-knock' jokes always follow exactly the same sequence. They derive their humour from the fact that many English names sound like other words or parts of phrases.

Work with a partner and practise telling 'knock knock' jokes using the names below.

Ivor (I've a present for you.)
Phil (filter coffee)
Rose (roast beef and yorkshire pudding)
Hugo (... you going to open this door?)
June (Do you know it's cold out here?)
Len (Lend me a hand with these bags.)
Uri (You really need a doorbell.)

Here are some more names, but this time YOU have to work out the rest of the joke for yourself!

Ann Carrie Shirley Harold Isabel

If you are really stuck, there are some clues on page 162.

Can you make any 'knock knock' jokes using names in your language?

Final task

11 *The popularity questionnaire*

In this unit we have looked at three aspects of popular culture: fashion, pop music and humour. Now you are going to find out what is most popular in your class.

Work in pairs. Make two copies of the questionnaire below. Choose any five of the following categories and write them on the top line of your questionnaire. Fill in the first line with your own prediction of what will be most popular and then take your questionnaire around the class, asking as many students as you can and writing in their replies.

pop song	pop group	pop singer	pop album
type of film	film	film star	film director
TV show	fashion designer	fashion item	comedian
magazine	type of humour	musician	TV personality

POPULARITY QUESTIONNAIRE *Who/What is your favourite...?*					
	categories				
names	1	2	3	4	5

When you have finished, work out what is most popular in each of your chosen categories and prepare to present your results to the class.

Unit 18   The Art of Selling

Introduction

1 *Yesterday's luxury is today's necessity.*

How do the photographs illustrate this well-known saying?

- Do you agree that the car is now a necessity?
- Can you think of any other things that illustrate the saying?

Work in pairs. Decide if the objects listed are luxuries or necessities. Only tick one of the first two columns in the chart at this stage.

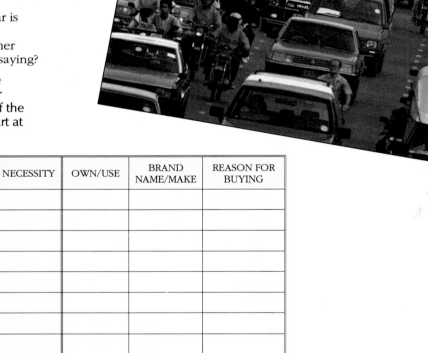

OBJECT	LUXURY	NECESSITY	OWN/USE	BRAND NAME/MAKE	REASON FOR BUYING
car					
deodorant					
shampoo					
shaving foam					
perfume					
toaster					
personal stereo					
wristwatch					
television					
sunglasses					
telephone					

Now compare your decisions with another pair.
Agree on a definition of *luxury* and *necessity*.

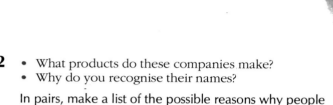

2
- What products do these companies make?
- Why do you recognise their names?

In pairs, make a list of the possible reasons why people choose to buy one particular brand and not another, as in the examples below.

It was recommended by a friend.
A salesperson persuaded them.

Now complete the chart in Exercise 1 by asking your partner if he/she owns or uses any of the objects listed. Ask about the brand name or make of the object and why your partner bought that particular brand.

When you have finished, compare your charts in small groups. Which reasons are the most influential?

Listening skills

3 *Listening to check information*

A You are going to hear an interview with Hamish Pringle, an account director at Leagas Delaney, a leading London advertising agency. In the interview Hamish uses some advertising jargon – some specialist words which are used with reference to a particular field or subject.

🖳 Listen to the first part of the interview and decide if the explanations of jargon below are correct. Write down any corrections that are necessary.

market research finding out what people want
focus groups people on street corners with clipboards
empty nesters children who have left home
segmentation establishing particular groups of people who want particular things
niche defined segment of products
brand name a badge or trademark
brand a brand name which has added value because it costs more
media planning and buying establishing which media are read by, listened to or watched by minorities
position a product find out how a product fits into people's lives and place it relative to other products they are already using

B
- Do you think that advertising is influenced by cultural or national stereotypes?

Later in the interview Hamish uses the following adjectives to describe the advertising of cars in different countries. In pairs, match the adjectives with the countries you think they apply to.

humorous shiny aggressive chic jokey whimsical glossy elegant poetic irreverent surrealistic rational facts-based

1 Germany 2 France 3 Italy 4 England

C 🖳 Now listen to the second part of the interview and check your answers.

- Do you agree with Hamish's observations?
- Can you think of any examples of advertisements that illustrate your opinion?

Speaking skills

4 False starts

A ▦ Listen carefully to the short extracts from the interview and complete the underlined gaps in the transcript below.

1 Uh, brand names are clearly trademarks _____ , … or yes … trademarks or _____ for a particular product or service.
2 Anybody can have a brand name um _____ … there's a brand name sitting here isn't there – Abbey Well mineral water.
3 Does the product they're using … _____ in some way?

B In each extract in Exercise 4A, Hamish changes what he is saying in the middle of a sentence. Underline the exact place where he changes direction. In pairs, discuss questions 1 – 4.

1 In each of the extracts, for which of these reasons did Hamish change what he was saying?
a He wanted to change the meaning.
b What he had started by saying was going to lead him into saying something grammatically incorrect.
c He had started by using an unsuitable word.
2 Are there any other reasons why people change what they are saying in mid-sentence? If so, what are they?
3 Should you try to avoid this when you are speaking English?
4 How can knowing about false starts help you to speak English more fluently?

Pronunciation

5 Linking sounds

A ▦ Listen to the extracts from the interview with Hamish Pringle and decide whether you hear the sound /j/ (you), /w/ (we) or /r/ (red) where you see the asterisks.

1 *I could be selling a packet of these, or * I could be selling an idea …*
2 *… are there * any special techniques or methods that you can use to achieve that?*
3 *… we've established who they * are and where they * are …*
4 *… what they're already buying vis-a-vis the product that we * are trying to sell them …*
5 *… the sort of people who * are going to watch American football …*
6 *… how * are you actually going to persuade them to buy that product or service …*

Use the examples above to answer the questions below.

• What happens when a word ending in:
a /r/ is followed by a word beginning with a vowel?
b /eɪ/ (they) or /iː/ (we) is followed by a word beginning with a vowel?
c /uː/ (who) or /aʊ/ (how) is followed by a word beginning with a vowel?

B ▦ Listen to these examples on the tape and decide whether they follow rule b or c from Exercise 5A.

1 /aɪ/   I often lie * awake at night.
2 /əʊ/   Go * over this exercise again please.
3 /ɔɪ/   I bought him a toy * aeroplane.
4 /ɪ/   He's already * in the house.

C Write in the linking sounds in these short sentences.

1 My mother and I took the car over the Channel.
2 Did I tell you about the bird that flew away?
3 The other boy organised the trip.
4 Please go in and turn the radio on.
5 Don't say anything about the evening we spent together.
6 Is there anyone more efficient than my secretary?

▦ Now listen to the phrases on the tape, check your answers and repeat the phrases for practice.

Reading skills

6 Finding evidence for an argument

Look at the four extracts from books about marketing and advertising. Complete the chart below by matching the points with the extracts they come from.

POINT	EXTRACT
1 Advertising makes us dissatisfied with our present life.	☐
2 Advertising encourages unnecessary spending.	☐
3 Advertising gives consumers freedom of choice.	☐
4 Many newspapers and magazines depend on advertising.	☐
5 Advertising exploits the weaknesses of certain groups in society.	☐
6 Without advertising many products and jobs would disappear.	☐
7 Advertising gives consumers the knowledge to enable them to make choices.	☐
8 Advertising is based on anxiety.	☐
9 Most television stations could not exist without advertising.	☐
10 Advertising suggests that if we buy something we will become richer although we will actually become poorer.	☐

Now decide which points are critical of advertising and which points support it.

A

A dramatic commercial could be made showing how much we would all miss advertising. The first few incidents would be easy. Posters and billboards would disappear. Most of the world's television stations would vanish. Many newspapers and magazines would cease to exist and those that remained would be much smaller and more expensive. Yet such deprivations would be nothing compared with the effect the disappearance of advertising would have on the process of mass production and mass consumption, on the price and range of goods in the shops, on the economy and on employment. Without advertising, many products, companies and jobs would simply cease to exist.

B

Marketers have had to channel enormous sums of money into commercial campaigns in order to achieve their current position of dominance in this country. But as a result of their long-term efforts they are now able virtually to dictate the foods we eat, the soda or beer we drink, the cigarettes we smoke, the clothes we wear, the cars we drive, even the presidents we elect.

Contributing little of tangible value to our society, advertising's primary objective is to reap the financial rewards of the manic and often unnecessary public purchasing it induces. To keep us spending, spending, spending. At the heart of Madison Avenue's new system of persuasion lies one fundamental premise: each group in our society has its weaknesses and deep-seated emotional needs. Advertising agencies can make big money by identifying these vulnerabilities, transforming their products into magic panaceas and then targeting their therapeutic sales pitches at the right group.

C

The consumer has spending power nowadays for many goods and services over and above the necessities of life. Industry responds by offering a wide variety of such products to suit as many tastes as possible. No one could ever want, or can afford, them all. People have to choose. There is in fact a strong case for arguing that advertising is an essential facility if there is to be freedom of choice for consumers. Such freedom implies the necessity for businesses to have efficient means of placing their products and services before the public so that the choice can be made based on knowledge of what is available.

D

Publicity images propose to each of us that we transform ourselves, or our lives, by buying something more. This more, it proposes, will make us in some way richer – even though we will be poorer by having spent our money. The purpose of publicity is to make the spectator dissatisfied with his present way of life. It suggests that if he buys what it is offering, his life will become better. All publicity works upon anxiety. The anxiety on which it plays is the fear that having nothing, you will be nothing.

Publicity turns consumption into a substitute for democracy. The choice of what one eats or wears or drives takes the place of significant political choice.

7 Complete the asterisked gaps in the chart below with words from the extracts indicated. Then use your own knowledge or a dictionary to fill the other gaps.

EXTRACT	VERB	NOUN	ADJECTIVE
A	dramatise		*
		*	deprived
		*	dominant
B	*	dictator	
	persuade	*	
	*	transformation	
C	*	response	
	*		implied
		*	chosen
D	publicise	*	
	*		proposed

Language work

8 *Participles in adverbial clauses*

A Study these extracts from the passages in Exercise 6.

1 *… having nothing, you will be nothing.*
2 *Contributing little …, advertising's primary objective is to reap the financial rewards of the … public purchasing it induces.*

Re-write the extracts without using participles.

- What does the use of participles in adverbial clauses allow us to do?
- What do you notice about the subject of the main verb and the subject of the participle?

B Write sentences using participles, as in the examples below.

Because we see commercials so often, we rarely notice them.
Seeing commercials so often, we rarely notice them.

Advertisements are expensive. Thus they increase the cost of products.
Being expensive, advertisements increase the cost of products.

1 Because they exploit weaknesses, advertisers take advantage of certain people.
2 If we lose advertising, we will lose freedom of choice.
3 Advertisers suggest things can be better. In this way they make us dissatisfied with our lives.
4 Because they contain intangible values, brands tend to cost more than other exactly similar products.
5 Advertisers establish segments of consumers. As a result they are able to market their products more effectively.
6 Because they compete with each other, companies are forced to be more efficient.
7 Advertisers spend a lot of money. Thus they can virtually dictate the products we buy.
8 Italian advertisers love elegance. Because of this they tend to show cars as pieces of sculpture.

Writing skills

9 *Writing a discursive essay*

A Study the short essay on the right written by a student.

Answer the following questions.

1 The student has divided her essay into three parts. Can you identify these?
2 She has taken three points from Exercise 6 and added two new points. What are these?
3 She has used quite a formal style of writing. Can you find any examples of this in the essay?

B Now write a similar essay. Follow the style and layout but instead of disagreeing with the title you should support it, using some of the points from Exercise 6 and adding one or two points of your own. You can use the same introductory paragraph if you wish.

"Here's a programme to interrupt the commercials."

Do you agree that there should be no advertising on TV?

In recent years the amount of advertising on television seems to have increased dramatically. As a result many people feel that their enjoyment of the programmes has been spoilt by the constant interruptions by commercials and that therefore advertising should be banned or at least reduced in quantity.

There are several reasons why I disagree with this suggestion. Firstly, it must be remembered that television companies rely on the income from commercials to pay for the programmes. Without advertising television companies would go out of business or would have to rely on government subsidies, and this would lead to political control over news and current affairs programmes. Secondly, advertisements increase our knowledge of different products and this enables us to make better choices as consumers. Finally, television advertising encourages competition between manufactures who each try to produce the best quality products at the cheapest prices. It is well-known that countries which do not have advertising produce goods which are expensive and of poor quality.

As a result of these points I feel that we should keep commercials on television and therefore I disagree with the suggestion that 'there should be no advertising on TV'.

10 *Assessing advertisements*

A   In pairs, look at the three holiday advertisements. Decide which are the special features of each advertisement and complete the chart below with ticks.

SPECIAL FEATURES	JAMAICA	EGYPT	CYPRUS
climate			
natural beauty			
wildlife			
local culture			
special atmosphere			
sports			
accommodation			

- In your opinion, which is the most effective advertisement?
- Can you explain why?

PAPHOS is the south western district of popular Cyprus. The Birthplace of Aphrodite, Goddess of Love, it provides a mixture of sandy beaches, stunning coastline, monuments and fascinating History.
Combined with the warmth of local hospitality, make this, your ideal holiday location. Our Hotels will provide the rest...
Welcome to **CYPRUS**

Jamaica

JAMAICA
"NO PROBLEM"

And In our Opinion undoubtedly the most perfect of the Caribbean Islands. Convenience first. Scheduled Air Jamaica Services have started from Orlando to add to the daily connecting Miami services and the flight is just 1 1/2 hours. When you get there you will find a tropical climate, exquisite forests, lazily flowing rivers from the mountains and of course soft sandy beaches lapped by the warm Caribbean Sea, which hides a spectacular Underwater World.
The Jamaicans have also helped out by bringing these Natural attractions closer to you. Try the Unique river rafting on the Martha Brae, White or Rio Grande Rivers, let yourselves be guided up the Spectacular Dunns River Falls, go horseriding in the Mountains, through a Plantation or Swimming in the Sea, "Great" Plantation Houses are to be explored - hear the legend of the White Witch, snorkel over the coral reefs, try an excursion to Cuba! Noel Coward and Ian Fleming lived here. Dr. NO was filmed on the island.

NOWHERE LIKE EGYPT

Egypt offers attractions modern as well as ancient. One can follow its history through the magnificent palaces, churches and mosques, the Pharaonic Pyramids and not least through its arts. The major attractions in Egypt are Cairo, Alexandria and the Northern Coast, Nile cruises, Luxor, Abu Simbel, Aswan and the Pharaonic treasures, the Sinai, and the fabulous Red Sea coastline including Sharm El Sheikh and Hurghada. Egypt's beach resorts and ancient heritage make it one of the most exciting holiday centres near Europe.

Egyptian State Tourist Office
168 Piccadilly,
LONDON
W1V 9DE

Reading skills

11 *Skimming and matching*

A   Although publicity and advertising play a major part in persuading us to buy things, salespeople working in shops or travelling around to customers can have an even greater effect.

- What techniques do you think salespeople use?
- Can you remember any time when a salesperson persuaded you to buy something you didn't really need? Think about the last time you were in a clothes shop!

B   Successful salespeople often write books explaining the secrets of their selling techniques. The most important point in any sale is 'the close', that is to say the moment when the customer may decide to buy the product. Below is a list of techniques used to achieve the close.

1   the inflation close
2   assuming the sale
3   the planned pause
4   the attempted close
5   give the customer the product
6   the step-by-step technique

Now quickly read the paragraphs below and head each of them with one of the techniques 1 – 6.

A ...
The salesman does not necessarily wait until the end before he attempts to close. He may make his move at any time during the presentation. He may ask 'What colour do you prefer?' If the customer says 'Blue,' he has indicated a willingness to buy. If he is not ready, you can easily say, 'Sorry, I didn't mean to push,' and carry on with your presentation.

B ...
This ploy works best with timid people who find it hard to say 'yes' or 'no'. You simply assume agreement – taking it for granted that your prospect has decided to buy – and start writing up the order.

C ...
However tempted he is, the prospect can't quite bring himself to agree to buy. Tell him that, with the cost of labour and raw materials going up because of inflation, this may be his last chance to get your product at its present price. This gives him a justification for acting right away.

D ...
Many people find it difficult to make a major decision but quite happily make a minor one. Ask the prospect a series of questions which he will find easy to answer, e.g. 'Would you like it in black or green?' 'Do you want to take advantage of our easy credit terms?' Gradually, step by step, the rest of the decisions are made until the whole transaction is completed.

E ...
If you can't clinch the deal on the spot, offer to let him try out your product for a week or so. If you are selling, say, a computer to a first-time buyer, he may find, at the end of the week, that he has grown so used to its benefits that he will gladly sign the order.

F ...
It often pays to remain silent after you have asked the closing question and leave the prospect to make the next move. Few people can stand silence for long and by pausing you may force him to say something. He may agree to go ahead. If he is evasive, try to establish just what it is that he needs to think over. This will give you another chance to identify the objection, deal with it, and attempt to close.

12   Have you ever experienced any of these techniques?

Which techniques are the most effective? Put them into rank order 1 – 6.

Compare your list with a partner.

The effectiveness of these techniques often depends on the character and preoccupations of the prospect. In pairs discuss which techniques would be most effective for the following people.

1   a person who finds it hard to make decisions
2   a person who worries about costs
3   a person who is sceptical about the product
4   a person who is easily manipulated
5   a person who likes to dominate situations

Now compare your answers with another pair.

Vocabulary

13 *Buying and selling*

- Which word in the paragraphs means *potential customer*?

Find and underline these words and expressions in each of the extracts in Exercise 10. Then use the context to work out the meaning of each of them.

EXTRACT A *I didn't mean to push*
EXTRACT B *ploy*
          take something for granted
EXTRACT C *tempted to*
          bring oneself (to do something)
          last chance
EXTRACT D *easy credit terms*
          transaction
EXTRACT E *clinch a deal*
          try (something) out
EXTRACT F *make the next move*
          evasive
          think something over

Now select the most appropriate words and expressions from the list above to complete sentences 1 – 8. Use a dictionary if necessary.

1 Shy people are often … when you ask them personal questions.
2 Today is the last day of the sale; it's your … to buy!
3 However hard I try I can never … to apologise when I'm wrong.
4 It's so easy to take good health … when one is young.
5 That computer game looks interesting. Let me … it … .
6 Our boss always takes us out for dinner when we successfully … with a new client.
7 In my experience tax cuts are a typical … used by governments when an election is approaching.
8 I'm not sure about that, I'll have to … it … .

Language work

14 *Concessive clauses*

A Study this sentence from Extract C in Exercise 11 above.

However tempted he is, the prospect can't quite bring himself to agree to buy.

What are the two facts which this sentence combines?

However tempted he is is a concessive clause. Here are some more examples of these clauses. Study the construction in the examples below and decide which emphasise the degree of contrast most strongly.

However tempted (he is) (to buy), …
No matter how tempted (he is) (to buy), …
It doesn't matter how tempted (he is) (to buy), …
Although (he is) tempted (to buy), …
Even if (he is) tempted (to buy), …

B Combine the sentences below using concessive clauses as in the examples.

My parents are reluctant to buy new things.
They are usually talked into buying things by persuasive salesmen.
Although (they are) reluctant to buy new things, my parents are usually talked into it by persuasive salesmen.

1 Salesmen are paid to talk about their products. They spend most of their time talking about themselves.

2 People are unwilling to spend a lot of money. They will always spend a lot of money if they think they are getting a 'bargain'.

3 TV viewers say they never watch the commercials. They can always remember the names of the most heavily advertised brands.

4 Pushy shop-assistants are unpopular. They always sell more than their colleagues.

5 British people are often dissatisfied with the products they buy. They rarely complain about them.

6 People who know when to keep quiet often make successful salesmen. This seems very unlikely.

7 High-technology products are often unreliable. They are always more expensive than less sophisticated items.

8 Advertising is very expensive. Advertising actually helps to make products cheaper by stimulating competition between manufacturers.

Final task

15 *Writing advertisements*

A Work individually. You are a copy-writer for an advertising agency which has been asked to prepare an advertisement for the Tourist Authority of Thailand. Your designers have prepared the layout of the advertisement and your job is to write the 'copy'. Look at the unfinished advertisement on the next page and then study the Thailand information sheet on page 162. Decide which features are most important. Think of a good headline which will catch people's attention and then prepare your 'copy' on a piece of paper. You should write no more than 120 words.

B   Now work with a partner. Compare your 'copy' and together decide on the best version. You may decide to combine the best parts of each version. Complete the advertisement below by writing in the copy you have agreed on.

C   Work in groups of four to six and exchange advertisements with students from other groups.

You are the directors of the Tourist Authority of Thailand. Look at the advertisements you have been given and together decide which one you prefer. Consider and discuss these points as you reach your decision:

- What techniques have been used?
- Are the important points included?
- Will the advertisements appeal to the right people?
- Could any improvements be made?

When you have finished, be ready to explain your choice to the rest of the class.

Introduction

1 Are you aware of the space and buildings around you? For example, can you describe the architectural style and the size in square metres of the building you are in now?

You are going to take part in a short experiment. Work in pairs.

Student A: Spend a few seconds looking at your surroundings and then close your eyes. Your partner is going to ask you some questions.

Student B: Turn to page 175.

Did you find the results surprising?

B   All the buildings in photographs A – E are in Britain. Different countries usually have their own particular architectural styles. In which three countries are buildings 1 – 3 typical?

 • What are the typical architectural styles of your country? Can you name examples or describe what they look like?

Vocabulary

2 *Architectural styles*

A   Buildings come in a variety of shapes, styles, sizes and colours. Look at pictures A – E and match the buildings with the architectural styles listed below. Then answer the questions that follow.

> *classical modernist post-modernist gothic baroque*

 • Which building is the oldest and which is the newest?
 • If you had to live or work in one of these buildings, which would you choose? Do you think its architectural style would influence your daily life and moods? If so, how?
 • Which style is the most popular in the class?

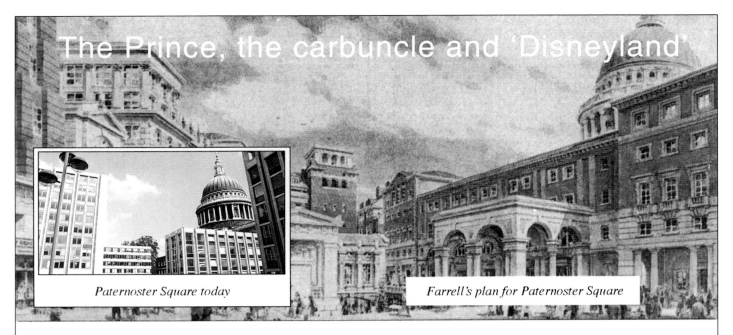

The Prince, the carbuncle and 'Disneyland'

Paternoster Square today

Farrell's plan for Paternoster Square

From our London correspondent

England, home of picturesque villages and historic towns, is now reeling from the effects of an architectural debate unequalled in its ferocity and intensity. The debate is at its fiercest in London, for the once-elegant capital is now a city of choked streets, overloaded subways and a motley collection of architectural masterpieces rubbing shoulders with the decaying products of the post-war rebuilding boom.

For years there had been an undercurrent of public frustration and dismay at the faceless new buildings which were springing up all over the city. The modern movement with its unornamented facades, its rigorous simplicity and its love of concrete and steel had never been a big hit with the British public. But that famous British reserve kept anyone from speaking out against the architectural profession and its outmoded beliefs. Until, that is, the Prince of Wales entered the scene.

Looking at prize-winning plans for a modernist extension to London's classical National Gallery, the Prince declared the proposed building 'a monstrous carbuncle on the face of a well-loved and elegant friend.' Such language had rarely been heard from royalty, and although the architectural profession let it be known they would rather the Prince stuck to subjects he knew something about, his words struck a chord with the public, and the media were quick to turn the Prince's statement into a challenge against all modernist design. Following unprecedented public pressure the plans were quietly dropped and replaced with a traditional pseudo-classical design.

Architects who had been used to bulldozing old buildings and erecting concrete towers had to face up to a new mood of public enmity. As a result the British profession has split into two camps: those who cling to the modernist philosophy and would rather be unpopular than renounce their beliefs, and those who seek to give the people what they want – traditional 'styles' such as classicism.

Now the debate is centering on an area to the north of St Paul's Cathedral. Designed by Britain's greatest architect, Sir Christopher Wren, this 17th century baroque masterpiece was once the dominant feature of the city's horizon; now it is dwarfed by steel skyscrapers. Developers seek to pull down the surrounding post-war office blocks and recreate the cathedral's original surroundings with a variety of traditional-looking buildings. Critics have called the scheme anachronistic and say the developers' architect, Terry Farrell, is acting as though he were living in Disneyland. Others argue that the question of style is irrelevant, good design is good design, whatever the style it is dressed in. But, for once, the critics are not going to have the last word. The drawings for the proposal are going on public display and it is the public, claim the developers, who will decide between building Farrell's 'Disneyland' and retaining the existing steel and glass monoliths.

Reading skills

3 Finding evidence

A   People often have strong feelings about architectural styles. An architectural debate about proposals to rebuild the area around St Paul's Cathedral in London is the subject of the article above from an American magazine. Read the article and explain the significance of the title *The Prince, the carbuncle and 'Disneyland'*.

B   From the article, find evidence to prove or disprove the following statements.

1   People in London don't like modern architecture.
2   Most people agreed with the Prince of Wales.
3   British architects generally agree with each other.
4   St Paul's Cathedral is in danger of being demolished.
5   Terry Farrell was the designer of Disneyland.

C   If you had to decide between Terry Farrell's scheme and retaining the 1960s office buildings, what would be your choice? If you can, explain your reasons.

Vocabulary

4 *Matching and expanding*

A Find and underline these words and phrases in the magazine article and study their contexts. They are in the same order as in the text.

> *picturesque ferocity motley undercurrent*
> *rigorous hit* (noun) *outmoded*
> *strike a chord with unprecedented pseudo*
> *renounce anachronistic monoliths*

Now use some of the words and phrases to replace the words in *italics* in the text below.

The Classical Revival

Since the birth of the modern movement in the early years of the 20th century most designers have regarded the classical style of architecture as (1) *out of date* and unsuitable for the modern industrialised world. Architects (2) *rejected* a style which was seen as being (3) *no longer in fashion* and looked for an aesthetic they believed to be more in keeping with the spirit of the 20th century. It was only when modern architecture provoked (4) *previously unrivalled* disillusionment in the 1970s and '80s that critics noticed an (5) *underlying movement* of interest in more traditional styles. Those who still believed in the (6) *strict and severe* philosophy of modernism attacked the revival of classicism with great (7) *aggression*, arguing that the style was totally innappropriate to the modern age and was merely intended to (8) *appeal to* people in a sentimental way similar to the way in which the fake buildings at Disneyland appeal to them.

B Using words from Exercise 1, the newspaper article, and your own knowledge, add at least five words to each of these lists:

ARCHITECTURAL STYLES	BUILDING MATERIALS	BUILDING ELEMENTS
classical	concrete	wall
gothic	brick	window

Reading skills

5 *Identifying bias*

A The article in Exercise 3 does more than simply explain the facts behind the architectural debate in England. The writer indirectly reveals her attitude towards the subjects she is describing.

Read through the article again and complete the chart at the top of the next column.

SUBJECT	ATTITUDE			EXAMPLES
	POSITIVE	NEGATIVE	NEUTRAL	
London		✓		once-elegant choked streets, over-loaded subways a motley collection
New buildings in London				
The British architectural profession				
St Paul's Cathedral				
Terry Farrell's scheme				
The existing buildings around St Paul's				

Were there any other subjects that you think the writer showed a particular bias towards? Add them to the chart. What parts of speech are most commonly used to show a writer's attitude to a subject indirectly?

B The existence of a large number of 'near synonyms' (words with only a slight difference in meaning) in English makes it easy for writers to express their bias subtly. Compare these pairs of sentences.

1 a Some architects maintain the philosophy of modernism.
  b Some architects cling on to the philosophy of modernism.

2 a The Prince of Wales denigrates modern design.
  b The Prince of Wales criticises modern design.

The sentences within each pair have almost exactly the same meaning, but each expresses a different attitude by the writer. Match the sentences with these attitudes.

1 I have no particular opinion on the Prince of Wales' views.
2 I think modernism is out of date.
3 I have no particular opinion for or against modernism.
4 I think the Prince of Wales' opinions are too negative.

Writing skills

6 Expressing attitude indirectly

A   Here are two lists of words. Each word in **A** has a similar meaning to a word in **B**. Find the matching pairs and decide which word in each pair has a positive or neutral connotation, and which has a negative connotation.

A *generous   a riot   sophisticated
the masses   slim   a terrorist   to flatter
respectful   an enemy   to debate*

B *skinny   subservient   a popular uprising
an opponent   a freedom fighter
affected   the people   to compliment
to argue   spendthrift*

B   Work in pairs. Using words from the lists above, write two sentences for each of the following situations. The first has been done for you.

1   You are describing your sister's boyfriend, who is rather underweight for his height.
   a   You only like well-built men. *Mike's terribly skinny.*
   b   You think thin men are attractive. *Mike's really slim.*

2   A mother is commenting on her son's participation in a violent demonstration on behalf of a minority group.
   a   She strongly disapproves of her son's behaviour.
   b   She knows her son feels he is fighting for a just cause.

3   You are explaining how a friend is always telling your sister how intelligent, beautiful and talented she is.
   a   You think your friend is being honest.
   b   You think your friend is exaggerating.

4   You are describing a classmate who often quotes poetry and talks about art and music.
   a   You think she is just trying to impress people and isn't really very cultured.
   b   You think she is a very cultured person.

5   You are explaining how your father's assistant at work always calls him 'sir' and asks for permission before he does anything.
   a   You think this behaviour is unnaturally polite.
   b   You think this is the appropriate way for an assistant to behave.

Compare your sentences with other pairs.

C   Below are five more groups of words with similar meanings.

1	emulate	copy	plagiarise
2	teach	brainwash	enlighten
3	fascinated	obsessed	interested
4	fanatical	enthusiastic	committed
5	inspire	influence	overawe

Work in three groups.

Group A: Choose one word from each group and prepare five sentences with a negative attitude.

Group B: Choose one word from each group and prepare five sentences with a positive attitude.

Group C: Choose one word from each group and prepare five sentences with a neutral attitude.

Get together and compare your sentences when you have finished.

Language work

7 would rather/sooner, as if/though + *unreal past*

A   Look at these extracts from the magazine article in Exercise 3 and answer the questions below.

a   … the architectural profession let it be known they would rather the Prince *stuck* to subjects he knew something about.
b   Critics … say the developers' architect, Terry Farrell, is acting as though he *were living* in Disneyland.

1   Do the words in italics refer to past time?
2   Which phrase introduces a comparison which is hypothetical or unreal.
3   Which phrase introduces something you wish would happen?

Now study these sentences.

a   That man talks as though he has visited the building.
b   That man talks as though he had visited the building.

Which sentence describes something you *know* is not possible? Which sentence describes something which *may or may not* be possible?

B   Re-write these sentences using *would rather/sooner* or *as if/though* without changing the meaning.

1   He would prefer architects to study the classical style.
2   Most people wish St Paul's were surrounded by traditional-style buildings.
3   Some architects act like dictators.
4   I wish members of the royal family wouldn't get involved in architectural debates.
5   From the way he is acting I think he must have seen the plans.
6   She talks like a person who has lived in a palace, but I know she never has.
7   I'm not sure, but from looking at them I would guess that these drawings were done by an architect.
8   She thinks it is a pity that the British are so obsessed with old-fashioned styles.

Now use your imagination to complete the following sentences.

9   Most people in my country would rather … .
10   Some architects act as if they … .
11   I would rather architects … .
12   My house looks as though it … .

Listening skills

8 *Identifying speakers*

A Look at the photographs. What kinds of building do they illustrate?

🖭 Listen to five extracts from interviews. The people being interviewed are talking about where they live. Match each speaker with the correct photograph.

B 🖭 Listen again and answer these questions.

1 Which speaker complains about architects?
2 Which two speakers complain about a similar problem? What?
3 Which speaker came from another country?
4 Which speaker moved recently for health reasons?
5 Who seems the most contented with their home?

C Have you ever experienced any problems like those described by the speakers?

Do you agree with the last speaker that community spirit and nosiness are two sides of the same coin? How could architects design flats to give people more privacy?

Language work

9 Wish + would/*past simple/past perfect*

A Look at these three extracts from the interviews in Exercise 8.

a *I often wish they'd mind their own business.*
b *I sometimes wish I lived in a town.*
c *You know, I wish we'd never moved here.*

Match sentences a – c with descriptions 1 – 3.

1 a regret for an action in the past
2 a desire for something to change
3 a regret about a present situation

Do any of the three forms express annoyance? Which of the three forms can only refer to an action or situation outside the control of the speaker?

B Re-write these sentences using suitable structures with *wish*.

1 I regret the fact that I bought such an expensive house.
2 I don't like living in a flat. I would like to live in a house with a garden.
3 I get annoyed with people complaining about modern design all the time.
4 My sister says that if she could have her life all over again, she would never have studied architecture.
5 My neighbours keep interfering in my private life, which really gets on my nerves.

Speaking skills

10 *Expressing annoyance and regrets/complaining*

A   Work in groups of three.
You all live in this old block of flats, Grimethorpe House. Using your imagination, briefly discuss the following.

1   the reasons why you have to live here, such as losing your job, being evicted from a previous home
2   the problems you have living in this building, such as lack of privacy, damp, lack of space, noise
3   possible improvements, such as repairing the lifts, putting on a new roof, building garages, planting trees, installing sound insulation in the walls

B   Using the structure from Exercise 9, express your feelings about living in Grimethorpe House to the rest of the group.

Student A: Talk about how you regret the circumstances and events which led up to your living in the building.
Student B: Talk about all the things which annoy you and you wish were different.
Student C: Talk about all the external things which annoy you and how they could be improved.

C   Tell the group about your own home. Describe anything which annoys you and things which you would like to change.

11 The speakers in the interviews in Exercise 8 had typically British views on how much privacy they were entitled to in their own homes. In other countries people often have a very different attitude to privacy. In their book *Watching the Dragon* Charles and Jill Hadfield recount their experiences as English teachers in a remote part of China in the 1980s. The authors were particularly fascinated by the different concept of privacy in China. In the extract on the next page the authors consider this subject. Read the extract and answer questions 1 – 4.

1   What point do the stories of the slippers and the bank statement illustrate?
2   What reasons does the author give for Chinese curiosity about Westerners?
3   Why does the author tell the story of her interview with a student who had fallen behind with his work?
4   What is the purpose of describing the various incidents in the extract?

12 Work in pairs. Find phrases a–e in the text and together try to write definitions of the phrases in your own words. Then compare your ideas with another pair.

a   *an ardent stamp collector*
b   *natural nosiness*
c   *a rather drab and monotonous daily life*
d   *seen as public property*
e   *an unwarrantable intrusion*

13 Jill Hadfield considers that a conversation between a student and his teacher is something private and confidential. Do you agree?

Working in pairs, look at this list of situations and decide whether they are considered private or not in your culture, in other words, would the people involved be happy to have a third person listening?

- discussing an illness with your doctor
- discussing your salary with your boss
- discussing your bank account with your bank manager
- discussing your exam results with a teacher
- discussing problems with your husband/wife/ boyfriend etc.
- discussing your religious beliefs

Can you think of any situations which you consider to be completely private?

Certain types of information are often considered to be confidential. Do you agree that the following items are private? Would it be acceptable to publish them in a newspaper, for example?

- a letter from a friend
- someone's medical records
- someone's telephone number and address
- someone's income
- someone's age
- someone's political views

Is there anything which you personally would never discuss?

Nothing is secret here. People wander into our house without knocking at all hours of the day and night, the most personal questions are asked without embarrassment, and any decision, however private and personal is subject to group discussion and analysis.

I'm sure our post is sometimes opened. Letters often arrive stuck down with tape, but of course we can't be sure if it's British tape or Chinese. A parcel from an ex-student was handed to me with the words, 'Do you remember Li? His wife has sent you some slippers.' A fat packet was handed to me by one of the admin staff, an ardent stamp collector, with the words 'Open it, open it. I want to see what's inside.' So I opened it, and of course had to give her some of the stamps it contained, but I'm convinced she knew all along what was inside. But best of all was the envelope handed to Charlie with the words, 'You've got six thousa..., er, I think this must be your bank statement.'

These small incidents, of which there have been many more, have caused a range of reactions in us, from indignation through mild annoyance to, on better days, amusement. I refuse to see anything sinister in them (though I don't like the thought that my post might be opened). I think the Chinese interest in our activities is made up in equal parts of a genuine concern for our welfare, a desire to be in control, and natural nosiness. Add to this a very different concept of privacy and a rather drab and monotonous daily life, and it is not surprising that the affairs and actions of ten Westerners in a college in the heart of China are seen as public property. What we see as an unwarrantable intrusion into our private lives, they see as a form of caring. Adjustments have been made on both sides.

Maybe, as foreigners, our personal affairs are the subject of more curiosity, but the Chinese themselves draw different boundary lines between what is private and what is not. At the end of last term, I was having an interview with a student about what, in Western terms, would be a sensitive subject: he had fallen behind the rest of his group and I was advising him to go down a level. In the middle of our conversation, another student walked into the room. I explained that I was talking to Chen about his work, thinking that he would apologize and go out again, but he just drew up a chair and got involved in the discussion. A couple more of Chen's friends came along and joined in, too. What in Western terms was a private matter, was, to them, a matter for group discussion and analysis.

Final task

14 *Decision making*

Work in groups of four to six.

Do you remember Grimethorpe House from Exercise 10? You are members of the Residents' Committee. The government has recently set up a special fund to improve buildings like Grimethorpe House. Your local council has told you that they will be able to give you £500,000 if you can present them with a well-argued and costed plan of works. You asked a firm of architects to submit a summary of costs for various suggestions you made.

Your job now is to discuss the summary and work out the best way to spend the money, remembering that you will only have £500,000. When you have finished you should present your proposals and reasons to the class. The class will then vote to decide which group should receive the government grant.

McGrew Horston Leech Associates
Architects and Surveyors
Maudsley House
London SW3

ESTIMATE FOR PROPOSED WORKS AT GRIMETHORPE HOUSE

1	Sound insulation to floors and ceilings	£320,000
2	Sound insulation to internal walls	£175,000
3	Removal and replacement of roof covering	£250,000
4	Installation of entryphone system	£15,000
5	Installation of video entryphone system	£25,000
6	Building garage block	£100,000
7	Installing communal laundry facility in basement	£65,000
8	Installation of double-glazing to all flats	£180,000
9	Damp-proofing treatment to external walls	£30,000
10	Cleaning of exterior walls	£12,000
11	Re-painting of exterior and hallways	£22,000
12	Replacement of all entrance doors to flats with high-security metal doors	£90,000
13	Building of children's protected play-area	£110,000
14	Planting of trees and providing window-boxes	£10,000
15	Re-plastering and decorating of walls in all flats	£112,000

TOTAL   £1,516,000

Unit 20 A Changing Language

Introduction

1 Do you know how widespread the English language is today? On the right is a list of countries in which English is spoken either as the mother tongue (M), as a second or official language (S), or learnt as a foreign language (F). Decide in which way English is used in each of the countries and identify the countries on the map to complete this chart. Finally, complete Exercise 1 Key on the map.

Reading skills

2 *Finding specific information*

A Read the text on the next page and check the answers to Exercise 1. (Not all the answers are in the text.)

B Complete Exercise 2 Key on the map, to show the development of English and its spread around the world.

COUNTRY	M/S/F	MAP REF.	COUNTRY	M/S/F	MAP REF.
Australia	M	26	Kenya		
Burma			Madagascar		
Cameroon			Mexico		
Canada			Morocco		
Denmark			New Zealand		
Ghana			Pakistan		
Guyana			Philippines		
Hong Kong			Saudi Arabia		
Iceland			Singapore		
India			Spain		
Indonesia			South Africa		
Ireland			Thailand		
Israel			United Kingdom		
Jamaica			United States		
Japan			Zimbabwe		

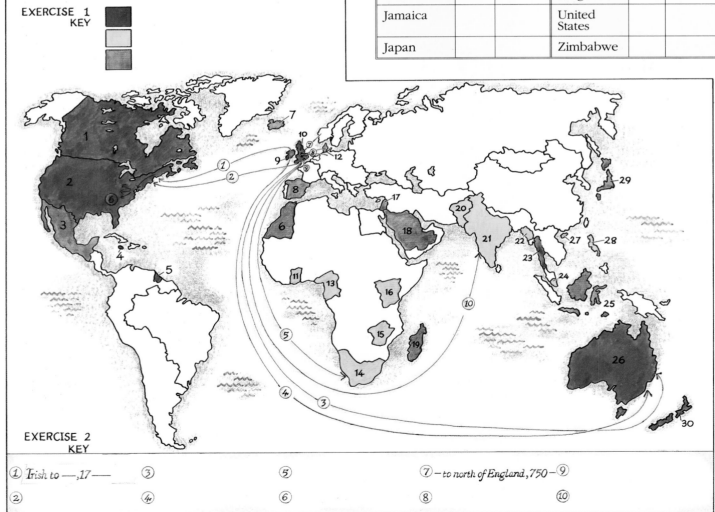

EXERCISE 1
KEY

EXERCISE 2
KEY

① Irish to —,17—— ③ ⑤ ⑦ —to north of England, 750—⑨

② ④ ⑥ ⑧ ⑩

1   The development of English

English is spoken by over a billion people around the world: in other words, by more than a quarter of the world's population. It is spoken as a mother tongue in the UK, in former colonies such as Australia and New Zealand, and of course, by the vast majority of the North American population. It is a second or official language in most of the former Empire, for example, Ghana and Singapore, and of course, it is studied as a foreign language all over the world, but particularly in Europe now. This has made it a truly international language: it is the language of shipping and aviation, of science and technology, and of commerce. But how did the language spoken by the population of a small island in the Northern Hemisphere reach such widespread use? Let's start from the beginning.

English has not always been the language of the British Isles: until the fifth century AD the British Isles were populated by a race called the Celts, whose language lives on in Celtic languages such as Gaelic and Welsh, the former being spoken in Scotland and the latter in Wales. In 449 AD the British Isles were invaded by warlike Germanic tribes from the coast of what is now north Germany and Denmark. One of these tribes – the Angles – gave their name to the language that was to become English. During the next 150 years these warriors drove the Celts to the western and northern extremities of the islands and settled in the area now known as England. For nearly three hundred years their language spread and became the vernacular.

Between 750 and 1050 AD the Vikings, from present-day Norway, colonised the north of England; while it is difficult to evaluate the effect of Norse on Old English because of the similarity of the languages, certain traces remain, such as place names ending in *-wick,* and words starting with *sk-,* such as *sky.* The Norman invasion of 1066 changed the course of the English language by bringing to England both Norman French and Latin, thus dividing the country linguistically between the educated classes with French or Latin at their disposal and the common people with only English. As a result of this linguistic mix, English has become a language with a huge vocabulary full of nuances, often with three or four ways of expressing the same idea, as in *rise/mount/ascend* or *time/age/epoch.*

2   English in North America

Its introduction to the New World in the 17th century resulted in this hybrid language becoming the second oldest version of English – and the most widely spoken – American English. In 1620 the Pilgrim Fathers, escaping to a land of religious freedom, left Plymouth on *The Mayflower* and settled in Massachusetts. Many other migrations followed and more settlements were founded on the north-eastern seaboard. In the 1720s another large group of immigrants arrived on the New England coast from the northern part of Ireland, fleeing from religious discrimination. These rough-and-ready farmers were not well received in New England, and moved further south to Pennsylvania, from where they moved once more to the western frontiers, this time to buy their own farmlands. After this the two Englishes – in the British Isles and in America – developed along their own paths, giving us the two distinct dialects we know today.

3   English in the Southern Hemisphere

Early pioneers did not only head west; they also went east and south. In 1770 James Cook sailed *The Endeavour* into what is now called Queensland, Australia. In 1788 the first group of immigrants from England – mostly convicts – arrived and set up the first colony. In the late 18th and 19th centuries a large number of Irish also emigrated to Australia. Also in the 1700s pioneers travelling south established a colony in the southern lands of Africa, where English remained the dominant imperial language until the late 19th century, when the Boer War established the predominance of Afrikaans in South Africa. English is now considered a second language for the majority of the white population in South Africa.

4   Commercial expansion

The colonisations of America, Australia, New Zealand and South Africa were all very much at the expense, linguistically as well as in other ways, of the indigenous races, American Indians, Aborigines, Maories and Zulus respectively. However, a different type of colonisation – based on commerce rather than immigration – took place in other areas, particularly South-East Asia. In India settlements were first established in 1600 by the East India Company, and by the end of the 18th century it controlled most of the commercial life in India. In the early 19th century the company was dissolved, but by this time India had become the keystone of the British Empire, and the Indian population had begun to learn English in order to find employment in the new order. In India, English now shares the status of official language with Hindi, and it is spoken by over 70 million people – more than the entire population of the British Isles.

C   The text you have just read does not deal with the rise of English in chronological order, but according to the part of the world under discussion. Use the information in the text to write a chronology of the development and spread of English, starting like this:

date	event	result
449 AD	British Isles invaded by tribes from Denmark and Germany	Language of the Angles became vernacular

Vocabulary

3 *Scanning a text for specific words*

A Find words in the text that have the following meanings:

1 survives (*section 1*)
2 aggressive (*section 1*)
3 local language (*section 1*)
4 available for them to use (*section 1*)
5 subtle variations (*section 1*)
6 of mixed origins (*section 2*)
7 coast (*section 2*)
8 uncouth, hard-living, uncivilised (*section 2*)
9 prisoners (*section 3*)
10 local, native (*section 4*)
11 foundation (*section 4*)
12 revised social structure (*section 4*)

B Find the following in the text.

1 five uses of English around the world today
2 nine languages
3 three ways of expressing 'started an enterprise'
4 three ways of expressing a concept which was unknown at the time described in the text, for example, *… what is now north Germany … .*

Language awareness

4 *Similarities in words*

A *Words with similar meanings*
The text tells us that the development of English from a number of languages has given us different ways of expressing the same concept. It gives two examples:

time/age/epoch
rise/mount/ascend

These words have subtle differences, or are used in different ways. Use a dictionary to help you find out the differences and write definitions of each of the words.

Look at the twelve words below. Some of them have similar meanings. Work in groups of four and divide the words into four meaning groups. Each student should take one group and write definitions of the words. Then find another student who has defined the same group of words. Do you agree?

animal beast chase creature effective hunt influential journeys powerful pursue tours travels

B *Homonyms, homographs and homophones*
As well as having a lot of words with similar meanings, English has a lot of words with the same spelling or pronunciation, but with different meanings.

• *Homonyms* have the same spelling and pronunciation but have different meanings:
bear (animal, to endure)
saw (tool, past tense of *see*)

• *Homographs* have the same spelling but different pronunciation and different meanings:
tears (/tɪəz/ water droplets, /teəz/ rips)
lead (/liːd/ to go in front, /led/ metal)

• *Homophones* have the same pronunciation but different spellings and different meanings:
praise/prays   steal/steel   aloud/allowed

Student A: Look at page 168.
Student B: Below is a list of words. Decide whether each one is a homonym, a homograph or a homophone and list them under these three headings. Then do the following:

homonyms: find the two meanings and write them down.
homographs: find the two pronunciations.
homophones: work out what the other spelling is.
Compare your answers with Student A.

address desert fair flour ground lead pear plane poor pound rowed wind

C Read this text and choose the correct word for each gap from the list below the text. Some of the alternatives are homophones, and others contain nuances of meaning or usage. Compare your decisions with your partner and explain your choices.

English is still a changing (1) … . Because (2) … are several different varieties of English, each one is bound to have (3) … on the others, especially in these days of international television and radio (4) … . British English is probably most influenced by American English, and it is common to find American words (5) … the language, such as (6) … for *men* and *truck* for *lorry*. Sometimes, we can also notice changes in (7) … , such as the American pronunciation of *schedule* with a hard /sk/ rather than the British soft /ʃ/.   I suppose it is (8) … that these changes will take place, as Britain is becoming ever more (9) … on the United States in so many different (10) … .

1	a	tongue	b	language	c vernacular
2	a	their	b	there	
3	a	an effect	b	power	c an influence
4	a	emissions	b	outputs	c broadcasting
5	a	entering	b	infiltrating	
6	a	guise	b	guys	
7	a	pronunciation	b	dialect	c stress
8	a	necessary	b	unavoidable	c inevitable
9	a	dependant	b	dependent	
10	a	weighs	b	ways	

Listening skills

5 *Understanding arguments*

A   We have just been looking at the way one language changes because of the influence of other languages. It can also change for other reasons.

This is a very common riddle in English. Can you explain it?

A man and his young son are involved in a serious car accident. On the way to hospital the man dies, but the child remains in a stable condition, although his injuries are extremely bad. As it happens, the ambulance arrives at the hospital at the same time as the mayor arrives, about to open a new wing, and the two groups of people meet at the entrance. On seeing the child's injuries, the mayor exclaims, 'Oh, no! That's my son!' What relation is the mayor to the child?

B   ▣ Listen to the first part of the panel discussion on tape. Did you get the right answer to the riddle?

C   Whose opinion is summarised by each of these statements?

1   The issue of language change is not important.
2   Language is part of our heritage and should not change.
3   Language should reflect the society it serves.
4   The English language is harmful to women and should therefore be changed.

D   Discuss the following questions.
Whose opinion do you most strongly agree with?
Do you have any similar problems in your language?
(Think about pronouns, job titles etc.)
Can you think of other problems not mentioned in the dialogue? (Think about articles, for example, as in the Spanish *los padres*, meaning parents.)

Language work

6 *Reference within a text*

A   The people in the panel discussion talked about the possibility of changing the English language to reflect society. British and American writers, editors and journalists follow a code of conduct that adheres to this principle. Look at these examples from the discussion, say what could be argued to be wrong with each of them and suggest an alternative.

1   *mayoress*
2   *chairman*
3   *man in the street*
4   *the working man*
5   *Anyone who says that needs his head examined.*
6   *Anyone who says that needs their head examined.*

B   Look back at the text on page 149 and find these words.

1   *It* (line 3)
2   *the former Empire* (line 6)
3   *This* (line 9)
4   *whose* (line 16)
5   *the former* (line 17)
6   *the latter* (line 18)
7   *thus* (line 34)
8   *Its* (line 41)
9   *their* (line 53)
10   *this* (line 54)
11   *where* (line 65)
12   *respectively* (line 74)

Work out exactly what each word or phrase refers to.

• One of items 1–12 refers forward, to something yet to come in the text, rather than back. Which one?
• One of them assumes a certain amount of knowledge about history. Which one?

C   Rewrite the text below to do the following.

1   Change generic nouns and pronouns, for example, change *chairman* to *chairperson*.
2   Change repeated nouns or clauses replacing them with text references.

Refer to the work you did in Unit 7 as well as B above. Then compare your text with your partner.

Someone – I don't know who the someone was – once wrote something very interesting about language. He wrote that men's language and women's language were actually quite different because men's language reflects the world of the working man while women's language reflects the world of the housewife. The idea that men's language and women's language should be different may have been true some years ago, when many professions were very male dominated and men only mixed with each other, but the professions that were very male dominated, for example, firemen, policemen, barmen, are now rather more mixed, and anyone can join them if he wants. Whatever else can be said about language, I think that it is man's use of language that makes him different from animals in that man's use of language is unique. Use of language is also essential to live life as a full human being – just imagine a person – this person is deaf and dumb: everyone treats him like an idiot. But whatever language a person speaks, however he speaks the language, he is accepted into society.

7   Formal and informal verbs

🖭 During the course of this book you have done a lot of work with multi-word verbs. These are usually used in informal contexts. Extracts 1–8 from the text and the listening all use multi-word verbs. Read and listen again and complete each sentence with a multi-word verb. Then match each verb with its more formal equivalent from the list below, and rewrite the sentence accordingly.

establish originate progress solve specify survive talk excessively understand

1   … the Celts, whose language _____ in Celtic languages such as Gaelic and Welsh.
2   In 1788 the first group of immigrants arrived from England and _____ the first colony.
3   Did any of you _____ it (*the riddle*) _____?
4   There's no reason at all why we should _____ that a particular mayor is a woman.
5   I think people do _____ about relatively trivial things.
6   … there have been university studies which have shown that children can't _____ the exclusion of women in certain phrases, …
7   I can understand how these phrases _____ originally.
8   Perhaps we could _____ now to the influence of American English on the language …

Pronunciation

8   Sound-spelling correspondences (2)

In Unit 15 you studied the different ways in which we can spell the eleven full vowel sounds of English. This exercise looks at the diphthongs.

A   🖭 This chart shows eight diphthongs in English. Practise each one after the tape.

/eɪ/	bay	
/aɪ/	by	
/ɔɪ/	boy	
/əʊ/	bow	
/aʊ/	bough	
/ɪə/	beer	
/eə/	bare	
/ʊə/	boor	

B   🖭 Say each of the following words aloud and write them down in the appropriate row of the chart. Then check by listening to the tape. You now have a record of the most common spellings of these words.

aisle break brooch cow dour during dye eight either fear fewer gauge gaol here high home idea late lie mauve noise out pair pear road sew sure they though time toe train weird year

C   Work in pairs.
Student A: Turn to page 168.   Student B: Turn to page 175.

Writing skills

9   Using textual references

A   Look at the summary below of the development of the language in Sierra Leone. Work with a partner. Underline all the textual references and say what they refer to. Then look at all the expressions in *italics* and match them with the function they perform.

a   expressing the start of something
b   expressing sequence
c   expressing the result of something
d   expressing duration
e   expressing what is happening now

THE EMERGENCE OF A NEW LANGUAGE

Krio is the language spoken by approximately two million people in Sierra Leone, West Africa. The name derives from 'creole' – the word used to describe a language formed by the mixing of two or more language communities.

It has developed *over hundreds of years, as a direct result of* the slave trade in the 18th century. The need for a common language for West Africans *originally* came about as the captured tribespeople were taken to the coast to board the slave ships bound for America and the West Indies. The pidgin they *initially* created was *subsequently* altered by contact with a number of European languages, notably English, French and Portuguese, on the long sea voyage. The latter two languages diminished in influence as the majority of slaves were put to work on plantations owned by the British or Americans; *consequently* English became the greatest influence and the unifying factor in the pidgins being spoken at that time.

The next stage in the development of Krio came in the early 19th century with the abolition of the slave trade. *This meant that* Britain returned a large number of slaves from the West Indies to Sierra Leone. Naturally, they took their language back with them, where it became accepted as a lingua franca. *Its final influence* was that of Yoruba, the predominant indigenous language.

The current position of Krio is that of a flourishing language. Whereas many African governments have discouraged the use of creole, the government of Sierra Leone has always encouraged the acceptance of Krio as an official, albeit only oral, language in the country.

B   Use your chronological chart from Exercise 2C to write a brief summary of the development and spread of English, as in the example below.

The language originally spoken in the British Isles was that of the Celts, but the islands were invaded in 449 AD by tribes from what is now Denmark and Germany, and consequently, the language of one of these tribes – the Angles – became the vernacular.

Speaking skills

10 *Giving a formal speech*

A 🖭 Listen to the four panellists from Exercise 5 summarising their feelings about language change. How many features can you find in their speeches that are the same as in the written summary in Exercise 9A? Note them down. What do they express?

🖭 Now listen again or look at the tapescript on page 183. Write down phrases which express the following.

1 sequencing   2 result   3 conclusion

B Check your answers in pairs. Then choose two of the discussion topics below. Discuss your feelings about them, making notes. Take one topic each and prepare a short formal speech about it.

a Note down your opinion and your arguments.
b Organise your speech into an introduction, a sequence of two or three points and a conclusion.
c Note down expressions you can use from Exercise 10A.

Give your speech to the class.

Topics
- Everybody should speak their language perfectly, without grammatical errors and dialect forms.
- Everybody should be taught a foreign language in primary school.
- English should become the 'world language'.
- A language should not be allowed to change.

Final task

11 *Different styles of writing*

A So far we have looked at the ways in which language can change with time and because of pressure from groups in society. However, our own use of language changes all the time, according to the person speaking/writing and the person they are addressing. Consider the following questions.

- Do you speak in exactly the same way to your mother, your best friend, your manager or head teacher, an elderly relative and a child? What changes do you make?
- Do the following people express themselves in exactly the same way? Why/Why not?
  a university lecturer   a writer   a politician
  a manual worker   a child

B Work in groups of three. You are each going to read a text. As you are reading, make a note of the following: the events in the story, who is telling the story, what kind of language he/she is using and why.

Student A: Read the text below.
Student B: Turn to page 175.
Student C: Turn to page 180.

C In your groups, discuss the story and try to reconstruct exactly what happened. Build up a description, as far as is possible, of the characters in the story, then choose a character and write their version of the story.

It was approaching one o'clock on a sultry summer's day in an overheated London. Trafalgar Square was crowded, hot and sweaty with office workers eating their lunches, people crossing the city, tourists, police keeping the peace. At precisely one o'clock another bus full of tourists arrived and the bus disgorged its contents into the Square – fifty more flushed, irritated tourists into the already pulsating crowd. A rolled-up newspaper appeared from the middle of the new group and fifty sheep followed the newspaper into the centre of the throng. Suddenly, a cry went up from somewhere in the middle of the crowd. Every head turned to find the source of the anguish and a frisson of excitement verging on fear ran through the crowd. Then an awareness arose of a scuffle in one corner of the square: a policeman seemed to be wrangling with a passer-by – no one appeared to know why. Then the policeman marched the passer-by off down a side street and calm descended once more on a disappointed crowd.

Particle	Verb	Type	Meaning/Example
on	carry on	1	(General meaning: starting/continuing/progressing) to continue e.g. Carry on until you find the colour you prefer.
up			
off			
down			
through			
out			
in			
over			
away			

Unit 4

10 Speaking skills

Jane Eyre: Extract D

'I dreamt another dream, sir – that Thornfield Hall was a dreary ruin. On waking, a light dazzled my eyes. I thought, 'Oh, it is daylight!' But I was mistaken. It was only candlelight. The maid, I supposed, had come in. There was a light on the dressing table. And the door of the closet, where before going to bed I had hung my wedding dress and veil, stood open. I heard a noise there. I asked, "Sophie, what are you doing?" No one answered, but a shape emerged from the closet. It took the candle, held it high, and looked at the garments hanging from the door. "Sophie! Sophie!" I again cried and still it was silent. I had risen up in bed. I bent forward. First surprise, then bewilderment came over me and then my blood went cold in my veins. Mr Rochester, this was not your maid, Sophie. It was not even that strange woman, Grace Poole.'

'Describe it, Jane,' demanded Mr Rochester.

'It seemed, sir, a woman, tall and large, with thick and dark hair hanging long down her back. I know not what dress she had on.'

'Did you see her face?'

'Not at first,' I replied. 'But then she took my wedding veil from its place. She held it up, stared at it and then put it on her own head and turned to the mirror. At that moment I saw the reflection of her face and features quite distinctly in the dark oblong glass.'

'And how were they?'

'Fearful and ghastly to me. Oh, sir, I never saw a face like it! It was a discoloured face – it was a savage face. I wish I could forget the roll of the red eyes and the horrible distorted features!'

'But ghosts are usually pale, Jane.'

'This, sir, was purple. The lips were swollen and dark, the brow furrowed, the black eyebrows widely raised over the bloodshot eyes.'

'What did it do?'

'Sir, it removed my wedding veil from its horrible head, tore it in two parts, and flinging both on the floor, trampled on them.'

'Afterwards?'

'It took the candle and came to my bedside. The creature bent over and her fiery eyes glared upon me. She thrust up her candle close to my face and extinguished it under my eyes. I was aware of her lurid face close to mine and then I lost consciousness. I fainted with terror.'

Unit 9

1 Introduction

- Dish: Spotted Dick
- Ingredients: sponge pudding   in batter

14 Final task

You run a restaurant called Grandma's Kitchen. Make a notice with this name and put it on your desk. Use the following information to answer questions from customers.

GRANDMA'S KITCHEN

MENUS   A range of traditional English dishes, especially roast beef, steaks, and lots of vegetables. Your chef received a special award in the 'Great British Cuisine' competition last year.
A special vegetarian menu is available.

DRINKS   All drinks are available.

FACILITIES   Banqueting suite sitting up to 45 people is available with set menu for four-course meal with drinks costing £18.50 per person.
Garden with outdoor tables available in summer.

PROBLEMS   You do not have a no-smoking area.
Because the building is old with narrow doors, the fire regulations do not allow wheelchairs.
You have no facilities for young children.
You don't accept credit cards.

Unit 17

1 Introduction

16 an Austrian bodybuilder who became a Hollywood star
17 an American singer who is also a comedienne and film actress
18 the Englishman who used to be the drummer in the rock group Genesis and is now an internationally successful solo singer
19 the American film director who made *Jaws*, *Close Encounters of the Third Kind*, *E.T.*, *Raiders of the Lost Ark* and *Hook*
20 the English shoe manufacturers whose training shoes became the biggest fashion of the nineteen eighties

Answers
s The Sex Pistols   t *Twin Peaks*
u Jean-Paul Gaultier   v Bryan Adams
w *Monty Python's Flying Circus*   x *Star Trek*

THE ROUND THE WORLD GAME

HEATHROW AIRPORT – LONDON

FOLLOWING WIND

MOVE FORWARD TO ROME

TEST BOX

CAPITAL CITIES

AIRCREW STRIKE!

GO BACK TO LONDON

PARIS

Play this game in small groups of three or four.
Aim To be the first back to Heathrow Airport.
Rules Take it in turns to throw the dice and move your token to the box indicated. There are three types of boxes:
1 *Destination boxes*. You have arrived somewhere. Leave your token on the box until your next turn.
2 *Forfeit or bonus boxes*. Something has happened. Follow the instructions to move your token.
3 *Test boxes*. The other players have to get together to ask you a question on the topic indicated in the box. If you answer correctly you can move your token to the next destination box. If you answer incorrectly you must move your token back to the previous destinations but one.

Example questions are on page 160.
Good luck!

TEST BOX

RIVERS & MOUNTAINS

NEW YORK

AIR TRAFFIC STRIKE !

GO BACK TO LOS ANGELES

TEST BOX

PAINTERS OR POLITICIANS

SAN FRANCISCO

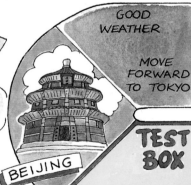

BEIJING

GOOD WEATHER

MOVE FORWARD TO TOKYO

OIL PRICE RISE!

GO BACK TO BANGKOK

TEST BOX

WRITERS & NOVELS

MONSOON

GO BACK TO DELHI

TEST BOX

MULTIWORD VERBS

HONG-KONG

STORMS !

GO BACK TO BANGKOK

TOKYO

TEST BOX

CLASSICAL OR POP MUSIC

PASSPORT STOLEN!

GO BACK TO RIO DE JANEIRO

PLANE CRASH !!

GO BACK TO HAWAII

HOLLYWOOD

LOS ANGELES

TEST BOX

ANIMAL OR PLANT VOCABULARY

TEST BOX

KINGS & QUEENS

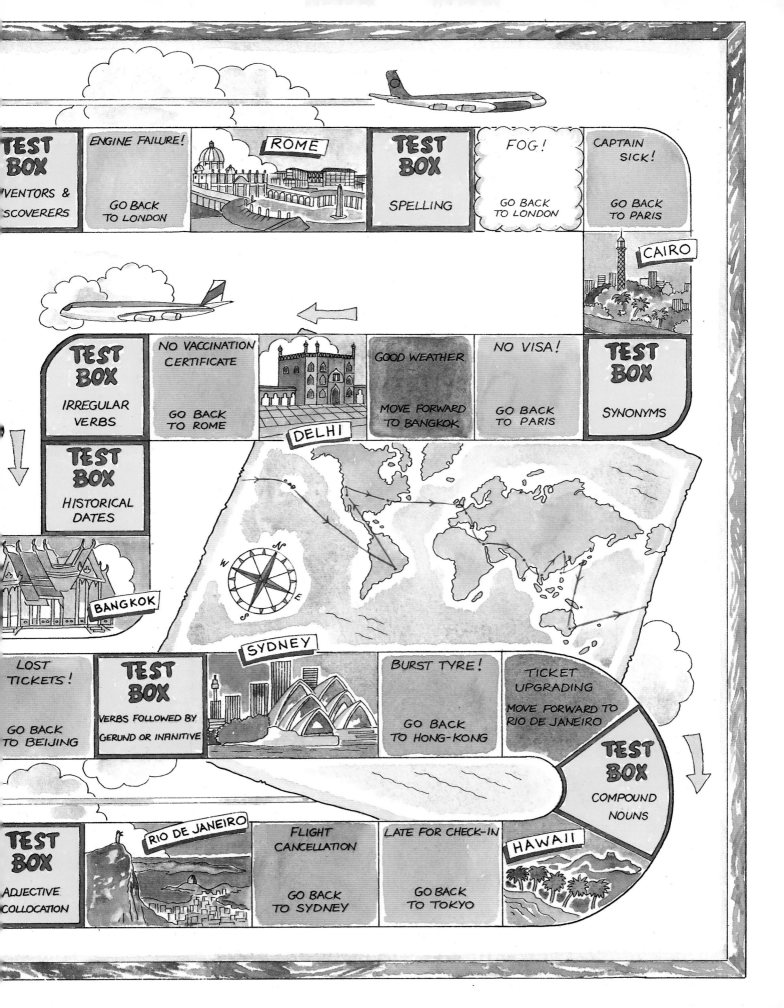

Unit 3

1 Introduction

1b Japan has the lowest rate of heart disease of any developed nation. If you live in Britain or the USA you are about five times more likely to develop heart disease than if you live in Japan.

2b Health research has shown that being of low socio-economic status is the only major common cause of stomach cancer.

3a Figures show that the majority of road accidents occur within 2 miles (3km) of people's homes. Statistically, motorways are the safest roads of all.

4a Statistics for the European Community have shown that Britain has the least dangerous roads of any member country.

5a A 1 in 10 chance may seem high but remember that this is an average. Some people may have many accidents in a lifetime, others may have none.

6b Every year in Britain, about 90,000 people are admitted to hospital casualty units as a result of DIY accidents. The most common injuries are cuts caused by using knives.

7a Few people realise that their home is far more dangerous than any other place.

8b In the last 20 years, 23% of all fatal crashes have been over Latin America. This compares with 7% over Africa and only 6% over the Middle East.

9a These statistics are explained later in this unit.

10c Deep-sea fishing has a 1 in 360 risk of death at work. The figure for coal mining is 1 in 5,000. For construction workers it is 1 in 7,000.

11b Research has shown that there are about 36 injuries for every 100,000 hours of football played. The rate for rugby is 30 and for boxing around 2.

12c Research by the Royal Society for the Prevention of Accidents in Britain showed that 34.7% of drownings were in rivers, 25% in the sea, and only 5% in swimming pools.

Unit 4

1 Introduction

1 The rooms are the same size. Room B looks bigger because the colour on the back wall is recessive (it looks further away than it really is) and the red wall in Room A makes it look smaller because red advances (it looks closer than it really is).

2 Both lines are the same length. This illusion is called the Muller-Lyer illusion.

3 The three men are all the same height. This illusion is caused by our mental expectation that drawings always follow the rules of perspective representation.

4 Line B is both in front of and behind line C. It all depends whether you think you are looking at the box from above or below. This illusion is known as the Necker Cube and is often used by psychologists to show how the brain perceives and processes visual information.

5 You should be able to see four faces: two formed by the tree trunks and two formed by the sides of the vase.

6 No, it is a painting of concentric circles. This illusion is known as the Fraser Spiral and shows the way our minds make false assumptions when we are confronted with complex images.

7 Both hallways are the same size. These pictures illustrate the advancing and recessive effect of red and blue tones.

Unit 4

11B Writing skills

'Miss,' said the servant who met me in the lobby, where I was wandering like a troubled spirit, 'a person below wishes to see you.'

I ran downstairs without inquiry. I was passing the sitting room, to go to the kitchen, when someone ran out.

'It's her, I am sure!' exclaimed the stranger, stopping my progress and taking my hand.

I looked. I saw a woman attired like a servant: matronly, good-looking, black hair and eyes, and a lively complexion.

'Well, who is it?' she asked.

Unit 5

1 Introduction: clues

A Four of the languages are from the Indo-European family (two Latin, two Germanic).
Two of the languages are from the Sino-Tibetan family.
Two of the languages are from the Afro-Asiatic family.

B This list gives some of the areas in which the ten languages are spoken, in the correct order.
1 China, Hong Kong, Taiwan
2 Australia, United States, Britain, New Zealand, South Africa
3 Spain, Latin and South America
4 India
5 The Gulf, North Africa, Iraq, Jordan, Syria
6 Bangladesh
7 Russia
8 Brazil, Portugal
9 Japan
10 Germany, Austria, Switzerland

C Three are from France, three from Germany, three from Holland, three from India and three from Spain, one comes from Mexico and one from Russia.
See page 159 for the answers.

 Unit 5

1   Introduction: answers

A   French, English, German and Romanian are all from the
Indo-European family; French and Romanian are from
the Latin branch, and English and German are from
the Germanic branch.
Cantonese and Thai are both from the Sino-Tibetan
family.
Arabic and Hebrew are both from the Afro-Asiatic
family.

B   1   Chinese (1,000 million speakers)
2   English (350 million)   3   Spanish (250 million)
4   Hindi (200 million)   5   Arabic (150 million)
6   Bengali (150 million)   7   Russian (150 million)
8   Portuguese (135 million)   9   Japanese (120 million)
10   German (100 million)

C   France   *café, garage, menu*
Germany   *blitz, poodle, quartz*
Holland   *dollar, gin, yacht*
India   *bungalow, pyjamas, shampoo*
Italy   *influenza, studio, violin*
Mexico   *tomato*
Russia   *vodka*
Spain   *canyon, hurricane, potato*

 Unit 6

2   Introduction

Here are the scores for the quiz. Work out the scores
for your friends and yourself and then find out below
how moral you are!

Scores

1 a0 b2 c3	7 a3 b1 c2 d0	
2 a1 b0 c1 d2	8 a2 b0 c2 d3	
3 a1 b0 c1 d2	9 a0 b1 c2	
4 a3 b2 c0	10 a0 b2 c3	
5 a0 b3 c1 d2	11 a3 b2 c1 d0	
6 a1 b0 c2 d3	12 a0 b2 c3 d2	

What did you score?

Below 10 You really are immoral! It is unlikely that
you would ever find yourself in a moral dilemma
because you don't know what they are! You live life
for yourself and yourself alone. Haven't you ever
wondered why you don't have any friends?
11-19 You understand what morals are, but you
are rather lacking in them. When faced with a moral
dilemma you are likely to consider yourself first and
others afterwards. You are quite a selfish person.
20-28 You have a strong sense of morals, which
occasionally weakens. Don't worry, this happens.
When you are faced with a moral dilemma you look
at all sides and you generally try to take a course of
action which is best for all concerned.

Above 29 – If you have answered this quiz truthfully
you are entirely selfless! When faced with a moral
dilemma you consider everybody else before
yourself. You must be a very nice person, but there
are times when we have to put ourselves first, and
you should do that sometimes.

5A   Vocabulary

It's a verb. The general context is that it has an abstract
subject and an inanimate object – the object is a treaty
of some kind, therefore it is likely to be a verb in
slightly legal use. There is a clue in the prefix *up*,
which in some cases has the meaning *support*. In this
case, *uphold* means *agree with and support*.

13   Listening skills

Marion has been under me for some time now, since she was
admitted to hospital suffering from depression during her
mother's illness. A few months ago, after her mother's
death, she decided to take on a new job – much too soon, I
thought, but I persuaded her to agree to come back and see
me if anything started going wrong again. Six weeks ago she
started coming to see me every week again – apparently
things are going badly wrong at work and she's getting very
depressed again. She's obviously very worried about losing
her job but does not want anyone at work to find out about
her illness. She believes that they would use it as an excuse
to dismiss her if they discovered that she had lied about her
illness.

 Unit 7

2   Introduction

A   4   Queen Elizabeth II   D   6   Margaret Thatcher
B   3   Meryl Streep   E   5   François Mitterand
C   1   Adolf Hitler   F   2   Sting

 Unit 8

9   Reading skills

clothing items	non-clothing items
six shirts	towel
six pairs of socks	sponge bag
six pairs of	various
underpants	pharmaceuticals
three T-shirts	Sony walkman
swimming trunks	six cassettes
short-sleeved sweater	radio
three pairs of long	diary
trousers	dictaphone
two pairs of shorts	camera
one pair of sports	Kingsley Amis novel
shoes	'Learn Arabic' book
jacket and tie	address book
panama hat	mints
	inflatable globe

Unit 8

14   Final task: Round-the-World Game

The board game is on page 156.

Example test box questions

- capital cities
  What is the capital of Spain? (Madrid)

- inventors and discoverers
  Who invented radio? (Marconi)

- spelling
  Spell 'embarrassing'. (EMBARRASSING)

- synonyms
  Give a synonym for 'reticent'. (reluctant)

- irregular verbs
  Give the past participle of 'drink'. (drunk)

- historical dates
  When was the Battle of Waterloo? (1815)

- writers and novels
  Who wrote 'Don Quixote'? (Cervantes)

- multi-word verbs
  What is the multi-word verb meaning 'to offer accommodation'? (to put someone up)

- verbs followed by gerund or infinitive
  What follows 'to deny'? (gerund)

- compound nouns
  Give a compound noun meaning a 'small clock worn on the arm'? (wristwatch)

- adjective collocation
  Does 'sensitive' collocate with 'dog'? (Yes)

- kings and queens
  Which English king had six wives? (Henry VIII)

- animal or plant vocabulary
  Which animal looks like a horse and has stripes? (zebra)

- classical or pop music
  Who made a record called 'Thriller'? (Michael Jackson)

- painters or politicians
  Who painted the Sistine chapel ceiling? (Michelangelo)

- rivers and mountains
  Which river runs through Paris? (The Seine)

Unit 9

1   Introduction: Student E

- dish: Welsh Rarebit
- ingredients: sausages   on toast

14   Final task: Customers

There are four restaurants in the High Street of your town. Your task is to choose the best restaurant for each of the following situations. Start by working out the questions you will need to ask.

1   Your aged aunt is coming to visit you at the weekend. You want to take her out for a meal. You know that she is a fanatical anti-smoker. She also rather likes good wine. She is slightly deaf and uses a walking-stick.

2   One of your colleagues has asked you to arrange a restaurant booking for his next marketing conference. There will be ten people attending the conference. You have been told that two of the guests are vegetarians; your colleague will be paying for the meal with his company American Express card.

3   You are organising an end-of-exam celebration for your brother's class. There are 30 students in the class, they are all in their late teens and enjoy rock music. Two of the students are vegetarians. One of the students is disabled and uses a wheelchair.

4   You and a colleague want to take your boss and her husband out for a meal. You know that your boss's husband dislikes noisy places and is rather snobbish. Your boss is a vegetarian and rather enjoys French wines.

5   Your sister is getting married next month. Your parents have asked you to organise a restaurant booking for the wedding reception. Forty people have been invited. You want to spend no more than £20 a head, and you expect drinks and a three-course meal to be included. Some of the guests will be vegetarians.

6   You want to organise a birthday celebration for your best friend and her family at a local restaurant. She has two young children aged two and three. You know that she is on a strict diet and is strongly anti-smoking.

Unit 10

14A   Final task

the Threarah   chief rabbit
silflay   to eat outside
ni-Frith   noon
hrududu   motor vehicle

Three things described: metal cylinders/containers, hosepipes, poisonous gas.

Unit 12

1   Introduction

1A   REAL 'The Birth of Venus' (detail) by Botticelli, 1485.
1B   FAKE 'Madonna of the Veil' painted by an unknown forger sometime in the 1920s. It was bought for $25,000 in 1932 and believed to be genuine until the 1950s when scientific tests revealed that the paint was modern.
2A   REAL Queen Elizabeth II.
2B   FAKE Impersonator of Queen Elizabeth.
3A   FAKE Schloss Neuschwanstein, Bavaria, fake medieval castle built by King Ludwig II in 19th century.
3B   REAL The Alcazar, Segovia, Spain. Built in 14th century.
4A   REAL Rolex oyster perpetual diver's watch.
4B   FAKE Rolex watch bought from a street market in Bangkok

Unit 12

4   Reading skills

Further information
From 1912 until the late 1940s Piltdown Man was generally accepted as the 'Missing Link'. In 1936 a memorial was erected on the site of the discovery and the area was later declared a national monument. However, in the 30s and 40s the discovery of fossils in China, Java and Africa showed that early man in fact had an ape-like skull and a human-like jaw, not the other way round. In the 1950s further investigations were carried out and it was discovered that the teeth of Piltdown man had been filed down artificially.

Recently, radio-carbon tests have revealed that both the skull and jawbone are less than 1,000 years old, and had been stained with potassium dichromate to make them look older. It seems that Professor Smith Woodward was the victim of an elaborate fraud perpetrated by Charles Dawson, who had ingeniously taken advantage of the professor's enthusiasm in order to mastermind what has become known as 'the greatest scientific fraud of the twentieth century'.

Unit 13

1   Introduction

Answers and extra information
1a The October 1987 storm in the southern parts of England. This arrived in the early hours of the morning with winds of up to 167 km/h, leaving 19 people dead and huge amounts of damage, including the destruction of many forests and hundreds of trees.

2d Snow fell in the Canary Islands – very unusual for that particular time of the year. Britain was enjoying mild spring weather at the time – also very unusual!

3b The winter of 1989-90 was the third in succession with far less snow than normal in the Alps. The lack of snow created huge problems for the ski resorts, many of which could provide golf, canoeing and hiking, but not skiing!

4f Abnormally heavy rain through 1988 to 1990 on the eastern side of Australia resulted in flooding which created an 'inland sea' bigger than Britain. Four people were drowned and many sheep were lost.

5c In July 1990 record temperatures of 40°C were recorded near Toulouse in the South of France. The heatwave caused problems with water shortages and a number of elderly people died of sunstroke.

6g In August 1990 temperatures of 37°C were recorded in towns in the south-west of England. The heat caused Big Ben to stop working and the surface of several motorways to melt.

7h Touggourt, an Algerian town in the northern Sahara, recorded 115mm of rain in 72 hours in August 1990. The normal amount of rainfall *per year* for this part of the Sahara is 100mm.

8e The drought and famine in Ethiopia which was extremely well publicised in the 1980s (mainly due to World Aid and Band Aid) still persists in the northern provinces of Tigre and Eritrea.

16C *Final task*

Unit 14

14A *Final task*

Physiological changes
1 We could be shorter and less muscular.
2 Our legs could be much shorter and weaker.
3 There should be no difference in the strength of men and women.
4 Sexual difference could be less noticeable.
5 We could lose all our head and body hair.
6 We should all have dark skin to protect us from the sun, especially our hands and faces.
7 Our eyes should become more powerful.
8 Our hands and feet should become smaller.
9 We should produce less adrenalin when under stress.
10 We could lose all our teeth. Hard gums would be more efficient and less likely to cause trouble.

Unit 16

6   Vocabulary

Here are the missing words in jumbled order.

discrepancy digest numerous hardened bestseller cursory voracious recipients

11B *Pronunciation*

This shows the stress patterns for the first four lines of the poem. Notice that the lines are broken up into units of two syllables and that every second syllable is stressed.

She is / not fair / to out / ward view

As ma / ny mai / dens be

Her love / li ness / I ne / ver knew

Un til / she smiled / on me.

## Unit 16

12C *Final task*

Macavity: The Mystery Cat   by T.S. Eliot
Macavity's a Mystery Cat: He's called the Hidden Paw–
For he's the master criminal who can defy the law.
He's the bafflement of Scotland Yard, the Flying
                                        Squad's despair:
For when they reach the scene of crime – *Macavity's not*
                                        there!

Macavity, Macavity, there's no one like Macavity,
He's broken every human law, he breaks the law of
                                        gravity.
His powers of levitation would make a fakir stare,
And when you reach the scene of crime – *Macavity's not*
                                        there!
You may seek him in the basement, you may look up in
                                        the air –
But I tell you once and once again, *Macavity's not there!*

Macavity's a ginger cat, he's very tall and thin;
You would know him if you saw him, for his eyes are
                                        sunken in.
His brow is deeply lined with thought, his head is
                                        highly domed;
His coat is dusty from neglect, his whiskers are
                                        uncombed.
He sways his head from side to side, with movements
                                        like a snake;
And when you think he's half asleep, he's always wide
                                        awake.

Macavity, Macavity, there's no one like Macavity,
For he's a fiend in feline shape, a monster of depravity.
You may meet him in a by-street, you may see him in
                                        the square
– But when a crime's discovered, then
                                Macavity's not there!

He's outwardly respectable. (They say he cheats at cards.)
And his footprints are not found in any file of Scotland
                                        Yard's.
And when the larder's looted, or the jewel-case is rifled,
Or when the milk is missing, or another Peke's been
                                        stifled,
Or the greenhouse glass is broken, and the trellis past
                                        repair –
Ay, there's the wonder of the thing! *Macavity's not there!*

And when the Foreign Office find a Treaty's gone astray,
Or the Admiralty lose some plans and drawings by the
                                        way;
There may be a scrap of paper in the hall or on the stair –
But it's useless to investigate – *Macavity's not there!*
And when the loss has been disclosed, the Secret
                                        Service say:
'It must have been Macavity!' – but he's a mile away.
You'll be sure to find him resting, or a-licking of his
                                        thumbs,
Or engaged in doing complicated long division sums.

Macavity, Macavity, there's no one like Macavity,
There never was a Cat of such deceitfulness and suavity.
He always has an alibi, and one or two to spare:
At whatever time the deed took place – *MACAVITY*
                                WASN'T THERE!
And they say that all the Cats whose wicked deeds are
                                        widely known
(I might mention Mungojerrie, I might mention
                                        Griddlebone)
Are nothing more than agents for the Cat who all the
                                        time
Just controls their operations: The Napoleon of Crime!

## Unit 17

10   *Speaking skills*

Clues
- Carry my bags in please.   • How old are you?
- Is a bell better than knocking?
- Surely you're not serious?
- And what makes you think I want to come in?

Unit 18

15   *Final task*

HOLIDAYS IN THAILAND: Information Sheet

CLIMATE
Hot and sunny all year round. Average temperature 28° C.

NATURAL BEAUTY
Tropical jungle and mountains in the north. Fertile plains with wide rivers in the centre. Excellent white sand beaches in the south. Long coastline with warm tropical sea and coral formations.

WILDLIFE
Many varieties of tropical animals, especially elephants, crocodiles, lizards, snakes and giant turtles.

LOCAL CULTURE
Many ancient Buddhist temples. Authentic tribal villages in the mountains. Famous dancing tradition. Well-known spicy local cuisine. Established silk-weaving industry. Thriving street markets.

SPECIAL ATMOSPHERE
Thai population are very hospitable and like foreigners. Buddhist philosophy and tradition make people very easy-going, tolerant and relaxed. Country combine fascinating ancient civilisation and customs with modern tourist facilities and resorts.

SPORTS
Good watersports facilities: scuba diving, fishing, water-skiing, snorkelli swimming, parascending etc.

ACCOMMODATION
Full range of tourist accommodation from luxury five-star hotels to very ch pensions and beach huts.

6D *Pronunciation*

You believe that a sport is played with equipment of some description, usually a ball and a racket, or something similar.

1 *Introduction*

Find completions for sentences a – c. Then use the other phrases to help complete the remaining sentences.

a   The original 'Dracula' was a fifteenth century Romanian prince, ...
b   President John F. Kennedy ...
c   Gilles de Rais, known as 'Bluebeard', ...

... by Jack the Ripper.
... was started by the Emperor Nero, ...
... who cut off his ear and sent it with their ransom note.
... assassinated US president Abraham Lincoln ...
... conducted medical experiments without anaesthetic ...
... in the Tower of London in 1495.

6 *Review of past tenses*

Dr Crippen's life

1910 July	Captain of the Montrose, sailing from Antwerp to Canada, sends telegram to police describing his suspicions of two passengers he thinks are Dr Crippen and his girlfriend, Ethel, in disguise. Inspector Dew of Scotland Yard boards a fast ship bound for Canada.
August	Inspector Dew arrives in Canada. He arrests Crippen and Ethel when the Montrose arrives in port.
November	Crippen is found guilty of murder in court and hanged at Pentonville Prison. Ethel is found not guilty and released, then changes her name and disappears.
1967	Ethel Le Neve dies in London aged 84.

7 *Speaking skills*

You are an expert on swimming pool safety. Use the information below to give advice to your partner.

MINIMUM LEGAL SAFETY REQUIREMENTS IN PUBLIC SWIMMING POOLS

Lifeguards   One qualified lifeguard per 30 swimmers. Max. single shift: 90 minutes.
Diving   Minimum depth for diving: 2 metres. All pools to have clearly marked diving zones.
Depth of water   Sudden changes of depth are dangerous. Slope of bottom of pool to be gradual and depth to be marked clearly on side.
Safety equipment   Clearly marked alarms at both sides of pool. Minimum of two rescue poles. Provision of first aid equipment.
Water quality   Bacteriological content to be tested every 12 hours. Approved testing kits to be used. Water authority inspection every 3 months.

11B *Final task*

AT HOME – DAYTIME
- Call the fire brigade by the nearest available public or private telephone. Do not use a telephone in your home.
- Leave the room with the other occupants, closing windows if safe to do so.
- Leave the house, taking all the occupants with you.

AT HOME – NIGHT
- Wait at the window for the fire brigade to arrive.
- Roll out of bed on to the floor, keeping low.

10A *Speaking skills*

Jane Eyre: *Extract A*

My wedding was just about to begin when two men burst into the chapel. The first one spoke.

'The marriage cannot go on. I declare the existence of an impediment.'

The priest looked up at the speaker and stood silent.

'My name is Briggs. I am a lawyer. Mr Rochester already has a wife and she is still living. I have a witness to the fact. Mr Mason, please step forward.'

The second stranger came forward and spoke.

'She is now living at Thornfield Hall,' said Mason. 'I saw her there last April. I am her brother.'

'At Thornfield Hall!' ejaculated the clergyman. 'Impossible! I am an old resident in this neighbourhood, sir, and I never heard of a Mrs Rochester at Thornfield Hall.'

I saw a grim smile contort Mr Rochester's face. For a few moments he was speechless, then he spoke.

'Enough! There will be no wedding to-day. Bigamy is an ugly word! I admit I meant to be a bigamist, but fate has out-manoeuvred me. What this lawyer and his client say is true: I have been married, and the woman to whom I was married lives! You say you never heard of a Mrs Rochester at the house up yonder, but I expect you have heard gossip about the mysterious lunatic kept there in a locked room. Some have whispered to you that she is my bastard half-sister; some, my cast-off mistress. I now inform you that she is my wife, whom I married fifteen years ago. Bertha Mason is her name. Bertha Mason is mad and she came from a mad family: idiots and maniacs through three generations! Her mother was both a madwoman and a drunkard, – as I found out only after I had married the daughter: for they had deceived me about their family secrets! Bertha, like a dutiful child, copied her parent in both points. But I owe you no further explanation. I invite you all to come up to the house and visit Mrs Poole's patient, and my wife! You shall see what sort of a being I was cheated into marrying, and judge whether or not I had a right to seek happiness with a new wife.'

 **Unit 5**

7   Pronunciation

Your words are: *record, protest, permit.*

15A   Final task

What do you think are the best ways of a) learning grammar and b) practising listening? Rank each item from 1 (very effective) to 5 (totally useless) for you and for two other students, B and C below.

GRAMMAR	YOU	B	C
working out rules from examples	☐	☐	☐
learning the rules by heart	☐	☐	☐
doing written grammatical exercises	☐	☐	☐
playing games/having discussions which use a certain structure	☐	☐	☐
doing grammatical drills	☐	☐	☐
reading about grammar	☐	☐	☐
LISTENING			
listening to the teacher	☐	☐	☐
listening to cassettes in the language lab	☐	☐	☐
listening to other students	☐	☐	☐
listening to the cassette in the classroom	☐	☐	☐
listening to the radio (e.g. BBC World Service)	☐	☐	☐
watching TV/films/videos	☐	☐	☐
listening to pop songs	☐	☐	☐

 **Unit 6**

15   Language awareness

Below are the definitions of all the words on the left on page 51.

principle (n) moral rule, general truth
stationary (adj) not moving, standing still
serial (n) a number of things in order, e.g. parts of a novel (adj) relating to a series of things, e.g. serial killer
precede (v) to go before someone or something
canvass (v) to determine opinions/feelings, usually by a survey
affect (v) to influence, change
currant (n) dried grape, often used in cakes
des'sert (n) sweet course of a meal

19A   Final task

Discuss these questions, but add more points of your own.

- Does everyone have the right to have children?
- If people are desperate to have children will they look after them well?
- Do older people or younger people bring up children better? (Remember that older people – i.e. in their thirties – in the UK cannot adopt babies.)
- Should children have an equal chance of life, wherever they come from?
- Should people be allowed to use money to adopt children? Can adoptive parents give enough love?
- Should government money be spent on orphanages?

Unit 7

4   Speaking skills

Check this information with your partner.

1 The author says that in literary circles people ask you if you went to university.
2 She claims that 93% of the population went to university.
3 She says that Anne Wintour still feels self-conscious about not going to university.
4 The author says that a classic liberal education is rather useless.

14B   Final task

PART - TIME TEACHERS	SUBJECTS	HOURS AVAILABLE
Mr Sutton	Biology and Physics	Every afternoon
Ms Bingham	Chemistry and History	Every morning except Tuesday
Ms Terry	Economics	Mondays and Fridays only
Mr Carlton	Music and Literature	Tuesday and Wednesday mornings only

Unit 8

2   Introduction

Trailfinders' itineraries
Take a few minutes to check that you can find all the places on the map on pages 60 – 61 and that you understand the routes on the next page.
Your partner will describe his/her ideal route to you. Find the itinerary which is closest to your partner's plan and is within his/her budget.
If this itinerary does not exactly match his/her plan, try to persuade your partner to fit in with the standard itinerary or to select one of the alternatives.

LONDON LOS ANGELES TOKYO KUALA LUMPUR BANGKOK LONDON	LONDON NEW YORK SAN FRANCISCO HONOLULU FIJI SYDNEY BANGKOK DELHI LONDON	LONDON TORONTO or VANCOUVER HONOLULU FIJI SYDNEY BANGKOK DELHI LONDON	LONDON JOHANNESBURG own land arrangements to HARARE PERTH SYDNEY LOS ANGELES own land arrangements to SAN FRANCISCO LONDON
£763	£1,003	£900	£1,086
LONDON BANGKOK PHUKET SYDNEY BRISBANE FIJI HONOLULU SAN FRANCISCO NEW YORK LONDON	LONDON LOS ANGELES HONOLULU CAIRNS SYDNEY PERTH HONG KONG BANGKOK LONDON	LONDON DENVER LOS ANGELES TAHITI RAROTONGA AUCKLAND BALI JAKARTA SINGAPORE LONDON	LONDON DELHI KATHMANDU HONG KONG BANGKOK own land arrangements to KUALA LUMPUR AUCKLAND TAHITI LOS ANGELES LONDON
£1,187	£1,066	£1,203	£1,399
LONDON NEW YORK SAN FRANCISCO own land arrangements to VANCOUVER HONOLULU CAIRNS SYDNEY BANGKOK HONG KONG own land arrangements to BEIJING LONDON	LONDON NAIROBI own land arrangements to HARARE MAURITIUS SINGAPORE PERTH ADELAIDE SYDNEY AUCKLAND HONOLULU LOS ANGELES own land arrangements to MEXICO CITY LONDON	LONDON RIO own land arrangements to LIMA SANTIAGO EASTER ISLAND TAHITI FIJI AUCKLAND SYDNEY own land arrangements to PERTH BALI SINGAPORE DELHI LONDON	LONDON DELHI SINGAPORE SYDNEY AUCKLAND HONOLULU LOS ANGELES RIO JOHANNESBURG NAIROBI LONDON
£1,358	£1,599	£1,965	£1,990

11 *Speaking skills*

Extract A
A Force 8 wind blowing from East North East is covering the sea with spray. We're lying 1453 nautical miles from New York, a little more than halfway to Europe, Newfoundland is 580 miles North-West and the Azores archipelago 600 miles South-East. It's a warm 61 degrees but very wet.

Extract B
In the midst of Europeans of all nationalities, there were Persians with pointed bonnets, Bunhyas with round turbans, Sindes with square caps, Armenians in long robes and Parsees or Ghebers, direct descendants of the followers of Zoroaster who are the most industrious, most highly civilized, most intelligent and most austere of the Hindus, and who at that time included the richest native merchants of Bombay. That day they were celebrating a sort of religious carnival, with processions and entertainments at which dancing girls, dressed in pink gauze decorated with gold and silver, danced, gracefully but with perfect modesty, to the sound of viols and the beating of tambourines. Rarely had he seen such a curious spectacle.

Extract C
The Desert Wind is made up of Amtrak Superliners, two-tiered coaches in silver, red and blue livery. Its interior, like the bullet train in Japan, but unlike the trains in China and India, owes much to aircraft design. A lightweight shell, moulded seats in open coach formation, inadequate but neatly designed lights, fold-down tables. There are also sleeping cabins, utilising the space quite skilfully but failing to disguise the fact that there isn't much of it.

Unit 9

1 *Introduction*
- Dish: Toad in the hole
- Ingredients: sausages   in a pastry shell

14 *Final task*
You run a restaurant called New York, New York. Make a notice with this name and put it on your desk. Use the following information to answer questions from customers.

NEW YORK, NEW YORK

MENUS   Burgers, pizzas, fried chicken, french fries, various vegetables and desserts.
A range of vegetarian dishes.
A special low-calorie menu is available.

DRINKS   No licence to sell alcoholic drinks, but customers can bring their own drinks into the restaurant.

FACILITIES   Large no-smoking section.
High-chairs for young children.
Rock groups play in the restaurant every evening.
You accept VISA and American Express cards.

PROBLEMS   Steep stairs and no lift.
Maximum number of customers at one time is 35. No facilities for large groups.

Unit 10

9B *Speaking skills*
Read the text below and the definitions on the next page. Tell your partner about the text, including the factual information and your opinions about it. Explain anything your partner does not understand.

The British are renowned for their love of animals and for their ability to domesticate any animal. A favourite pet is the rabbit, which leads a very different existence in captivity from in the wild. Wild rabbits make their home in a burrow, which is often part of a warren, and surface to graze whenever possible. They live on grass, only occasionally finding other types of food. However, in captivity, a rabbit usually lives in a hutch and is fed on all sorts of tidbits, such as lettuce and carrots.

One of the most unusual pets, and one which is becoming much more common in urban areas, is the fox. In Britain, the fox has become an urban scavenger: areas which were once farmland and are now becoming densely populated present the fox with a dilemma. The average fox chooses to stay and to forage for its food amongst the rubbish tips and dustbins of the outer city areas. Some people attempt to make pets out of these displaced animals, but the fox is not easily tamed and those who try are destined for disappointment.

Definitions

burrow   hole underground, dug out by rabbits for shelter

warren   number of burrows all joined by tunnels, where a group of rabbits live

graze   eat grass

hutch   wooden box, often used for housing domestic rabbits

tidbit   small piece of luxury food

scavenger animal that feeds on waste food of others

forage   search for food

Now listen to your partner. Ask about anything you don't understand and make a note of any new vocabulary you learn.

12   *Pronunciation*

Write two relative clauses from the information below, then dictate them to your partner. Check that your partner's sentences are the same as yours, especially the punctuation.

1 Your dog is both very clever and very helpful. It can tell the sound of your car and waits at the door with your slippers.

2 You have three pedigree cats. You entered them all for a cat show recently. The cat with one blind eye won first prize.

 Unit 11

1   *Introduction*

You have an answer to each question in the quiz, but only some of your answers are correct. In your group, decide on each correct answer.

1 Alexander Graham Bell	8 *Citizen Kane*
2 One or two minutes	9 Steven Spielberg
3 American	10 Italy
4 Type	11 *Ran*
5 John Wayne	12 Paris
6 Richard Nixon	13 *Fantasia*
7 Marlon	14 Hitachi

Unit 12

6B   *Speaking skills*

Picture 1

• The photograph is very hazy (unclear).
• It could be a trick photograph.
• It could be a model floating in the water.

Picture 2

• The sculpture looks like other genuine Greek statues.
• The quality of the carving is very good.
• The marble used comes from a quarry near Athens.

Unit 13

6C   *Listening skills*

Ask Student B about the geographical features in the chart. Student B will ask you about the environmental terms. Here are some definitions to help you.

global warming increase in temperature of the Earth's climate

environmental pollution releasing into the air gases which pollute and damage the atmosphere (also known as greenhouse gases) e.g. carbon monoxide from cars

greenhouse effect pollution in the atmosphere reflects and 'holds in' the hotter air, making the atmosphere act like a greenhouse

deforestation cutting down trees for commercial purposes, thereby destroying forests and reducing the amount of oxygen released into the atmosphere

the hole in the ozone layer the ozone layer shields us from the dangerous ultra-violet rays of the sun. The 'hole' is an area above northern Europe where the ozone layer appears to be thinning and therefore is not as effective. There is also a much more serious one over the Antarctic.

Unit 14

5B   *Language work*

A sings like a bird.

B ranks the highest.

C is better-looking than E.

D has been married more often than the others.

E is the least famous in this group.

F probably exercises the most frequently.

Unit 15

2   *Introduction*

Below are five linguistic 'rules' explaining the things children do when they are learning English. Match them to the pictures, then check with your partner.

a The child follows the rules of the language but uses them wrongly, e.g. with past tenses.

b The child omits the subject pronoun.

c The child uses words that sound like the object/animal.

d The child uses verbs but does not use tenses.

e The child omits articles and prepositions.

Unit 12

13   *Final task*

ST AGNES HOME FOR RETIRED OFFICERS
CANTERBURY

Thursday 25th March, 1886

Dear Mr Holmes,

Thank you for your letter of yesterday. Yes, I remember Dr John Watson very well from our meeting in Calcutta eight years ago. 'Honour or Death' is the motto of the Norfolk Regiment. As you know from Watson, I was Watson was correct when he told you that 'Honour or Death' is the regimental doctor with the Norfolks while they were stationed at Mulahabad in northern India between 1856 and 1872.

You asked me in your letter if I can identify an ex-soldier of the Norfolks with two bullet wounds in his chest, one near the heart. Yes, I know the man well. Corporal Tom Cabmoll is his name, and he received those wounds during the great Indian rebellion against the British in 1857. I remember the day that Cabmoll was carried into the field hospital outside Delhi with the blood pouring from his chest and the two bullets still inside him. It took me all night to extract the bullet which was near his heart: I was so tired when I finished that I couldn't walk and the nurses had to help me to my bed. It was the most difficult operation of my life and I will never forget it.

During his convalescence I got to know my patient. I liked Cabmoll and thought he was a good and honest soldier, but three years later I discovered I was wrong. Next to the camp in Mulahabad there was a Hindu temple which was famous for its treasure, and in particular for ten big blue diamonds. One morning in 1860 the Hindu priests arrived at the temple and found that all ten diamonds had disappeared. Orders then came from Colonel Tosh, who was commanding officer of the Norfolks, to search all the soldiers. The ten diamonds were found in Cabmoll's bed. He was immediately arrested and the diamonds were held as evidence by the military authorities.

Cabmoll's court martial took place a month later. He admitted that he had stolen the diamonds and Colonel Tosh sentenced him to 25 years in military prison. But that wasn't the end of the story. When the diamonds were returned to the Hindu temple after Cabmoll's court martial, the priests discovered they were fakes - imitation diamonds made of paste. Colonel Tosh said that Cabmoll must have planned to substitute the fake diamonds for the real ones, but that he was caught before he could do so. Cabmoll had hidden the real diamonds somewhere. When I visited him in prison Corporal Cabmoll said that this wasn't true, and that the diamonds in his bed were the same ones he had stolen from the temple. He told me he knew nothing about the false diamonds.

Cabmoll spent the next 25 years in Calcutta Military Prison, where I visited him several times. The diamonds were never found, but on three occasions magnificent diamonds, very similar to those stolen in Mulahabad, were sold anonymously on the London market. The first time in 1865, when two diamonds were sold; in 1872 another two were sold; and at the beginning of last year two more were sold. All of them were the same light blue colour as the Mulahabad stones but, as you know, you can change a diamond very easily just by cutting it a bit. So it was impossible to prove that the diamonds sold in London were those which had been stolen in India in 1860. The police never found out who was selling them, but Scotland Yard and the military police were working on the theory that Cabmoll had given the real diamonds to an accomplice before he was arrested, and that the accomplice was now selling them. Each time these diamonds appeared on the London market, military police officers visited Cabmoll in Calcutta Military Prison and offered him his liberty if he would tell them who had the Mulahabad diamonds. Each time Cabmoll said he didn't know.

Cabmoll was freed last August and arrived in London in October. I have seen him a couple of times and in fact helped to get him a job as a gardener.

If there is anything else you would like to know, please tell me. Meanwhile my best wishes to John Watson.

Dr I Brown

Dr Ignatius Brown,
Captain, Royal Army Medical Corps (retired)

Unit 15

11C *Pronunciation*

Look at the chart of words below. Say these words to Student B, in random order, so he/she can write them in a similar chart. Be careful to pronounce the vowels clearly. Student B will then give you some words to put in your chart.

/iː/	/ɪ/	/e/	/æ/	/ɑː/	/ɒ/	/ɔː/	/ʌ/	/ɜː/	/ʊ/	/uː/
cheap	chip	check	chap	chart	chop	chalk	chuck	church	–	choose
peek	pick	peck	pack	park	pot	port	punt	pert	put	poodle
steal	still	stealth	stack	star	stock	stall	stuck	stern	stood	stoop

Unit 16

12B *Final task*

Missing lines

- Or when the milk is missing, or another Peke's been stifled,
- And when you think he's half asleep, he's always wide awake.
- And they say that all the Cats whose wicked deeds are widely known
- You would know him if you saw him, for his eyes are sunken in.
- You may meet him in a by-street, you may see him in the square –
- And when the loss has been disclosed, the Secret Service say:

Unit 17

1   *Introduction*

1 a famous Swedish pop group from the nineteen seventies
2 the French fashion designer who worked for Madonna
3 a famous Spanish film director from Madrid
4 an American comedian and film director from New York
5 an American soap-opera about a family which owns an oil company

Answers

a *The Wall*   b Gerard Depardieu
c Luciano Pavarotti   d   Bette Midler
e U2   f Reebok

Unit 20

4B   *Language awareness*

Below is a list of words. Decide whether each one is a homonym, homograph or homophone and divide them into three groups.

> *arms   coach   fare   flower   pair   plain   pour
> read   refuse   road   sow   suit*

Now do the following:
- homonyms: find the two meanings and write them down.
- homographs: find the two pronunciations.
- homophones: work out what the other spelling is.

Compare your answers with Student B.

8   *Pronunciation*

Look at the chart of words below. Say these words to Student B, in random order, for him/her to write in a similar chart. Be careful to pronounce the diphthongs clearly. Student B will then give you some words to put in your chart.

/eɪ/	raid, shade
/aɪ/	ride, shied
/ɔɪ/	royal, soil
/əʊ/	road, showed
/aʊ/	round, sound
/ɪə/	rear, sheer
/eə/	rare, share
/ʊə/	lure, sure

 **Unit 1**

6 D *Pronunciation*

You believe that a sport has to be competitive and that it has to involve skill.

7 A *Reading skills*

The History of Trivial Pursuit

The current best-selling board game, Trivial Pursuit, owes its origins to the success of another board game, Scrabble. It was invented one winter night of 1979 by Chris Haney and Scott Abbott, two journalists, in Montreal, Canada. The pair were playing Scrabble when they started to wonder whether they could devise a game to rival the then best-selling game in the world. They claim it took them just 45 minutes to invent the game we now know as Trivial Pursuit, originally named just Trivia Pursuit. Haney and Abbott were so convinced of the potential of their invention that they raised $40,000 from their friends and strangers to finance its development – most of which took place on a Spanish beach in 1980 and '81!

They returned to Canada in 1981 with everything (i.e. 6,000 questions and answers) ready to take the game into production, at which point the project began to look unviable because of the technical problems of colour printing and of collating the 1,000 question cards. Eventually they found a way of doing it and by the end of the year 1,100 sets were ready for sale. Despite the fact that the games didn't follow the marketing wisdom of the time – they cost far too much at $30 each and the box did not give any idea of the contents – the partners got down to the job of selling the first batch and were soon touring the games shops and drumming up custom. For a long time it looked as though the games weren't going to be successful, but after several weeks the games were selling, money was coming in, and thousands more sets were being produced.

The next step was to break into the lucrative American market. The game was sent to American distributors and was accepted by Selchow and Righter. Once again, it looked for a while as though Trivial Pursuit was set to founder, but then proof of the game's popularity was received with the news that the casts of the popular TV drama series *St Elsewhere*, and the film *The Big Chill*, were playing the game on the set between takes. From there, Haney and Scott never looked back.

Trivial Pursuit soon became a worldwide phenomenon. Indeed, in 1984, only two years after its launch on the American market, a copy of the game was buried in a time capsule alongside a copy of Michael Jackson's *Thriller* album. Now, only ten years after its initial production, the master game is selling across the world and several different versions of the game have been produced. Personalities such as Ronald Reagan and the British Royal Family are devoted to the game, and its originators have succeeded in their ambitions in a way that they never thought possible. Who knows, in a few years' time, a cast of a film or TV show may well be acting the story of Chris Haney and Scott Abbott.

Unit 2

1 *Introduction*

Help to complete sentences a – c, find completions for sentences d – f and help to complete sentences g – i.

d Five women prostitutes were severely mutilated and killed ...
e Paul Getty III, grandson of the world's richest man, ...
f King Richard III of England ...

... who also murdered his mother Agrippina and his half-brother Britannicus.
... who fought alongside Joan of Arc, ...
... known as Vlad the Impaler ...
... in a theatre in Washington in 1865.
... on Jewish prisoners at Auschwitz concentration camp during World War II.
... was assassinated by ...

6 *Review of past tenses*

Dr Crippen's life

1861	Crippen is born in Michigan USA.	Crippen in USA
1885	Crippen marries Belle Elmore, an actress.	
1890	The Crippens move to London. Crippen starts work as a dentist.	Crippen in London
1908	Crippen employs a young secretary, Ethel Le Neve, and secretly begins a love affair with her.	

Unit 2

13   *Final task*

14 Sea View,
Batterfield,
London E4.

Sunday 5th September, 1884

Dear Mr Holmes,

My name is Justin Milt, and I am writing to you about a very curious
thing that happened to me yesterday – Saturday. I would appreciate it
if you treated my letter as confidential, as I would not like my wife
to find out about this matter.

Yesterday evening I told my wife that I was going to have a drink
in the pub, but instead I took the underground to Soho to visit the
London Moulin Rouge Club. I go there every Saturday evening, without
telling my wife.

Yesterday, as usual, I handed in my umbrella in exchange for a
numbered ticket at the cloakroom of the club. I noticed then that Bill,
the regular attendant, wasn't there. Instead there was a young man who
quite clearly had had too much to drink. When I asked about Bill, the
young fellow blew alcohol fumes all over me and told me that Bill was
ill.

The show was as interesting as usual, with some very extraordinary
dancing which I enjoyed very much. Some of the young ladies were
particularly pretty, I thought.

When I left at about 10.25, I saw that the young man in the
cloakroom was even drunker. As I handed in my ticket and collected my
umbrella he nearly fell over.

It was in the underground on my way home that I noticed that the
stupid young attendant had given me the wrong umbrella. It seemed bigger
than mine, fatter than mine, and so I decided to roll it again so that
my wife wouldn't notice that it wasn't mine. As I opened the umbrella,
out fell notes – £50 notes! There were 20 of them – a total of £1,000!
I'd never seen so much money in my life.

Now I don't know what to do, Mr Holmes. If I go to the police they will
ask questions and my wife will find out about my Saturday evenings at
the London Moulin Rouge club. But it's not honest just to keep the
money, and I am a gentleman. What do you think I should do, Mr Holmes?

Yours sincerely,

Justin Milt

PS Incidentally, it says 'made in Germany' on the umbrella I was given
at the London Moulin Rouge club.

Unit 3

11   *Final task*

> **AT HOME – DAY-TIME**
> - Close the front door.
> - Keep low, because smoke and heat rise to the
>   ceiling.
>
> **AT HOME – NIGHT**
> - Shout for a passer-by to call the fire brigade.
> - Crawl back to the bed, remove the bedding and
>   place it at the foot of the door. This helps to hold
>   back the fire.
> - Crawl to the bedroom door and feel it with the
>   back of your hand for heat.

Unit 13

6C   *Listening skills*

Ask Student A about the environmental terms in the
chart.
Student A will ask you about the geographical
features. Here are some definitions to help you.

ice caps   the large masses of ice at the North and
  South Poles, the Arctic and the Antarctic ice caps
archipelago   a group of islands
delta   the place where a river meets the sea, creating
  a marshy area of waterways
desert belt   the region of the world where the
  climate has resulted in desert areas where little
  vegetation can grow, notably the Sahara region of
  North Africa

Unit 4

10   *Speaking skills*

Jane Eyre: Extract B

'Is Mr Rochester living at Thornfield Hall now?' I asked.

'No, ma'am. Oh, no! No one is living there,' replied the innkeeper. 'I suppose you are a stranger in these parts, or you would have heard what happened last autumn – Thornfield Hall is quite a ruin. It was burnt down just about harvest time. A dreadful calamity! The fire broke out at dead of night. I witnessed it myself.'

'Was it known how it started?' I demanded.

'They guessed, ma'am, they guessed. You see there was a lady – a – a lunatic kept in the house. She was kept locked up. No one saw her. They only knew by rumour that such a person was at the hall, and who or what she was no one really knew. But a queer thing happened a year ago – this lady turned out to be Mr Rochester's wife! The discovery was brought about in the strangest way. There was a young lady, a governess at the Hall, that Mr Rochester fell in love with. He tried to marry her.'

I had no wish to hear my own story. 'You shall tell me this part of the story another time,' I said, 'but I wish to hear all about the fire. Was it suspected that this lunatic, Mrs Rochester, started it?'

'That's right, ma'am. It's quite certain that it was her, and nobody but her, that set it going. She set fire first to the curtains in the room next to her own, and then she got down to a lower floor, and made her way to the chamber that had been the governess's and she set fire to the bed there, but there was nobody sleeping in it, fortunately. The governess had run away two months before and, although Mr Rochester had desperately searched for her, he was unable to find her.'

'Then Mr Rochester was at home when the fire broke out?'

'Yes, indeed he was, and he rescued the servants out of their beds and helped them down himself, and went back to get his mad wife out of her room. And then they called out to him that she was on the roof, where she was standing, waving her arms, above the battlements, and shouting out till they could hear her a mile away. I saw her and heard her with my own eyes. She was a big woman, and had long black hair; we could see it streaming against the flames as she stood. And then, ma'am, she yelled and jumped to the ground.'

'Was she dead?'

'Yes, as dead as the floor on which her brains and blood were scattered.'

'Were there any other lives lost?'

'No.'

Unit 5

7   *Pronunciation*

Your words are: *perfect, object, insult.*

15   *Final task*

What do you think are the best ways of a) learning vocabulary and b) practising writing? Rank each methods from 1 (very effective) to 5 (totally useless) for you and for two other students, A and C below.

VOCABULARY	YOU	A	C
learning x words a day by heart	☐	☐	☐
grouping words according to meaning	☐	☐	☐
keeping a bilingual vocabulary bank	☐	☐	☐
using new vocabulary actively, e.g. adding to sentences	☐	☐	☐
using images to retain vocabulary e.g. pictures	☐	☐	☐
reading, and looking up every new word	☐	☐	☐
WRITING			
doing written grammatical drills	☐	☐	☐
writing grammatical exercises	☐	☐	☐
writing to an English-speaking penfriend	☐	☐	☐
writing essays	☐	☐	☐
writing up your notes in English after a lesson	☐	☐	☐
writing in groups/pairs and helping each other/ correcting each other's work	☐	☐	☐

Unit 6

2   *Introduction*

Read the questions below and on the next page, write definitions for the words in *italics* and answer the questions for yourself. Then interview A and C.

5 You are an accountant working for a large company. You *dislike* the company and your direct manager but you are in a lot of debt and you need the job. One day you discover some papers in your boss's office which suggest that he is *cheating* the company. Do you:

a *blackmail* your boss into giving you a pay rise?

b go straight to the Managing Director with the evidence, at the risk of losing your job if you are wrong?

c *hint* that you know what your boss is doing, and give him or her a chance to stop?

d talk to your boss, at the risk of losing your job?

6 You discover a *code* that allows you to make telephone calls all over the world at no cost. Do you:
a use it as much as possible?
b tell all your friends about it?
c ignore it?
d inform the telephone company so that they can change the code?

7 A close friend has been through an unhappy experience. You are a writer and her experience would make a very good plot for a novel. Do you:
a decide that it is wrong to exploit your friend's situation?
b write the novel, but making some important changes?
c ask your friend first and only write the novel if she agrees?
d write the novel with all the details, so that it is unmistakably her story?

8 You are your elderly mother's only living relative. You live fairly close to her, and you see her quite often. You are offered a fantastic job overseas, which you really want. Do you:
a investigate the possibilities of providing a paid companion for your mother, or finding her some sheltered housing?
b take the job and leave her in her flat?
c take the job and take your mother with you?
d turn down the job in order to stay near your mother?

15 Language awareness

Below are the definitions of the words on the right on page 51.

principal (adj) main, most important
 (n) head of a school
stationery (n) writing materials, e.g. paper and pens
cereal (n) grasses which produce edible grains, e.g. rice, wheat
proceed (v) to continue
canvas (n) heavy material, used in making tents
effect (n) result
 (v) to make something happen
current (adj) present, up to date
 (n) flow of electricity/water
desert (n – 'desert) arid, dry, uncultivated area
 (v – de'sert) to leave or abandon, esp. army

Unit 7

4 Speaking skills

Check this information with your partner.

1 The author says that P.D. James is a bestselling novelist.
2 She says that Lisa St Aubin de Teran originally planned to go to Oxford university.
3 She says exotic experiences are just as useful as a degree to a novelist.

4 In the article Anne Wintour says that people without degrees are always more original.

14 Information

FULL-TIME TEACHERS	SUBJECTS	TIMETABLE	SUBJECT NOTES
Ms Lean	Computer Studies	Teaches the first form every afternoon	Art, Computer Studies and Sports lessons must always be double lessons (2 hours) because of the time needed for changing or preparation of equipment/clearing up.
Mr Denton	Geography and Art	Teaches the third form all day Mondays and Thursdays	
Ms Smith	Sports	Teaches the first year on Tuesday and Thursday mornings	

Unit 8

11 Speaking skills

Extract D
The carriage he occupied was a sort of long omnibus carried by two four-wheel bogies, which enabled it to take sharp curves. It had no compartments; two rows of seats lined its sides, and between them was an aisle which led to the lavatories and dressing-rooms with which each carriage was provided. Throughout the length of the train the carriages were linked together by gangways so that the passengers could walk from one end of the convoy to the other. There were saloon-cars, observation-cars, dining-cars and refreshment-cars at their disposal. The only things missing were theatre-cars, and these would come some day.

Extract E
When the *Henrietta* could not rise to a wave she went right through it, and her deck was swept from end to end. Sometimes, when a mountain of water raised her stern above the waves, her screw was lifted right out of the sea and beat the air with its maddened blades, but the ship still forged ahead. Never was it more than a gale, but unfortunately it stayed obstinately in the south-east, so that no sail could be hoisted.

Extract F
Today is a festival day called *Durga Puja*, the climax of a ten-day celebration of the triumph of good over evil. There are at least seven New Years in India, depending on when the harvest is brought in. Effigies up to 50 feet tall will be carried through the streets and destroyed to commemorate the killing of the evil king Ravenah of Sri Lanka by Lord Rama. The celebration of myth and the belief in the supernatural is an important part of Indian life, and on this festival day it is customary to bless whatever brings you your livelihood. So the soldier garlands his rifle and the photographer his camera and the farmer his plough and so on. This is called *Puja*, meaning worship.

Unit 9

1   *Introduction*

- Dish: Bangers and mash
- Ingredients: cheese and tomato   and mashed potato

14   *Final task*

You run a restaurant called Pizzeria Italia. Make a notice with this name and put it on your desk. Use the following information to answer questions from customers.

PIZZERIA ITALIA

MENUS   Speciality is pizza but also pasta dishes and Italian cuisine.
Several vegetarian pizzas available.

DRINKS   All drinks available, including large selection of Italian quality wines.

FACILITIES   Everything is on the ground floor, no steps.
Banqueting room is available, seating up to 50 people, three course meal available costing £25 per person, drinks not included.
Italian folk musicians play most evenings.

PROBLEMS   You don't have a no-smoking area.
You don't accept payment by credit card.
No facilities for young children.

Unit 10

9B   *Speaking skills*

Read the text and the definitions that follow it. Tell your partner about the text, including the factual information and your opinions about it. Explain anything your partner does not understand.

Second only to dogs, the most common pet in Britain is the cat – most often the common moggy. The British get their pet cats from all sorts of places: some people choose their cats from pet shops, friends' cats' litters or cats' homes. Others prefer to adopt feral cats or strays.

Life for the domestic cat in Britain is usually very pleasant – regular food, a warm place to sleep, pet humans and freedom provided by the catflap. It's surprising that we don't have an expression 'It's a cat's life', meaning a life of luxury.

However, this is only one side of the story. The pet shop kitten (or puppy) takes potluck when it is bought and taken from the pet shop. The incidence of discarded kittens and puppies is rising. These abandoned animals are found in rubbish dumps, on the side of motorways and on waste ground. They are usually put there by the caring human who bought them in the first place, who, having realised the true cost of day-to-day animal care, suddenly finds the new pet less appealing. This happens, not surprisingly, most often after Christmas: presumably the discarded cat is yet another Christmas present which the children have lost interest in after a few days.

Definitions

moggy   cat of mixed breeding, not a pedigree
litter   all the kittens born to a female cat at one time
feral   living in the wild
stray   a cat without a home
catflap   a small, swing 'door' built into a door or window to allow cats in or out when they wish
to take potluck   to take what is available, to take your chances
incidence   frequency of occurrence
discarded   abandoned

Now listen to your partner. Ask about anything you don't understand and make a note of any new vocabulary you learn.

Unit 11

1   *Introduction*

You have an answer to each question in the quiz, but only some of your answers are correct. In your group, decide on each correct answer.

1 Thomas Edison
2 Ten minutes
3 British
4 Male or female
5 Marilyn Monroe
6 Ronald Reagan
7 Uncle Sam
8 *E.T.*
9 Alfred Hitchcock
10 Spain
11 *The Seven Samurai*
12 Los Angeles
13 *Who Framed Roger Rabbit*
14 Panasonic

8A   *Language work*

Rewrite the text below in direct speech, then compare it with your partner's text.

He said that he remembered the first film he'd ever made, about fifteen years before. He said he'd been very young at the time and had been terrified, but he had been convinced even then that he was going to be a star. He told us that he'd come to Hollywood straight after that first film, as he'd been certain that Hollywood was the place to be. But he added that when he was living there that first time he'd got involved with a bad crowd and it hadn't been until 1985 that success had finally happened, after he'd left Hollywood. He remarked that when he'd come back in 1992, he'd known that he would be able to cope with it, and he concluded the interview by saying that he had signed a contract for two more, but then he would go back to Scotland, as he was missing it badly.

 Unit 12

6B Speaking skills

Picture 1

- Several witnesses saw the monster when the photo was taken.
- You can't make money out of this so why would anyone bother to fake it?.
- Over the years hundreds of people have seen the monster.

Picture 2

- The surface of the marble is too smooth to be really old.
- The head is facing in the wrong direction, as if it was added on afterwards.
- There aren't any cracks or damaged areas which you would expect to find in something so old.

13 Final task

POLICE CRIMINAL INVESTIGATION DEPARTMENT
SCOTLAND YARD LONDON SW1

Tuesday 23rd March, 1886

Dear Mr Holmes,

I am writing to you about an extraordinary death which occurred in a most expensive and luxurious area of north London at three o'clock this morning. Do you know Shakespeare Road? It is an exclusive little street where the very rich and the very important live. Sir Hugh Drummond, Governor of the Bank of England, lives at number 40 Shakespeare Road. He and Lady Drummond were sleeping peacefully early this morning when they were suddenly woken by a violent knocking on the front door.

     The first person to get to the door was the butler. As he opened it, a man of about sixty, his face covered in sweat despite the cold night air, pushed his way into the hall.

'Quick, quick', cried the stranger, 'have you got an axe?'
'An axe? What for?' asked the astonished butler.
'Never mind what for!' exclaimed the man. 'I need an axe and it's a matter of life and death!'

'There's a small axe in the kitchen,' said the cook, hurrying into the hall. 'I use it to break bones to make soup.' Behind the cook came Sir Hugh and Lady Drummond, dressed in their pyjamas.
'What is going on?' demanded Sir Hugh.
The stranger ignored him. 'Where's the kitchen, then? Hurry, hurry!'

The butler helped the stranger, who could walk only with great difficulty, towards the kitchen, while the cook ran ahead to light the gas lights. Sir Hugh and Lady Drummond followed the party into the kitchen.
'The axe, the axe!' shouted the man hysterically.
'Give me the axe!'
'Wait a minute,' interrupted Sir Hugh. 'Who are you? What do you want?'
'I want the axe,' repeated the man, 'I must have the axe!'

The cook handed the man a small kitchen axe.
'Please God,' prayed the stranger, 'give me strength.'
He sat at the kitchen table and laid his right arm on the table in front of him. Then he took the axe in his left hand, raised it above his head, and, before anyone could stop him, brought the axe down as hard as he could on his right wrist. Lady Drummond screamed as blood flew through the air and spattered her pyjamas. The man at the table lifted his right arm. His hand hung from his wrist, only half severed. 'Oh no no no!' he cried, put his arm on the table in front of him again and once more brought the axe down as hard as he could on it. This time when he raised his arm there was no hand on the end of it. 'I've done it!' exclaimed the stranger in triumph before he fainted.

Meanwhile blood was pouring out from the man's wrist and was collecting in little pools on the floor. Sir Hugh held the injured arm up while the butler put on a tourniquet, but the blood continued to flow. By the time a doctor arrived fifteen minutes later their mysterious guest was dead.

The police arrived a few minutes after the doctor, but so far we have not been able to identify the dead man. He is aged between fifty and sixty, and his face and arms are dark brown, suggesting that he has spent a lot of time in the tropical sun. In addition the words 'Honour or Death' are tattooed on his upper arm. There are also two old bullet wounds in the man's chest. The police doctor says that one of them is very, very close to the heart. The doctor says that these wounds probably occurred many years ago.

Lady Drummond is in bed under sedation after the terrible shock she has had. Sir Hugh is very angry about the whole episode. He says the police should never let such horrible things happen. He says that if I don't solve this mystery within 24 hours he will go to the Commissioner of Police to complain. Naturally I would be very grateful for any help you can give me, Mr Holmes.

Yours sincerely,

T. Gregson

Tobias Gregson
Detective Inspector

Unit 14

5B *Language work*

A is as thin as a rake.
B is as tall as F.
C is the youngest in this group.
D has the worst weight problem.
E probably earns less than the others.
F is the most heavily built.

Unit 15

2 *Introduction*

Below are five linguistic 'rules' explaining the things children do when they are learning English. Match them to the pictures, then check with your partner.

f The child follows the rules of the language but uses them wrongly, e.g. with plurals.
g The child says only one consonant because it is too difficult to pronounce double consonants.
h The child uses only 'no' for negation.
i The child uses 'not' for negation but does not link it to a verb.
j The child omits the finite verb completely and uses incorrect word order.

Unit 16

12 *Final task*

Missing lines
* And his footprints are not found in any file of Scotland Yard's.
* You'll be sure to find him resting, or a-licking of his thumbs,
* His coat is dusty from neglect, his whiskers are uncombed.
* Just controls their operations: The Napoleon of Crime!
* Or the Admiralty lose some plans and drawings by the way,
* He's broken every human law, he breaks the law of gravity.

Unit 17

1 *Introduction*

6 an Irish rock group with a singer called Bono
7 an American fashion designer who created the perfume Obsession
8 an album and a film created by English rock group Pink Floyd
9 a hugely successful American TV comedy series about a black family
10 a Canadian rock singer and guitarist whose greatest hit was called '(Everything I do) I do it for you'

Answers
g Madonna   h Abba   i Arnold Schwarzenegger
j Phil Collins   k Pedro Almodovar
l Guns 'n' Roses

Unit 19

1 *Experiment*

Allow your partner a few moments to study the room they are sitting in. Then ask them some of these questions while their eyes are closed. (Only choose those questions which are relevant to your classroom.)

1 What colour are the walls of this room?
2 How many windows are there?
3 What is on the wall behind me?
4 What can you see through the centre window?
5 What is the floor covered with?
6 What colour is it?
7 How many desks/tables/chairs are there in the room?
8 How many students are there in the front row?
9 What is the ceiling made of?
10 Does the door open into the room or into the corridor?
11 How many lights are there?
12 What is on the left/right/rear wall?

When you have finished tell your partner how many they answered correctly.

Unit 20

8 *Pronunciation*

Look at the chart of words below. Say these words to Student A, in random order, for him/her to write in a similar chart. Be careful to pronounce the diphthongs clearly. Student A will then give you some words to put in your chart.

/eɪ/	fade, take
/aɪ/	fight, tight
/ɔɪ/	foiled, toiled
/əʊ/	foe, toad
/aʊ/	found, town
/ɪə/	feared, tear
/eə/	fared, tear
/ʊə/	fewer, tour

11B *Final task*

On 17th July 1992 I was on patrol at Trafalgar Square. It was very crowded. At 13.09 precisely I heard a shout from the middle of the crowd. I immediately jumped onto a nearby wall for a better view and noticed a young man making his way hurriedly from the centre of the crowd. I moved towards him and apprehended him at the edge of the crowd at 13.11. My colleague, PC Donne, located the tourist whose handbag had been stolen. We took the offender to Vine Street police station, where the victim identified her bag and the offender was charged with theft.

 **Unit 2**

1 *Introduction*

Help to complete sentences a – f. Then find completions for sentences g – i.

g The actor John Wilkes Booth ...
h A fire which destroyed half of ancient Rome ...
i Dr Josef Mengele, the 'Angel of Death' ...

... who brutally tortured and killed over 20,000 Turkish prisoners.
... was kidnapped by unknown criminals ...
... Lee Harvey Oswald in Dallas, Texas in 1963.
... is reported to have imprisoned and strangled his two young nephews ...
... in the Whitechapel area of Victorian London ...
... is believed to have tortured and killed 140 children.

13 *Final task*

6 *Review of past tenses*

Dr Crippen's life

1910 January	Crippen murders his wife, cuts up her body and then buries it in his cellar. He tells their friends his wife has gone back to America.	
February	Ethel Le Neve moves into Crippen's house. Crippen goes to a party with Ethel. Some guests realise she is wearing some of Mrs Crippen's jewellery.	Crippen in London
March	Crippen announces his wife has died in California. Friends are suspicious and contact police. Crippen and Ethel panic and travel to Belgium.	
April	Police discover Belle's body in the cellar.	

THE DAILY TIMES   Tuesday 7 September 1884

GERMAN DIPLOMAT EXPELLED FROM BRITAIN
Shoots attacker

Diplomatic Crisis

A German diplomat has been declared *persona non grata* and given 24 hours to leave the country following an incident in which he shot dead a 29-year-old Londoner.

The diplomat, Captain Hans Schweiger, the Imperial German naval attaché, fired three shots at Michael Roe when he attacked the diplomat outside the German embassy yesterday evening. Roe, who was armed with a knife, had been waiting outside the embassy all day. When Captain Schweiger came out of the building at 5 o'clock, Roe ran at him with the knife. The Captain pulled a revolver from his pocket and fired three times. Roe fell dead at his feet.

The Foreign Office are extremely angry about the incident. 'We understand that Captain Schweiger was acting in self-defence,' said a Foreign Office spokesman last night. 'However, this country cannot and will not allow diplomats in London to carry guns. It is absolutely against international law. We will not tolerate it.'

The motive for Roe's attack on Captain Schweiger remains a mystery. In a statement made to the press by the German embassy last night, the German ambassador said that Captain Schweiger and Michael Roe were total strangers.

According to the dead man's landlady, Mrs Winifred Bun, of Bayswater, London W2, Roe had been behaving strangely since he came home late on Saturday night. 'Mr Roe was absolutely furious when he came in,' Mrs Bun told this newspaper. 'I made him a cup of cocoa before he went to bed and he was so angry he wouldn't drink it. He kept repeating, "I'll get him, I'll get the double-crosser!" Then he picked up his umbrella and threw it across the room. I asked Mr Roe what the matter was, but he wouldn't tell me. When he'd gone out on Monday morning, I discovered he'd taken the kitchen knife with him.'

Officials at the Admiralty, where Mr Roe worked as a filing clerk, say he did not come to work on Monday.

Unit 3

7 *Speaking skills*

> **AT HOME – DAYTIME**
> - Wait outside in a safe position until the fire brigade arrives.
> - Close the door of the room on the fire after everybody is out.
> - Alert your neighbours.
>
> **AT HOME – NIGHT**
> - If the door is cold, open it carefully and check for smoke. If there is no smoke, wake the other occupants and follow the instructions for DAYTIME fire survival.
> - Crawl to the window, take a deep breath, stand up and open the window. If it will not open, break it with a chair.
> - If the door is hot, do not open it, but act as follows:

Unit 4

10 *Speaking skills*

Jane Eyre: Extract C

I had withdrawn to my own bedchamber for the night. I hardly know whether I had slept or not. At any rate, I suddenly heard a peculiar noise, which sounded, I thought, just above me. I wished I had kept my candle burning. The night was very dark; my spirits were depressed. I rose and sat up in bed, listening. The sound was hushed.

I tried again to sleep, but my heart beat anxiously. My inward tranquillity was broken. The clock, far down in the hall, struck two. Just then it seemed my chamber door was touched, as if fingers had swept the panels in groping a way along the dark corridor outside. I said, 'Who is there?' Nothing answered. I was chilled with fear.

All at once I remembered that it might be Pilot, Mr Rochester's dog. The idea calmed me and I lay down. Silence composes the nerves, and as an unbroken hush now reigned again through the whole house, I began to feel the return of sleep. But then suddenly I heard another noise. It was a monstrous laugh – low and deep, coming, it seemed, from the very keyhole of my chamber door. I rose, looked round, and could see nothing while, as I still gazed, the unnatural sound was repeated, and I knew it came from behind the door panels. My first impulse was to rise and lock the door, my next again to cry out, 'Who is there?'

Something gurgled and moaned. Then steps retreated up the corridor towards the third-storey staircase. I heard a door open and close, and all was quiet.

Unit 5

15A *Final task*

What do you think are the best ways of a) practising speaking and b) reading? Rank each methods from 1 (very effective) to 5 (totally useless) for you and for two other students, A and B below.

READING	YOU	A	B
reading with a dictionary	☐	☐	☐
reading texts from your English book	☐	☐	☐
reading real English books/ magazines	☐	☐	☐
reading other students' work	☐	☐	☐
studying simplified readers	☐	☐	☐
developing reading skills in your own language	☐	☐	☐
answering detailed questions	☐	☐	☐
SPEAKING			
doing pronunciation work with a teacher	☐	☐	☐
doing pronunciation work at home (or in front of a mirror)	☐	☐	☐
doing drills in language lab	☐	☐	☐
answering questions in class	☐	☐	☐
working in pairs/groups	☐	☐	☐
roleplays	☐	☐	☐
free discussion	☐	☐	☐

Unit 6

2 *Introduction*

Read the questions below and on the next page. Write definitions for the words in *italics*. Then answer the questions yourself, and interview A and B.

9 You have an exciting engagement for this evening but you can't find a babysitter for your children, aged nine and ten. Do you:
  a leave the children by themselves?
  b ask a neighbour to check them once or twice during the evening?
  c cancel your engagement and stay at home?

10 You have cooked a meal for some friends, including a vegetarian friend. At the last moment you discover that you have used beef stock. Your friend eats no meat or fish and is against the killing of animals for food. Do you:
  a serve the meal without telling your friend?
  b tell him/her about the stock and offer something else?
  c throw the meal away and take your friends out?

11 You are a famous athlete. You are offered £50,000 to sponsor a product that you do not use. Do you:
a refuse to sponsor the product at all?
b tell the company that you would like two weeks to think about it, in which time you decide whether you would use the product?
c agree to sponsor immediately and try the product afterwards?

12 A friend asks you to write a reference for a job that you feel he/she is unable to do. Do you:
a write a glowing reference because you like your friend?
b write a fairly non-committal reference?
c refuse to write the reference, telling your friend why?
d make up an excuse for not writing the reference?

19A *Final task*

Discuss these questions, but add more points of your own.

- Are children a commodity? Should people be able to buy them? Should we accept nature's decision if a couple are not able to have children?
- Do children need to have some sense of 'roots'? (e.g. where they come from, their ethnic background)
- Do children who have been in children's homes need more stability than others? Does this have any bearing on the people who adopt them?
- Does adoption encourage women to be irresponsible about having children they don't want?

Unit 9

1   *Introduction*

- Dish: Cornish pasty
- Ingredients: meat and potato   with currants

14   *Final task*

You run a restaurant called L'Escargot. Make a notice with this name and put it on your desk. Use the following information to answer questions from customers.

L'ESCARGOT

MENUS   You specialise in French haute cuisine. Your chef used to work in a top hotel in Paris.

DRINKS   You only sell French wines and mineral water. You don't allow people to bring their own drinks.

FACILITIES   Space for 200 people on two floors. (There is a lift.)
Banqueting Room for up to 100 people. Special wedding reception service with three-course meal and champagne costs £35 per head.
Large no-smoking area. You accept all credit cards.

PROBLEMS   All your dishes have meat in them. You don't allow children under five or customers wearing T-shirts or jeans.

Unit 11

1   *Introduction*

You have an answer to each question in the quiz, but only some of your answers are correct. In your group, decide on each correct answer.

1 James Watt
2 Half an hour
3 Australian
4 Intelligence
5 Marlon Brando
6 George Bush
7 Oscar
8 *Mary Poppins*
9 Orson Welles
10 France
11 *Throne of Blood*
12 Bombay
13 *Rain Man*
14 Sony

Unit 12

13   *Final task*

39 Shakespeare Road,
Highgate,
London,

Tuesday 23rd March, 1886

Dear Mr Holmes,

My name is John Tosh. I am writing to you in confidence because something very strange has happened. My father says it is not important and that we must not report it to the police, but I think there is a mystery here that needs to be solved.

I should begin by saying that I don't know my father very well. He was in the army in India for many years while I went to school and grew up here in England. He met my mother when he came back to London on leave from India in 1865, married her and took her back to the colony. She died when I was born the following year. In 1872, when I was six, my father brought me back to England and left me at a boarding school. He immediately returned to his regiment, the Norfolks, in India, and I didn't see him again until last year, when he retired from the army and came back to this country.

On my father's return in 1885, he bought an enormous house here in North London, where we now live together. I am a student, he is an old man, and we have very little in common. In many ways we are like strangers.

Two weeks ago my father fell in the street and broke his leg. He was taken to hospital. Naturally, when I heard what had happened, I hurried to his bedside.

As I sat down my father grasped my arm hard. His face was white with pain and he could only speak with difficulty.

'Listen, John,' he said 'this is very important. While I am in hospital you must look after the house. Check all the doors and windows before you go to bed. You must sleep in my bedroom. Keep a revolver under the pillow and—'

'A revolver, father? But why?'

'Burglars, my boy, burglars. In the cupboard in my bedroom there is a big wooden box with a small hole in the top with a lid. Every morning you must put two live mice into the box and then close the lid firmly again. You must never look inside the box and you must never, never, put your hand inside. Promise John.'

'I promise, father, but why?'

'No questions, my boy, only orders, just like the army. The mice are in a cage in my study. Do what I say and remember never, never, put your hand into the box.'

Well, Mr Holmes, I thought my father must be getting senile. As far as I knew there had never been a robbery in Shakespeare Road, where we live. But I did as he said. Every morning I put two live mice into the mysterious box in my father's cupboard and carefully closed the lid again. Every night I went to sleep with a revolver under my pillow, though I thought it was stupid.

Well, I thought it was stupid until this morning, when I woke up with a terrible headache. someone had hit me on the head as I slept. The cupboard door was open and the lid had been taken off the hole in the top of the wooden box. On the box itself were three drops of blood. As I walked round the rest of the house I saw

that every room had been searched very carefully: all the drawers had been emptied on the floor, and the armchairs had been cut open. Broken glass in the sitting room showed how the burglar had forced open a window. But in spite of all the chaos and confusion, as far as I could tell nothing had been stolen.

I hurried to the hospital to tell my father what had happened.

'And there was blood on top of the box, was there?' said my father and gave an old man's laugh. 'Oh, he won't be back again.'

'But shouldn't we tell the police, father?'

'Of course not, my boy,' said my father, suddenly serious again. 'I absolutely forbid it. Nothing has been taken, you say, and the police are very busy with more important things. Don't mention this to the police, do you hear, John? That's an order. And tell the servants you're sorry, you got drunk last night and broke everything in the house. Don't tell them about the burglar.'

And so I haven't told the police, Mr Holmes, I've told you instead. What is it, Mr Holmes, what is happening? Is my father a lunatic? What is going on?

Yours truly,
John Tosh

Unit 14

5 B *Language work*

A   is darker than the others.
B   is treated with the most respect.
C   often dresses like a top model.
D   is the oldest.
E   Of E and F, E is the funnier.
F   is as strong as an ox.

Unit 17

1   *Introduction*

11   an English TV comedy series which specialised in surrealistic humour
12   the American TV series set on board the spaceship Enterprise
13   an American pop singer who was married to actor Sean Penn
14   the English pop group which invented punk rock
15   A French film star who also appears in Hollywood movies

Answers

m Calvin Klein   n *Dallas*   o Steven Spielberg
p Yves Saint Laurent   q *The Cosby Show*
r Woody Allen

Unit 20

11 B *Final task*

Anyway, I'm really writing to tell you about something that happened yesterday. You know I'm doing this tour guide thing in Central London during the college holidays? Well, yesterday I was accompanying a load of tourists on one of these 'see London from a double-decker bus' tours. We stopped at Trafalgar Square at one-ish, to have lunch, feed the pigeons, marvel at Nelson's Column and all that. It was really crowded, and I'd have liked to stay out of it, but of course they wanted to see everything, so we pushed our way through to the centre. We'd just got there when one of the tourists – a middle-aged American woman – shrieked. Someone had pinched her handbag and run off! We could see a young bloke – English, I think – pushing through the crowd, but then he disappeared. A couple of minutes later a policewoman turned up and asked the American woman to accompany her to the station – it was just like in the films. I thought I'd better go as well, so the tour bus had to go on without me. I don't think the tourists were very pleased! At the police station the woman got her bag back and the bloke who'd pinched it was taken in. It was really exciting. Oh, the best bit, the woman gave me £10 for looking after her!

Unit 9

8 TONY And do you eat much of this kind of thing?

JANET I personally don't, no. Um I very rarely go to places like McDonald's or Wimpy or whatever – Burger King. I, I just don't know, I, sometimes I go, maybe once every six months and then when I eat the food I think, 'Oh, this is so disgusting I don't know why I came,' and then I remember why I haven't been there for six months. I very rarely eat that kind of food.

MARK But it's very convenient, isn't it? I mean ...

LOUISE Yes I'm a hu ..., I must say, I must confess to being a huge fan of fast food.

TONY Are you? Mm.

LOUISE I'm afraid so, yes.

TONY Which particular kind?

LOUISE Well I tend ... I've discovered this wonderful, um, pizza place called, er, Perfect Pizza – where you can ring up and within twenty minutes [Oh yeah] there's someone, there's a ring at your doorbell and someone is at the door carrying this steaming hot pizza which is just ready to eat.

TONY And is it perfect when you eat it?

LOUISE It is ...

MARK It lives up to its name!

LOUISE ... it is perfect.

JANET But I think that's a lot better than um, McDonald's the, the kind of thing, I don't know, rubbery meat burgers that they give you in those places I think ... [Well they, yeah] a nice pizza is OK ...

LOUISE I don't know, I, I think really you'd probably find, if you analysed what was in these things, that a McDonald's was actually better for you than a pizza, 'cos I mean, what's good for you in pizza? [Mm, mm] All that ...

MARK It's all cholesterol and fat, isn't it? Dairy products, all that cheese.

LOUISE Yes, heavy uh, base ...

MARK But you know I, I often have this same thing as you, Jan, I sort of, you know, after I've had it I think 'Oh God! It was horrible, don't know why I went for that McDonald's yet I also have cravings and every few months I really get a craving for a burger: [Yes, that's right, yes] burger and fries ... I just think that that's what I want to eat.

LOUISE And a stack of pancakes.

[Yeah, yeah]

DIANE I can't say I ever feel that I've had a burger and I feel ill afterwards. The only thing that makes me feel ill is fish and chips ...

JANET Fish and chips, I was just going to say exactly the same thing ...

DIANE I get the occasional craving [That's right] when I smell fish cooking. I think I must have fish and chips and then buy some [I agree with you] and I get half way through it and I feel really ill [I agree with you, yes] it's just the amount of fat [That's right] when normally I have quite a fat-free diet suddenly it's ... you're saturated with it and ... [Yeah]

MARK But what about things like, you know, Chinese take-aways, I mean, they're quite healthy really.

JANET Yeah.

DIANE Chinese? Healthy?

MARK ... vegetable dishes, you know.

DIANE Monosodium glutomate.

LOUISE I think that's a myth [Mm]

TONY Do you think everybody thinks that fast food is not particularly healthy and they just eat it for the sake of convenience?

DIANE I think people do probably think it's, it's even less healthy than it is, um, as Louise said earlier I don't actually think that the occasional burger is unhealthy. [Mm] I think if you analyse, I'm sure if McDonald's were to analyse ... [But they have] oh they have done ... quite um what goes into a burger ...

JANET Well, the occasional burger: that's not too bad but there are some people who go there regularly every day for their lunch, or like fish and chip shops or something, every single day and eat that kind of food and that's what I personally would object to.

LOUISE Is that any less healthy than having a sandwich every day for lunch?

JANET Well, I don't know. Earlier I was going to say to you if I'm out and about lunch time and I, I don't really want to go to a restaurant, than, rather than go to McDonald's I would probably go to a supermarket and buy sandwiches which I actually do think is better, yes.

LOUISE Do you?

JANET Mm, cos I, I feel that those ... that its a bit fresher somehow. I don't know why but that's just a feeling I have that the food is ...

LOUISE Yes, it would be interesting to know if that was true.

MARK But a sandwich really is the ultimate fast food, isn't it?

DIANE It is.

LOUISE Absolutely, yes, but we're not classifying sandwiches as fast food ...

MARK A burger is just a form of sandwich ...

LOUISE Yeah, [yeah], exactly.

Unit 11

6B JOHN CARR And here's Mary James with our weekly review of the new films.

MARY JAMES Thanks, John, and hello everyone. The first film I'm looking at today is the new blockbuster from the States, *The Silence of the Lambs*. This film is based on a very powerful and gruesome novel by Thomas Harris, and it could have been the most gory film of 1991 if it weren't for the expert direction of Jonathan Demme. This, and the performances of the two lead actors, make the film a slick, tense, psychological thriller, which leaves almost everything to the imagination.

In the film Jodie Foster plays Clarice Starling, a trainee FBI agent, who's put on the case of tracking down the killer of several women, known as Buffalo Bill. I won't say here why he's known as Buffalo Bill. Her boss asks her to visit Hannibal Lecter, another serial killer now safely behind bars, as he feels that she might get some useful information from this man. Lecter was a psychoanalyst before he turned to a life of crime and he does eventually give Starling some leads, which help her to find Buffalo Bill, but only after she has given him some very painful details of her childhood in an almost Faustian exchange.

This film is just as likely to become a box-office smash here as in the States. Obviously, the topic is fascinating, but the outstanding performances of both Foster and Hopkins is the other main attraction of the film. These are both well-respected actors, with a number of acclaimed films behind them, especially perhaps Foster's Oscar-winning performance in *The Accused*. I'll be very surprised if Foster isn't nominated for the Best Actress award, and if Hopkins doesn't win the Oscar for Best Supporting Actor. If you see this film, you'll find it very difficult to forget those soulless steel-blue eyes.

It's interesting that a film about a serial killer of women is being accepted as a feminist film. This is because of the focus on the character of Starling and what she goes through in her determined search for the killer. Foster plays this perfectly. Superficially, she's the hard-bitten FBI trainee but is also vulnerable enough to make the audience worry about her fate when she finally meets Buffalo Bill in his lair.

Audiences everywhere in the States are saying that this is the most frightening film ever, even though it's not particularly violent. It's refreshing to find a truly horrific film which doesn't depend solely on violence and shock tactics to win over its audience. I loved it, and if you only see one film this year, make sure it's this one.

Unit 12

7 B ANNOUNCER And now to discuss this week's book choice is journalist, Melanie O'Donnell.

MELANIE O'DONNELL As a citizen of a country which was not involved in the Second World War, I am usually bemused and untouched by the rampant fascination which the British and Americans seem to experience for anything connected with Nazism and the myth of Adolf Hitler. But, for once, I was held spellbound by a book dealing with that very subject. Robert Harris's *Selling Hitler* is more than another historical investigation of the Nazi legend. It is an exposé of almost unbelievable credulity and greed in modern international publishing. It describes in minute detail the tangled web of deception, intrigue and farce which gave rise to what may have been the greatest fraud of the century – the handing over of more than four million dollars for sixty totally worthless and ineptly forged notebooks masquerading as the 'lost diaries of Adolf Hitler'.

The story centres around Gerd Heidemann, an ambitious and unscrupulous journalist on Germany's *Stern* magazine, and Konrad Kujau, alias Konrad Fischer, a small-time forger and petty criminal working in Stuttgart. Harris's account begins in the dying days of the Third Reich when Adolf Hitler, who must have been trying to save his personal documents for posterity, sent a plane containing a mysterious locked trunk from the bunker in Berlin to a safe haven in Salzburg. That plane never arrived – it was shot down in the middle of a remote forest in what was to become East Germany. The story culminates in a courtroom in Hamburg in July 1985, almost exactly forty years later, with the sentencing of Kujau and Heidemann to prison for over four years for fraud. The trial had hinged on forensic test results published in May 1983, exposing the diaries, which had been purchased by over a dozen international press agencies, as amateurish and blatant fakes. The tangled web which links these events forms the plot of this gripping and barely credible tale of self-delusion.

The fact that Konrad Kujau's forgeries had fooled dozens of so-called experts is convincingly explained by Harris as the result of the obsessive secrecy and cut-throat competition in the magazine and newspaper publishing world. Because of this secrecy, none of the experts was allowed to examine more than one page of the diaries at a time. In 1982 handwriting experts in the United States and Switzerland confirmed the handwriting as being unquestionably that of Adolf Hitler. But, unknown to them, the originals with which they were comparing the diaries were also fakes, forgeries which Kujau had perpetrated earlier in his remarkable career. Similarly, the world-renowned Hitler scholar, Hugh Trevor-Roper, who confirmed the authenticity of the diaries in April 1983, was only allowed to look at the diaries in a bank vault in Zurich for a few minutes. He was unable to take any away or even make photocopies, all for the fear of a rival magazine getting the story.

How was it that the management of *Stern*, a respected and professional team of outstandingly successful businessmen and journalists, never smelt a rat; and were so easily duped into parting with millions of Deutschmarks on such flimsy evidence of authenticity?

It seems that gullibility is infectious. Heidemann had 'discovered' Kujau in January 1981 and heard his story about a fictional brother, a general in the East German army, who had come across peasants who had secretly retrieved the diaries from the smouldering wreckage of the plane carrying Hitler's documents to Salzburg. Following up an earlier story, in November 1980 Heidemann had set out for East Germany to search for the site of the crash and had eventually discovered a number of graves in the East German village of Boernersdorf. So few people had known about that secret flight that Heidemann became immediately convinced of Kujau's story. Heidemann had reached Kujau through a wealthy collector of Nazi memorabilia, Fritz Steifel, whom he had visited in 1979. Steifel's proudest possession was a Hitler diary which he had bought from an importer and antique dealer in Stuttgart. It was illegal to export Nazi documents from East Germany and Steifel was reluctant to give Heidemann the name of his dealer.

By discovering Kujau, Heidemann thought he had been a skilled detective, following clues to the source of a great secret, when he had, in fact, simply found a notorious forger.

Kujau's story of his brother illegally exporting documents from the East was a masterstroke of pure genius, for such were the severity of punishments in the East that he could rightly claim that any publicity or exposure would put the life of his brother in mortal danger. Thus he could justify his exorbitant conditions – all money to be handed over in cash, no legal contracts, no receipts, no viewing of the diaries by outsiders, and so on.

Starting in January 1981, Heidemann made 27 regular visits to Kujau, swapping suitcases full of cash for each instalment of the diaries. By April 1983 *Stern* had collected the full set and began secret negotiations for the international syndication rights with the world's leading publishing companies. But within a week of the publication of the first extracts in Germany, Britain and the United States the *Bundesarchiv* scientists had let out the secret and the diaries were exposed as forgeries.

This book is a must for any student of human fallibility. Harris masterfully unravels the causes, physical and psychological, and the labyrinthine train of events which made this fiasco, once it had gained momentum, almost unstoppable. And in so doing, he has once again proved the old saying that 'fact is stranger than fiction'.

ANNOUNCER *Selling Hitler* is published by Faber and Faber. Next week, well-known critic, Jason Lively, will be discussing …

Unit 20

10A INTERVIEWER Right, everyone. I'd just like you to summarise your ideas for the audience on the subject of language change. Let's start with you, Geoff.

GEOFF GRAHAM Right. Well, the point I'd like to make is that language has a very specific function, and that function is to serve its users, to serve its society. Consequently, if part of that society feels that it is not being served by the language, then we have a duty to change it in order to make it reflect society.

INTERVIEWER Thank you, Geoff. Melvyn.

MELVYN WINCHESTER I have just three points to make. My first point is that society has no right to change language; language should be allowed to change organically. My second point is that language is part of society, not just a tool. And my final point is that, in my view, we really should not accommodate all the crazy ideas that are put forward by minority groups. In essence, I think that we should not meddle with language.

INTERVIEWER Thank you, Melvyn. Now, Rachel.

RACHEL MACMILLAN My opinion is that the issue is unimportant. I feel that people who spend a lot of time worrying about language do so because they have nothing better to do, and, as a result, a lot of people spend their time on trivial issues and neglect important ones.

INTERVIEWER Thank you, Rachel, and finally, Arlene.

ARLENE SIMMONDS Yes. I feel rather strongly about this topic for two reasons. First, I think that language is used as a tool to subjugate women in society. Therefore, women feel less important than men and lack confidence. Second, the use of language is one of the first things that children learn, and it's one of the most powerful ways in which they learn about society, which has the inevitable result that language should be a true reflection of society. In conclusion, then, I feel that we have not only the right, but the obligation to change language for the right reasons.

ANDREW ANSELL Thank you very much, Arlene, and thank you, listeners, for being with us this afternoon. Any comments should be sent to us on a postcard and I'll read out a selection next Friday afternoon. So, for now, thank you to our panel this afternoon and goodbye.

 Unit 1

Continuous tenses

This is a summary of the main uses of the six continuous tenses.

1 Present continuous
* A temporary action in progress around a present time, possibly not completed.
  I'm working in the city at the moment.
* An action happening at the moment of speaking.
  Ssh – I'm listening to the radio.
* A future event which has already been arranged. (See Unit 4.)
  We're seeing Swan Lake *on Friday.*

2 Past continuous (See Unit 2.)
* A continuous action (often temporary) in progress around a past time.
  I was living in Edinburgh at the time.
* Describing a background situation to another event or story.
  It was a tumultuous time, wars were raging and lives were being wrecked all over Europe.
* A continuous action/situation interrupted by another action.
  I was watching TV when I heard a loud crash.

3 Present perfect continuous
* A continuous action (often temporary) leading up to the present time, possibly just finished.
  We've been living in this flat for two years.
  At last! I've been expecting this letter for days!
* A past action leading to present where the duration is emphasised.
  I've been ringing you all morning – where have you been?
  Compare *(I've rung you about ten times this morning!)*
* The main differences between the present perfect simple and continuous are that the continuous emphasises the duration of the action or the action itself, while the simple emphasis the result of the action, or a number of actions.

4 Past perfect continuous (See Unit 2.)
* An action or situation which continued until a specified time in the past.
  By 1900 Queen Victoria had been reigning for more than fifty years.
* As with the present perfect continuous, to emphasise duration.
  I'd been shouting for at least twenty minutes before someone unlocked the door.

5 Future continuous (See Unit 4.)
* Referring to something which will be in progress at a particular time in the future, either because it has been arranged or because it happens regularly.
  We'll be sitting on the beach this time next week.
  I'll post that parcel – I'll be going past the post office on my way to work.

6 Future perfect continuous (See Unit 4.)
* Referring to the duration of an action as seen from a particular time in the future.
  She'll have been teaching here for more than thirty years by the time she retires next spring.

 Unit 2

Past forms

This is a summary of the main forms used to express past meaning.

1 Past simple
* An action at a particular time in the past.
  She took her driving test yesterday.
* Repeated or regular actions in the past.
  They did a grammar test every morning.

2 Past continuous
* A continuous action or situation in the past.
  I was living in Edinburgh during the 1980s.
* Describing the background situation to another event or story.
  It was a tumultuous time, wars were raging and lives were being wrecked all over Europe.
* A continuous action/situation which was interrupted by another action.
  I was watching TV when I heard a loud crash.
* Expressing annoyance or criticism about a past situation with *forever* or *always*.
  He was forever complaining about the food.

3 Past perfect
* An action in the past which happened before another action in the past.
  When I got to the swimming pool I discovered I had left my costume at home.

4 Past perfect continuous
* An action or situation which continued until a specified time in the past.
  By 1900 Queen Victoria had been reigning for more than fifty years.

5 *Would* + infinitive
* A repeated or habitual action in the past.
  Harry would never sleep for more than two hours when he was a baby.

6 *Used to* + infinitive
* A repeated or habitual action, situation or state in the past.
  Germany used to be split into two countries.

 Unit 3

Substitution

A device used to avoid repetition by replacing a previously mentioned noun, verb or clause by a substitute word such as *one/s, do, so/not* and *same*.
Stephen broke his left leg when he was a child. He broke the other <u>one</u> when he went skiing in Austria three years ago.
The plates should be on the shelf. If <u>so</u>, bring me two of the large ones. If <u>not</u>, you'll probably find them in the cupboard.
Imogen has never been good at languages. Harry's <u>the same</u>.
Note
Reference words such as the pronouns *he/she/it* can often serve the same function as the substitute word *one*.
However, *one* can be modified whereas pronouns cannot.
He injured his left leg last week and his right <u>one</u> yesterday.
NOT ~~He injured his left leg last week and his right it yesterday.~~

Ellipsis

Omitting a noun, verb or clause when the meaning is clear from the context, in order to avoid repetition. (The omitted words are in brackets.)

- Ellipsis often occurs after *and*, *but* and *or*.
  She is poor but (she is) honest.
  Your glasses are either on the floor or (on) the desk.
  We must decorate our kitchen and (our) bathroom.
- Ellipsis often occurs with auxiliary verbs and with the verbs *be* and *have*.
  Will anyone be going to the club tonight?
  – I will (be going) / I will be (going).
  Have you finished your homework?
  – No, I haven't (finished it).
  Does anyone have an umbrella?
  – Yes, I have (an umbrella).
  My father is retired.
  – Oh, mine isn't (retired).
- Ellipsis is common with subject pronouns in short answers.
  Excuse me, do you know the way to the station?
  – Sorry, (I) can't help you.
  Do you think she'll win?
  – (I) Hope so!

Future forms

This is a summary of the main forms used to express future meaning.

1 Present simple
- A future event which is definite, usually referring to something on a timetable or schedule.
  The train departs at 1745.

2 Present continuous
- A future event which has already been arranged.
  We're seeing Swan Lake on Friday.

3 Future simple (*will* + infinitive)
- A prediction about the future.
  I think the Democrats will win the next election.
- A decision made at the time of speaking.
  Are you going? I'll get your coat.
- Threats and promises.
  Finish your dinner or I'll send you to bed.
  I'll never leave you.
- Offers and requests.
  I'll carry your bag.
  Will you give me a receipt please?
- Making a firm deduction about the present or future.
  Our team's losing. Dad won't be pleased!

4 Future continuous (*will be* + *-ing*)
- Referring to something which will be in progress at a particular time in the future, either because it has been arranged or it happens regularly.
  We'll be sitting on the beach this time next week!
  They'll be bringing in the wheat harvest next month.
- Making a firm deduction about the present or future.
  It's the soccer final on TV, my brother'll be watching this.
  Tomorrow is Sunday, so he'll be going to church.

5 Future perfect
- Referring to something which will be completed before a certain time in the future.
  He will have finished his exams by December.

6 Future perfect continuous
- Referring to the duration of an action as seen from a particular time in the future.
  She'll have been teaching here for thirty years by the time she retires next year.

7 *Going to* + infinitive
- A plan or intention for the future, which may or may not be arranged yet.
  Are you going to see him again?
- A prediction based on evidence in the present
  Watch out! He's going to fall in the water!

8 *Is/Are to* + infinitive
- Expressing a future arrangement, instruction or order in formal (usually written) English.
  The judge is to pass sentence tomorrow.

9 Future in the past (*was/were going to*)
- Referring to something which was planned for the future at a time in the past or a past intention which was not carried out or never happened.
  He was going to explain it to me yesterday but he didn't have time.

 **Unit 4**

Multi-word verbs

There are four types of multi-word verb.

Type 1
- Intransitive phrasal verbs: *to splash out, to watch out*.
- These verbs have no direct object.

Type 2
- Transitive phrasal verbs: *to do sth up, to pick sth up*.
- This is the most common form of multi-word verb. The meaning of these verbs is not usually obvious from the parts.
- The stress is usually on the particle.
- A pronoun object can only be put between the verb and particle. *I'm doing it up.* NOT *I'm doing up it*.

Type 3
- Prepositional verbs: *to pay for sth, to turn to sth*. The meaning of these verbs can usually be guessed from the combination of the meaning of the two parts.
- The stress is usually on the verb, not the particle.
- A noun object cannot be put between the verb and particle. *She's turning to the page.* NOT *She's turning the page to*.
- Pronoun objects must not be put between the verb and particle. *She's turning to it.* NOT *She's turning it to*.

Type 4
- Phrasal/prepositional verbs: *to come up with sth, to get away with sth*.
- This type always has three parts which cannot be separated except by an adverb which can be placed between the first and second particles.
  He came up eventually with a few suggestions.
- Noun and pronoun objects can only be placed after the second particle.
  He came up with a solution. NOT *He came up a solution with*. OR *He came a solution up with*.

Notes:
- Sometimes the same verb and particle combination can have more than one meaning and be a different grammatical type.
  take off (of an aircraft) leave the ground and rise (Type 1)

take sb off ridicule by imitation; mimic (Type 2)
see through sb not to be deceived by sb, aware of a trick
(Type 3)
see sth through continue/endure until something is
finished (Type 2).

- The position of *sb* or *sth* in the dictionary definition of
  multi-word verbs indicates which type it is.
- Some Type 1 verbs can add a second particle to become
  transitive Type 4 verbs. These are indicated in a
  dictionary with the transitive form in brackets: *break up
  (with sb), watch out (for sth)*.

Unit 5

Perfect tenses

This is a summary of the uses of the perfect tenses. (See
Unit 1 for information on the continuous forms of perfect
tenses.)

1 Present perfect
- An action started in the past and continuing to the
  present, either still continuing or just finished.
  I've worked in this company for 25 years.
  Oh, you're here at last. I've waited an hour for you! (Or
  I've been waiting …)
- An action in the past where there is an obvious result in
  the present.
  You look exhausted!
  Yes, I've just run back from the shops. (Or *Yes, I've just
  been running.*)
- A completed action in the past where the time scale is
  still continuing.
  Have you had breakfast this morning?
  Well, I've had a cup of coffee, that's all. (This morning is
  still continuing.)

2 Past perfect (See Unit 2.)
- An action in the past which happened before a second
  action in the past.
  *When I got to the swimming pool I discovered I had left
  my swimming costume at home.*
- An action in the past with a result at another time in the
  past.
  *When I finally arrived home I was exhausted because I
  had run from the shops.*

3 Future perfect (See Unit 4.)
- An action started in the present (or future or past)
  completed by a certain time in the future.
  He will have finished his exams by December.

Unit 6

The passive

This is a summary of the form and uses of the passive tenses.

Form
- The passive is formed by the verb *to be* and the past
  participle of the main verb. The **subject** of the active
  verb becomes the **object** of the passive verb. The subject
  of the passive verb is generally placed at the beginning
  of the sentence and the agent of the action (subject of
  the active verb) may or may not be used. The sentences
  at the top of the next column show the transformation
  from active to passive.

subject   active verb   object
The garage   has sold   my old car for £500.
My old car   has been sold   (by the garage) for £500.
subject   be   past participle   (agent)
                    passive verb

              subject   active verb   object
Do you think that someone can restore this table?
Do you think that this table can be   restored?
                subject   be   past participle
                        passive verb

(The last sentence is unlikely to have an agent, as the
original subject, *someone*, is not specific enough).

- The passive can be used in all tenses, but it is unlikely in
  the present perfect continuous, past perfect continuous,
  future continuous and future perfect continuous, where
  an active form or a simple (non-continuous) form would
  be preferred.
  ~~That magazine has been being prepared for months.~~
  They've been preparing that magazine for months.
  (impersonal *they*).
  That magazine has been in preparation for months.

Use
1 If the agent of the action is unknown.
   My house was burgled last night.
   (Active: *Someone burgled my house last night*).
2 If the agent of the action is known but unimportant.
   My car's being repaired at the moment.
   (Active: *The mechanic is repairing my car at the
   moment.*)
3 If particular emphasis is given to the object, rather than the
   subject of the active verb (i.e. it becomes the subject of
   the passive verb).
   That wonderful cake was cooked by my mother.
   (Active: *My mother cooked that wonderful cake.*)
   It is also possible to emphasise the subject of an active
   verb by making it the agent of the passive verb and
   giving it 'end-focus' of the sentence.
   This photo was taken by Man Ray.
4 In order not to attribute an action or feeling to a particular
   person/group of people.
   I see the washing up hasn't been done.
   It is thought that the crash was due to pilot error.
   Pilot error is thought to be/have been the cause of the crash.
5 With verbs such as *think, believe, consider, expect* etc. two
   passive forms are possible.
- With introductory *it* (See Unit 17.)
  It is thought that the crash was due to pilot error.
  *It was generally considered that he was the best writer of
  children's books.*
- With the subject of the subordinate clause becoming the
  object of the passive verb, and the subordinate clause
  introduced by an infinitive.
  *Pilot error is thought to be (to have been) the cause of the
  crash.*
  *He was generally considered to be the best writer of
  children's books.*
- These express a general feeling/belief, rather than the
  opinion of one person or group of people.

Connectives of contrast

(See Unit 15.)

Unit 7

Verbs + -ing or infinitive

A number of verbs are followed by the *-ing* form or the infinitive depending on meaning.

1 regret, go on, stop, remember, forget
*   When referring to an action/state that happened or began before the time of regretting, remembering etc. we use the *-ing* form.
    I stopped speeding when I saw the policeman.
*   When referring to an action/state that happens after the time of regretting, remembering etc. we use the infinitive.
    I stopped to ask for directions when I saw the policeman.

    allow, advise, forbid, permit
*   When there is no personal object we use the *-ing* form. When the verb has a personal object we use the infinitive.
    I forbid smoking in my classes.
    I forbid you to use dictionaries in this test.

2 Try
*   *Try* + *-ing* means doing something as an experiment.
    The car won't start. Try connecting those wires to the battery.
*   *Try* + infinitive means making an effort to do something which may be difficult.
    I've tried to give up sugar but it's too difficult.

Note
The following verbs can be followed by *-ing* or infinitive with little difference in meaning.
attempt begin bother cease continue deserve fear hate like love prefer start

Gerund/infinitive phrases

*   An infinitive or gerund phrase can be used as the subject of a sentence. Gerund phrases are usually used for general actions while infinitive phrases usually refer to a specific event/situation.
    Learning a foreign language requires a lot of effort.
    To compose an opera often took Mozart less than a month.
*   Infinitive phrases are usually only used in formal writing. In conversational English it is more usual to use an introductory *it* construction.
    It requires a great deal of effort to learn a foreign language.
    It often took Mozart less than a month to compose an opera.

Unit 8

Groups of nouns/compound words

1 Compound words
*   The first word classifies the second. We use this type to describe common well-known things. The two words can be written in one of three ways.
    a   as two separate words: *bank robbery dining table*
    b   as two words joined with a hyphen: *eye-opener, self-confident*
    c   as one word: *manservant classmate*
    The best way to check these words is to use a dictionary as there is no universally accepted definition of the difference between the three types.

*   In compound words the main stress usually falls on the first word. If this is a multi-syllable word, then the stress falls on the same syllable in the first word as it would if it were a word on its own: *a black bird / a blackbird She's cooking apples / cooking apples.*

2 The 's genitive
The first noun refers to something living, a particular place or person, or something closely related to human activity. e.g. *John's house.*

3 The of structure
This is used for something inanimate, it cannot be used where the subject is a particular person. e.g. *means of transport.*

Inversion after negative adverbials

*   Negative adverbial expressions can be placed at the beginning of a clause or sentence for added emphasis.
    I had never seen such an amazing storm.
    Never had I seen such an amazing storm.
*   The subject and auxiliary verb are inverted. If there is no auxiliary verb, *do/does* or *did* are used.
    I seldom go to parties.
    Seldom do I go to parties.
*   This structure is usually used in formal writing with the expressions below.
    never never before never again not (+ object) not since not until rarely seldom nowhere nobody hardly scarcely no sooner…than not only…but also only after only in only since at no time under no circumstances in no way on no account

Unit 9

Emphatic devices

In addition to inversion and the introductory *-it* (see above and below), there are a number of ways of adding emphasis to part of a sentence.

1   Emphatic reflexive pronoun
    It should be good. Theresa recommended it herself.
2   Emphatic use of auxiliary verb
    He does complain a lot.
3   Exclamations
    Oh Lord! I've left my homework on the bus.
4   Emphatic use of *so*
    Those students are so enthusiastic.
5   Question tags
    It's absolutely revolting, isn't it?
6   Repetition of intensifiers
    He's terribly, terribly overweight.

Actually and really

1   *Actually* is used to introduce something unexpected or to reinforce opinion.
    Although she failed the test, she is actually very bright.
    Yes, you were right, it was actually an excellent concert.

2   *Really* can be used to make a verb or sentence less emphatic and to make a verb more emphatic depending on its position.
*   Less emphatic
    They weren't interested in my photographs really. (sentence)
    They weren't really interested in my photographs. (verb)
*   More emphatic
    They really weren't interested in my photographs. (verb)

 Unit 10

Relative clauses

1 Defining relative clauses

- The subordinate clause in a defining (or restrictive) relative clause gives information about the a noun (subject or object) in the main clause which sets it apart from other, similar nouns (defines it).

  I'd heard a lot of bad things about the police in this town, but the police officer <u>who interviewed me</u> was very nice.

  In this example the relative clause (<u>underlined</u>) gives us information about the police officer which sets him/her apart from others.

- Defining relatives pronouns are:

  who for people.
  The dentist who saw me was very gentle.

  which for objects.
  That's the book which he wrote when he was only 17.

  that for objects and people.
  Have you seen the CD that I bought yesterday?
  She's the woman that takes takes my children to school.

  whose for possession.
  Is that the man whose wife works in the supermarket?

- These pronouns can be used to refer to both the subject or the object of the relative clause. In formal writing or speech the pronoun *whom* is often used to refer to the object of the clause.

  Shall I introduce you to the architect whom we employed to do the changes?

- The defining relative pronoun can be omitted from the clause when it refers to the object, but not when it refers to the subject.

  That's the book he wrote when he was only 17.
  Have you seen the CD I bought yesterday?
  Have you met the boy my daughter's been seeing?
  ~~She's the woman takes my children to school.~~

- It is possible to use the pronoun *what* in a defining relative clause. It can only refer to the object of the clause.

  I don't understand what you mean.
  My children always ignore what I say.

  The pronoun here means *the thing which/that*. Do not confuse *what* and *that*: ~~He's the man what I met yesterday.~~

2 Non-defining relative clauses

- The subordinate clause in a non-defining (non-restrictive) relative clause gives extra, non-essential information about the subject or the object of the main clause. The main clause can stand on its own without this extra information.

  I went to the police station to see the Chief Constable, who took all the details of the theft.

  The first clause here makes sense on its own.

- Non-defining relative pronouns are the same as those used for defining relatives with one difference: in non-defining relative clauses the pronoun *that* is never used. The pronoun may not be omitted in non-defining clauses.

- The pronoun *which* is often used to refer to the concept of the main clause.

  He never does any of the housework, which annoys his wife intensely.

  The *which* here means the fact that he never does any of the housework.

3 Punctuation

- Defining relative clauses do not take commas. Non-defining relative clauses always take commas. The comma may be the only part of the sentence in writing which tells you the meaning.

  I bought the blue car which cost £2,500.
  I bought the blue car, which cost £2,500.

  In the first sentence there were several blue cars but only one with a price tag of £2,500. I bought it.

  In the second sentence there was only one blue car and, incidentally, it cost £2,500.

- In speech, these commas are represented by pauses before the pronoun and after the clause if it occurs mid-sentence.

4 Prepositions in relative clauses

Prepositions can be put in a number of places in relative clauses.

That's the desk I work at. (informal)
That's the desk at which I work. (formal)
Also possible: *That's the desk where I work.*
She's the woman I sold the painting to. (informal)
She's the woman who(m) I sold the painting to. (informal)
She's the woman to whom I sold the painting. (formal)

 Unit 11

Reported speech

Reported (or indirect) speech is used every time we repeat what a person has said without using their exact words. The following guidelines may be useful.

1 The tense usually moves one 'step' back (backshift).
   present simple →*past simple*: spends →*spent*
   present continuous →*past continuous*: is doing → *was doing*
   past simple →*past perfect*: expected →*had expected*
   present perfect→*past perfect*: have grown →*had grown*
   will →*would*
   can →*could*
   The past perfect remains the same.

2 Pronouns change to refer to the correct person.
   I →*he/she*

3 Adverbs also change to refer to the correct time/ place.
   today →*that* day   here →*there*
   next week →*the next week*

   'Will you go to the shops today?'
   She asked if I would go to the shops that day.
   'He's leaving this evening but he won't get to Bangkok till Tuesday.'
   His secretary said that he was leaving that evening but that he wouldn't get to Bangkok till the following/next Tuesday.
   'I haven't seen you for ages. Are you going to stay here for good now?'
   She said she hadn't seen me for ages and asked if I was going to stay there for good.

4 It is not always necessary to change the tense in reported speech. It may not change in the following circumstances.

- After *when* (past simple and past continuous)
  'I was reading when you called.'
  She said she'd been reading when I called/had called.

- If the state expressed is a general truth
  'Madrid is the capital of Spain.'
  He said that Madrid is/was the capital of Spain.

- If the reporting verb is in the present
  'I'll be with you in five minutes.'
  She says she'll be with us in five minutes.
- If the state expressed remains the same
  'I'm staying here till the weekend.'
  She said she's staying here till the weekend.
  (reported before the weekend)
  She said she was staying there till the weekend.
  (reported after the weekend, in a different place)

5 There are a number of verbs that can be used to introduce reported speech or questions, for example *say, tell, ask, add, continue, exclaim.*

6 Many other verbs are used, often verbs which express the function of the direct words, for example, *offer, promise, suggest, refuse, deny, recommend, remind.* These verbs replace whole sections of the direct sentence, and are often more natural than verbs such as *say* and *tell.*
  'Would you like a cup of tea?'
  She asked if I would like a cup of tea. → *She offered me a cup of tea.*
  'It's a good film. You should see it.'
  She pointed out that it was a good film and said that I should see it. → *She said that it was a good film and recommended that I see it.*

7 These verbs take different complements and many of them do not take the *that* + verb clause construction.
  'Don't forget to lock the door.'
  He reminded me to lock the door.
  'We could go to the cinema tonight.'
  She suggested going to the cinema tonight.

verb + infinitive
agree to ...   offer to ...   refuse to ...
ask to ... *   promise to ...   threaten to ...
beg to ... *

verb + -ing
accuse sb of ...ing   deny ...ing   recommend ...ing
admit ...ing   regret ...ing suggest ...ing

verb + object + infinitive
advise sb to ...   implore sb to ...   remind sb to ...
ask sb to ... *   invite sb to ...   tell sb to ...
beg sb to ... *   order sb to ...   urge sb to ... (order)

verb + *that* + verb clause
advise sb that ... (i.e. inform) point out that ...
admit that ...   promise (sb) that ...
agree (with sb) that ...   reassure sb that ...
assure sb that ...   recommend that ...
complain that ...   remark that ...
deny that ...   remind sb that ...
exclaim that ...   repeat that ...
explain that ...   tell sb that ... (i.e. inform)
inform sb that ...   warn sb that ...

* ask/beg to = request permission to do something
  ask/beg sb to = want sb else to do something

Unit 12

Modal verbs expressing probability/certainty

1 Certain modal verbs followed by the infinitive without *to* are used to express the speaker's degree of certainty about present and future events and situations.
- Certainty *must, will*   • Possibility *may, might, could*
- Probability *should, would* • Impossibility *can't*

Imagine that you and a friend are at the cinema. Jack is supposed to be joining you but the film is starting in five minutes and he hasn't arrived yet.
It's getting rather late. Jack must be stuck in the traffic.
– No, he can't be. He told me he was coming on foot.
Well, he might be confused about the time we agreed to meet.
– No, he should be here on time. I saw him write down the time in his diary.

2 Certain modal verbs followed by the perfect infinitive are used to express the speaker's degree of certainty about past events and situations.
- Certainty   *must have*
- Probability   *would have*
- Possibility   *may have, might have, could have*
- Impossibility   *can't have, couldn't have*
  Imagine that you and your flatmate have just arrived at the airport and you can't find your flatmate's passport:
  You must have left it behind.
  – I'm pretty sure I would have put it in my bag when I packed.
  Well, you may have dropped it when we got into the taxi.
  – No, I couldn't have. My bag was locked.

Unit 13

Conditionals

This is a summary of the main conditionals and mixed conditionals.

1 **Zero conditional**
- Expresses general truths and actions.
  present, present
  If you don't water plants, they die.
  If I sit in the sun, I get a headache.

2 **First conditional**
- Expresses a situation that is possible.
  present, *will/won't/may/might*
  If you don't hold the baby, he'll fall.
  If you tell me in time, I might come.
  She won't come to the party if you don't ask her yourself.

3 **Second conditional**
- Expresses a situation in the present/future that is unlikely or contrary to known facts.
  past, *would(n't)* or *could, might*
  If I asked you, would you marry me?
  If I were 20 years younger, I'd play squash.

4 **Third conditional**
- Expresses a situation that was impossible, because it is contrary to known facts about the past.
  past perfect, *would/might/could* + *have* + past participle
  If I hadn't run into the road, the bus wouldn't have hit me.
  They might not have gone to the film if they'd known it was in German.

5 **Common mixed conditionals**
- Past perfect, *would* + infinitive: past conditional, present result.
  If he had paid his rent, he wouldn't be homeless now.
  (He didn't pay his rent. He is homeless now.)
- Past simple, *would* + perfect infinitive: as the second conditional, but the main clause refers to something which happened in the past.
  If I didn't respect her, I wouldn't have hired her.
  (I do respect her. I did hire her.)

- Present simple, future perfect: expresses the projected results by a certain time of present actions.
  If you don't stop eating sweets, you'll have lost all your teeth by the time you're twenty.
  (She does eat sweets. This will have serious consequences by a certain time in the future.)
- Where a conditional uses a particular tense (e.g. present), most tenses expressing the same time can be used (e.g. present simple, continuous, perfect).
  If you're staying, will you give me a lift home later?
  If you've finished your work, I'll start cooking the meal.
- The verb and subject can be inverted, omitting the *if*, in the third conditional and the second conditional with *were*. This is quite formal, literary style.
  Had he left school when he was sixteen, he might not have got such a good job.
  Were he a bit friendlier, he'd get on better.
- A similar inversion takes place in the second conditional with *should*.
  Should the sea level rise, many areas of land would flood. (formal)

Unit 14

Ways of comparing

1 Comparative adjective
   The Mercedes is more expensive than the Peugeot.

2 Comparative adverb
   I have been to New York more often than my friends have.

3 Superlative adjective
   Smoked salmon is the most expensive item in the supermarket.

4 Superlative adverb
   Of all the students, Mario ran the fastest.

5 Metaphor
   Sarah eats like a pig.

6 Simile
   Jim is as thin as a rake.

7 As ... as
   My car is as fast as yours.
   Films aren't as interesting as magazines.

Unit 15

The definite article

1 The definite article is used in the following situations.
- When identifying something defined by its uniqueness.
  Can you see the rainbow?
  He's the chairman of the company.
- When identifying something defined by its locality.
  Where's Mum? She's in the kitchen.
- When mentioning a noun for the second time.
  I've just got a new puppy?
  – Oh, what's the puppy's name?
- When identifying something defined by a phrase which follows it.
  That's the man who takes my swimming class.
  It's the door with the red handle.
- Before superlatives and adjectives used as a noun class.
  He's the best!
  I'm making regular donations to a charity for the disabled.

2 It is not used in the following situations.
- Before institutions except when referring to the building, rather than the concept.
  My mother goes to church every Sunday.
  It's a collection to renovate the church.
  (But note: *The Church is in agreement with the Government on this issue.*)
- Before abstract nouns except when they are followed by a phrase which makes them specific.
  We all need love in our lives.
  The love of parents for their children is totally undemanding.

3 There are a number of set phrases in which the definite article is used, often with geographical place names.
  The West Indies, the River Seine, the Alps.

Participle clauses

1 Participle clauses are formed with the present or past participle. The participle clause can precede the main clause when the participle refers to the subject of the main clause.
- Present participle
  The man sat there, staring at his empty coffee cup.
  (subject)
  Can you see the child playing behind the wall? (object)
  Dropping the tray, the waitress screamed in horror.
  (subject)
- Past participle
  Columbus, sponsored by the Spanish King and Queen, set sail.
  The athlete beaten in last week's race has just won the 1,000 metres.
  Designed by computer, this car is state-of-the-art technology.

2 Participle clauses are used to link two ideas which share the same subject or object.
  The man sat there. He was staring at his empty coffee cup.
- They often replace relative clauses.
  Can you see the child (who is) playing behind the wall?
- The present participle is used to express an *active* verb in the subordinate clause, either in the past or the present. The time is made obvious by the tense of the main clause or by time adverbials.
  The man sat there, staring at his empty coffee cup. (past)
  Living rough and sleeping under cardboard, she spends every day in a centre for the homeless. (present)
- The past participle is used to express a *passive* verb in the subordinate clause, either in the past or the present.
  Sponsored by the Spanish King and Queen, Columbus set sail. (past)
  Positioned carefully in the light, this picture gives the impression of moving water. (present)

Connectives of comparison and contrast

(The following connectives appear in Units 6, 14, 15 and 18.)

1 Comparison
- Phrases that introduce a sentence: *similarly, in the same way, by the same token.*
  Jogging is an effective aerobic exercise.
  Similarly,/In the same way,/By the same token, swimming is very good for you.
- Phrases that are followed by a noun: *it's the same for, it's equally true of*
  Jogging is an effective aerobic exercise.
  It's the same for/It's equally true of swimming.

2 Contrast

- Phrases which introduce a statement of contrast: *conversely, on the other hand.*
  Children generally love sweet things.
  Conversely,/On the other hand, they often dislike savoury tastes.
- Linking words which join two clauses: *while, whereas.*
  Many people enjoy taking exercise while/whereas they often hate the idea of doing it.
- *On the contrary* introduces a contrast which is unexpected.
  He says he doesn't actually like his job. On the contrary, he loathes it.
- *However* introduces an idea of concession. (See Unit 18, page 139.)
  The opera was very expensive. However, I decided to go.
- *Instead of* is used as a preposition.
  Instead of driving to work, you should consider walking.

 Unit 16

Sentence adverbials and adverbs

- The position of some adverbials in a sentence can change their meaning.
  A *The teacher clearly hasn't answered my question.*
  B *Clearly, the teacher hasn't answered my question.*
  C *The teacher hasn't answered my question clearly.*
  In A and B *clearly* is a sentence adverbial and indicates the speaker's attitude to the statement as a whole. In other words the speaker feels that the teacher hasn't answered his question, and he feels that this is obvious to the listener and cannot be disputed. In C *clearly* is an adverb of manner simply describing the way in which the question was answered.
- Here is a list of the most common sentence adverbials and their meanings.
  yet What follows is a surprising or contrasting additional piece of information considering what I have just said.
  understandably One can understand/sympathise with what I am about to say.
  similarly What I am about to say is similar to what I have just said.
  frankly What follows is my true opinion, although it may be shocking.
  incidentally The following is some information which is not directly connected with the previous information.
  superficially The following is how things appear on the surface.
  admittedly What follows probably contradicts what I have just said.
  apparently The following is something I believe to be true, but I'm not certain it is.
  ideally What follows is the perfect situation.
  naturally The following is what anyone would expect; it is not surprising.

Forms of adjectives and adverbs

- Adverbs modify verbs, other adverbs, adjectives and a number of other constructions, including whole sentences as explained above. Most adverbs are formed from adjectives by adding the suffix *-ly*
  beautiful beautifully
  Note: Some adjectives end in *-ly: friendly.*
- However, some adverbs (often connected with time, position and direction) look like adjectives.
  fast: a fast car (adjective) *He drove fast.* (adverb)

These are some of the most common adverbs which look like adjectives.
close dead direct fine hard high just late long low pretty short slow wide wrong
- Sometimes an adverb has two forms with a difference in meaning.
  He arrived late. (after the appointed time)
  I haven't been there lately . (in the previous few days or weeks)
- Sometimes the two forms have the same meaning, although the form which looks like an adjective is usually rather informal.
  They sell things very cheap in that shop.
  They sell things very cheaply in that shop.

 Unit 17

Order of adjectives before a noun

- The order of adjectives before a noun is as follows:
  defining adjective/determiner →opinion →size →age → shape →colour →origin →material →(compound) noun
  Two beautiful, large, 18th-century, oval, dark English mahogany dining tables.
- In fact it is unusual to use more than two or three adjectives before a noun. We prefer to give the information in other clauses or in additional sentences.
  Two beautiful, dark English dining tables which are oval, rather large, date from the 18th century, and are made of mahogany.

Introductory it

1 It is unusual to have an infinitive or a *that*-clause as the subject of a sentence in English. An alternative is to use introductory *it* as the subject and put the infinitive or *that*-clause later.

   That Americans are friendly is a common belief.
   It is a common belief that Americans are friendly.
   To be punctual is polite.
   It is polite to be punctual.

2 Introductory *it* is often used in the following phrases.
   It is true/not true that … It is probable that …
   It is likely/unlikely that …   It is better/best to …
   It is essential to …

3 We also use introductory *it* to introduce ideas we have just thought of.
   It occurred to me that … It struck me that …

4 We often use introductory *it* in formal writing when we wish to describe a generally held belief/theory/ argument, or when the person who originally put forward the statement/belief/theory etc. cannot be identified or is not important.
   Some people think that carbon dioxide is harmful to the environment.
   It is thought that carbon dioxide is harmful to the environment.
   Somebody, I don't know who, once said that diamonds are a girl's best friend.
   It has been said that diamonds are a girl's best friend.

5 Introductory *it* is used to give extra emphasis to the subject it introduces.
   Jim, not Jack, passed the test.
   It was Jim who passed the test.

Unit 18

Participles in adverbial clauses

Participles used as adverbial clauses allow us to combine two ideas or sentences in order to give a reason or result. The subject of the main verb and the participle must be the same.

If we lose advertising, we will lose freedom of choice.
Losing advertising, we lose freedom of choice.
She passed her driving test and then got a job as a chauffeur.
Having passed her driving test, she got a job as a chauffeur.
If it is used correctly, this drug will cure most headaches.
Used correctly, this drug will cure most headaches.

Concessive clauses

Concessive clauses are used to combine two contrasting ideas when the idea in the main clause is surprising in view of the information in the concessive clause.

1   A simple contrast can be introduced by *though, although,* or *even though.*
    Mary is very wealthy. She never gives money to charity.
    Though wealthy, Mary never gives money to charity.

2   A contrast which is particularly surprising can be introduced by *in spite of, despite,* and (very formal) *notwithstanding.*
    All the evidence was against him. He still denied the charge.
    Despite all the evidence, he still denied the charge.
    Simon has excellent qualifications but he can't find a job.
    Notwithstanding his excellent qualifications, Simon can't find a job.

3   Contrasting ideas which include the idea of a condition can be introduced by *even if.*
    You might invite her to the party. But if you do invite her, she won't come.
    Even if you invite her, she won't come.

4   A contrast which is true in a range of contrasting conditions can be introduced by *whatever, wherever, whoever, whenever, however, no matter/it doesn't matter how/what/where/who.*
    Sometimes the weather is good, sometimes it is bad. He never misses his daily run.
    Whatever the weather, he never misses his daily run.
    No matter how bad the weather, he never misses his daily run.

Unit 19

Would rather/sooner + *unreal past*

This construction is used to introduce an alternative action the speaker wishes somebody else would do. It is a polite form of *wish + would.*
    Clare has asked to borrow my car but I want her to borrow Michael's car.
    I'd rather you borrowed Michael's car.

As if/as though + *unreal past*

This construction is used to make a hypothetical comparison which you know is impossible.
(Your friend is describing a car he doesn't own.)
You talk as if you owned it yourself!

Note
When we are making a hypothetical comparison which may or may not be possible, we use the present or present perfect form.
(A colleague is describing a city. You don't know whether he has ever visited it.)
You talk as though you've lived there yourself.
(A stranger is describing a sports club. You don't know whether she is a member)
You sound as if you're a member.

Wish + would

This construction expresses a desire for something to change when the situation is outside the control of the speaker. It is often used to express annoyance.
I wish those students would stop talking.

Wish + *simple past/past continuous*

This construction expresses dissatisfaction or personal regret about a present situation.
(You are unhappy about being short.)
I wish I was taller.
(You are annoyed because it is snowing.)
I wish it wasn't snowing.
Note
Were is often used after *wish* in formal English.

Wish + *past perfect*

This construction is used to express regret for an action in the past.
(You failed an exam because you didn't work hard enough.)
I wish I'd worked harder for that exam.

Unit 20

Text reference

1   **Anaphoric reference**
    Anaphoric references are the most common ones. They look back in the text.
    The man walked into the shop. He was carrying a briefcase.
    He refers back to the *man.*

2   **Cataphoric reference**
    Cataphoric references are mostly used for stylistic effect, to create suspense. They look forward in the text.
    She was tall, graceful and charming, with long, blond hair. She wasn't what I had expected. When Mrs Grantham walked in the room I was taken aback.
    She refers to *Mrs Grantham.*

3   **Exophoric reference**
    Exophoric references are quite common. They refer to something outside the text, knowledge which is shared by the writer and his/her reader.
    The bells were ringing in St Paul's Cathedral as the Prince walked in to meet his bride.
    It might be understood here that *the Prince* refers to the Prince of Wales on his wedding day.